D0551233

The DMC Book of *Cross Stitch* *and Counted Thread Work*

The DMC Book of
Cross Stitch
and Counted Thread Work

ELEANOR VAN ZANDT

COLLINS & BROWN

First published in Great Britain in 1994
by Collins & Brown Limited
London House
Great Eastern Wharf
Parkgate Road
London SW11 4NQ

1 3 5 7 9 8 6 4 2

British Library Cataloguing-in-Publication Data:
A catalogue record for this book is available from the British Library.
ISBN 1–85585–167–9
ISBN 1–85585–227–6

CONCEIVED, DESIGNED AND EDITED BY
COLLINS & BROWN LIMITED

EDITOR *Catherine Bradley*
ART DIRECTOR *Roger Bristow*
DESIGNED AND STYLED BY *Carol McCleeve*
PHOTOGRAPHY BY *Sue Atkinson, Clive Streeter and Geoff Dann*
ILLUSTRATIONS BY *Coral Mula and David Ashby*

Filmset by Bookworm Typesetting, Manchester
Reproduction by J. Film, Singapore
Printed and bound in Italy by New Interlitho

Contents

Introduction

If you have never tried cross stitch embroidery, you'll be delighted to discover how simple it is. The basic stitch consists of two straight diagonal stitches forming an X. As the stitches are worked over a regular number of easily counted fabric threads, you never have to worry about keeping them even – the fabric does it for you.

Cross stitch is also an extremely versatile form of embroidery. It can be worked on a large scale in bold, striking, abstract designs, or on a small scale in delicate, intricate patterns. Although essentially angular, it can depict curves if worked finely. The most subtle shading effects can be achieved with this simple stitch, making it ideal for pictorial designs.

Cross stitch is just one member of a large family of embroidery techniques known as counted thread work. The name describes them perfectly: in each technique, stitches are worked over specified, counted numbers of fabric threads. The simplest of these techniques, pattern darning, consists of running stitches – the basic in-and-out sewing stitch – worked in regular patterns.

Blackwork offers the opportunity to create fascinating patterns, from simple, widely spaced ones to complex, more dense textures. These may then be combined for pictorial or abstract designs. For lacy effects, try pulled work, drawn thread work, or Hardanger embroidery, with its distinctively crisp, geometrical quality.

These techniques can be used for all sorts of projects, including home furnishings, personal accessories, and even clothing. You could, for example, work a cross stitch picture of your own house, making a chart from a photograph of it. Or you could work several rows of delicate drawn thread stitching on some lingerie for a bride. Experiment with colours and textures as you gain more confidence in each style.

You will find many project ideas in this book, along with suggestions for varying some of the projects to suit your own individual taste. All the techniques you need to create these projects are explained and illustrated with diagrams and photographs. A selection of motifs and stitch patterns for the different techniques is also provided, to encourage you to create your own original designs, while a section, "Materials and Equipment" will help you to choose correctly from the wide range available. All the threads and fabrics in this book are readily available from needlecraft shops and stockists.

I hope you will enjoy discovering the range of counted thread techniques described in this book, and use them to create attractive and practical articles.

Eleanor Van Zandt

A Living Tradition

Cross stitch is easily the most popular form of embroidery today. Samplers, cushions, pictures, paperweights and a host of other cross stitch items adorn homes in countries throughout the world, providing millions of people with a satisfying creative pastime.

Cross stitch is one of the family of popular and varied embroidery techniques known as counted thread work. As the name suggests, these techniques involve counting fabric threads. The fabric used in counted thread work serves as a grid for the stitching and always plays an integral part in the scale and appearance of the finished work. In surface embroidery, by contrast, the fabric serves as a background to the stitching, which is worked freely over it.

Most counted thread techniques are relatively easy to master. The main requirements are the ability to count threads, follow a chart or memorize a pattern, and work with an even tension. Although the techniques may be simple, the patterns produced are often highly complex.

CROSS STITCH

Cross stitch is found throughout the world. It is extremely versatile, has an appealingly crisp texture, and is well suited to pictorial and abstract designs. If worked on a small scale, it can produce fine detail, delicate effects, and subtle shading, as can be seen in the detailed naturalistic embroideries of Denmark.

The techniques of cross stitch can also be used to create solid areas of colour and pattern. The cross stitch embroidery of Thailand, for example, includes angular multicoloured border designs that cover the background completely. In the West, cross stitch is also sometimes used as a needlepoint stitch.

Below and detail above left: Modern three-panel cross stitch design of the Grand Canyon (Audrey Ormrod)

In the English-speaking countries cross stitch is most familiar in pictorial work, a tradition reaching back to the 18th century, when it became the favoured stitch for samplers. Early samplers were simply collections of different embroidery stitches, worked on long pieces of linen and kept by embroiderers as a reference. Gradually samplers became more pictorial in nature, consisting of motifs arranged within a border. Birds, flowers, trees, houses, and patriotic images, such as the American eagle, were popular motifs. Making a sampler soon became part of a young girl's education. Such samplers often included an alphabet, numerals, and a pious verse, as well as the date and the stitcher's name.

Although a variety of stitches might be used in these samplers, cross stitch tended to dominate. It was almost invariably used for the floral borders, which typically depicted an undulating stem or vine bearing stylized roses, carnations, or other blooms.

Stylized natural forms, sometimes altered beyond recognition, are worked in cross stitch on the native costumes of many peoples, including those of former Eastern Europe, Morocco, and parts of the Middle East.

In most cross stitch embroidery the stitches form the motif(s) and the background is left plain. This is reversed in Assisi work, an embroidery style that developed in Italy in the 16th century. The background of Assisi work is filled with cross stitch, or variant, and the motifs left void.

19th-century American cross stitch sampler (The American Museum in Britain)

PATTERN DARNING

Pattern darning may well have originated as a simple way of imitating woven patterns. Running stitches are worked across the fabric in a regular pattern to produce solid areas of colour. This technique lends itself especially well to geometric motifs.

The simplicity of pattern darning has ensured its popularity in many countries, including India, Mexico, and the former Yugoslavia, but it has especially flourished in Scandinavia. Icelandic embroidery includes fine examples of pattern darning, worked diagonally as well as in horizontal or vertical lines. In the Middle Ages diagonal darning was worked in wool threads on white linen to make complex interlaced designs, used on altar frontals and bed hangings. In the Telemark region of Norway, pattern darning was often used to embellish coffin cloths with multicoloured borders. Similar borders were also found on the necks and wristbands of shirts.

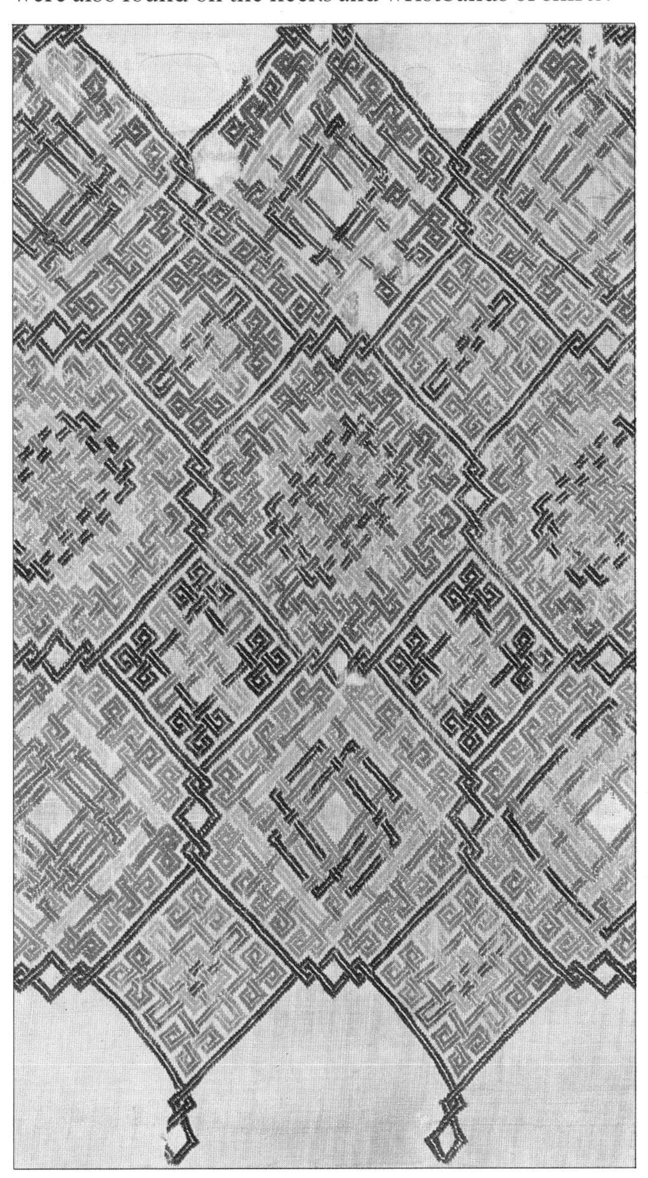

Example of pattern darning: centre panel of embroidered altar frontal (National Museum of Iceland)

BLACKWORK

The stitch used in outlining the motifs in Assisi work (double running or Holbein stitch) was used in the 16th century to create intricate linear patterns to adorn collars, sleeves, and other parts of ladies' and gentlemen's dress. Worked in black silk thread on white linen, this embroidery style later blossomed into extravagant all-over designs of swirling naturalistic shapes enclosing small repeating patterns. In England, Elizabethan blackwork was used on huge puffed sleeves.

Embroiderers today use the tonal contrasts of blackwork patterns to create highly imaginative pictorial work. They juxtapose patterns of different density to suggest distinct textures and varying colour tones.

Modern design of sheep worked in blackwork (Jenny Chippendale)

PULLED WORK

In the 18th century it was discovered that delicate openwork effects could be achieved without removing any fabric threads. Instead, the threads could be pulled together firmly in regular patterns, which left holes in the fabric. This technique was stimulated by the importation from India of fine muslin, which lent itself to such work.

Pulled work is a particular type of openwork. Each stitch pulls the fabric threads together to produce imaginative openwork patterns that can rival lace in their delicacy. Simple embroidery stitches are used in pulled work to add textural variation or to outline the motifs.

Pulled work is usually stitched on evenweave fabrics. The best quality work is stitched with threads of similar weight to threads of the fabric. In pulled work, the fabric threads are pulled back with special embroidery stitches to create attractive decorative holes.

The ultra-fine form of pulled work was made to imitate lace. This is also known as Dresden work, named after the city whose professional workshops produced the best examples. Gossamer bobbin laces, then the height of fashion, were extremely costly. Dresden work offered almost the same degree of fineness at a lower price.

The lacy fillings were enclosed within flowing shapes worked in surface embroidery. Master embroiderers, all men, did the surface embroidery in silk and gold. Women embroiderers, who were not guild members, were hired to do the Dresden work.

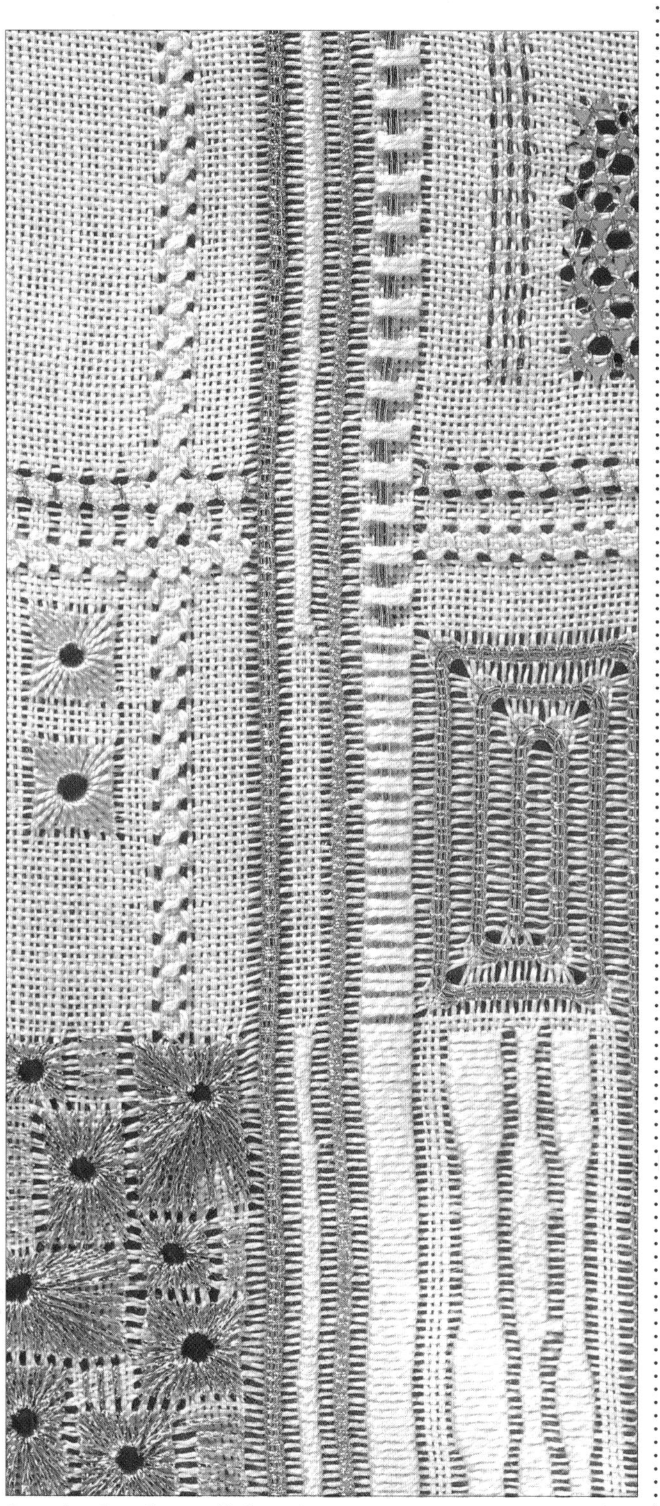

Sample of modern pulled work

DRAWN THREAD WORK

To create this type of openwork embroidery, certain warp and weft threads are drawn out from the fabric. The 16th-century fashion of needle lace owed its origins to an Italian form of counted thread work called *reticella* ("little net"). In *reticella*, most of the fabric threads were pulled out, leaving a grid over which additional, diagonal threads were laid; this delicate framework was then embroidered with buttonhole and other stitches. Stiff collars of lacy *reticella* appear in portraits of the time.

It was only a short step to eliminating the ground fabric entirely, laying the foundation threads over a parchment pattern and stitching over this foundation. With this *punto in aria* ("a stitch in the air"), needle lace was born.

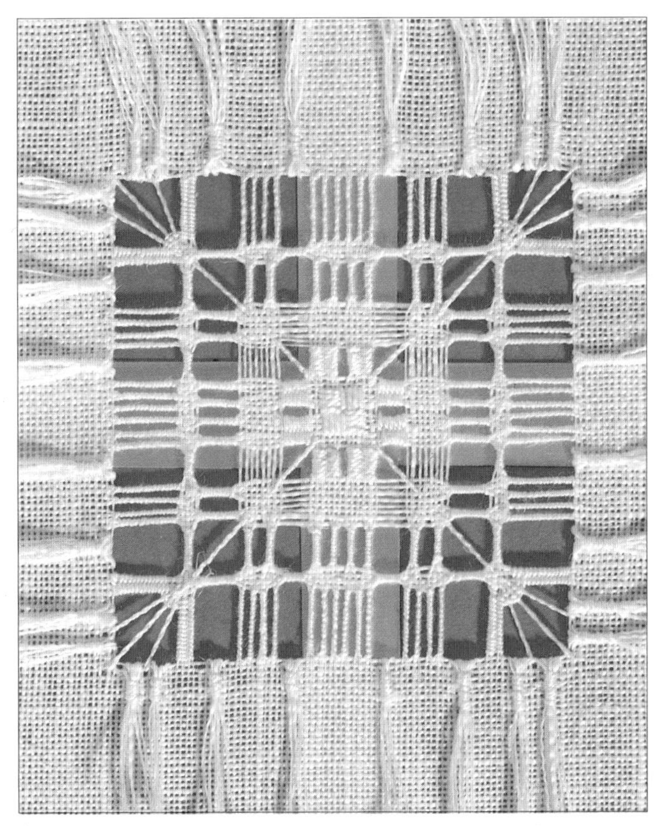

Cruciform design in drawn thread work. The threads are withdrawn from the filling and held down securely with the satin stitches

HARDANGER WORK

Another distinctive form of drawn thread work is Norwegian Hardanger. Distantly related to *reticella*, experts believe that it probably originated in Asia and came to Scandinavia by way of Persia and Italy.

Hardanger combines openwork squares, some decorated with filling stitches, and regular blocks of satin stitch. In Russian drawn ground work, the motifs are first outlined on the fabric in surface embroidery (typically satin stitch) then threads are removed from the background to leave a grid of pairs of threads. This grid is then covered with overcasting stitches. Needleweaving techniques are frequently used to enhance the open spaces, giving an appealing lacy effect. The areas around the openwork blocks can then be further decorated with geometric surface stitches.

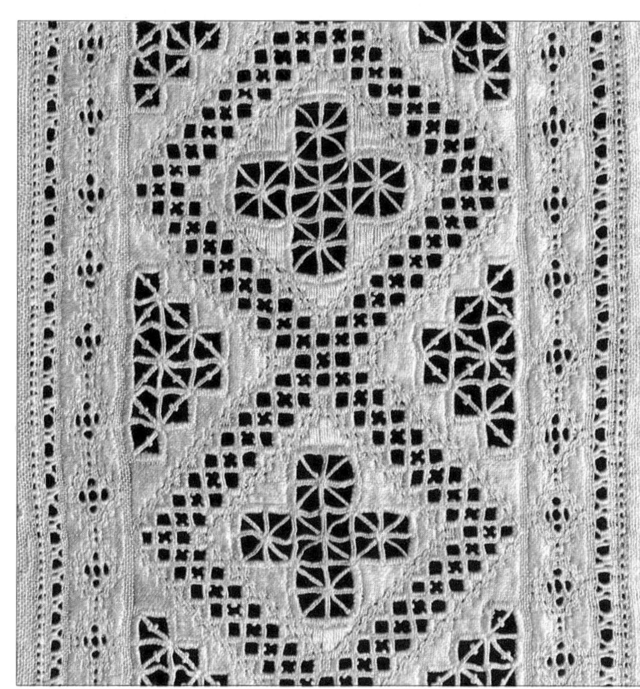

Detail of 19th-century Hardanger work on an apron border from western Norway (Norwegian Folk Museum, Oslo)

EXPLORING COUNTED THREAD WORK

Embroidery is no longer an essential part of a young girl's education; it is now, rather, a pastime to enjoy. All the variations of counted thread work offer a creative outlet without requiring formidable technical expertise. Cross stitch alone offers many different styles and cultural traditions to inspire you. Some attractive variations of the basic cross stitch are discussed and illustrated on pages 30–31. There are also suggestions for using these variations on the most suitable cross stitch projects.

You can use this book to discover a range of counted thread work skills as your confidence and experience develop. Pattern darning is a simple technique which uses running stitch to create its attractive designs.

If you enjoy cross stitch, you can also easily move on to blackwork. To finish a cross stitched tablecloth neatly, you can learn simple hemstitching, then progress to its many decorative variations. If you enjoy creating interesting textures, pulled work will appeal to you.

In time, you may become more adventurous and design your own original work. Many contemporary professional embroiderers have used the basic counted thread work as a basis for experimentation. It is one of the most versatile and creative forms of needlework.

Use this book to learn the different techniques. Each one is clearly explained to make it approachable and enjoyable. Develop new techniques and perfect old skills as you create these beautiful embroidery projects.

Materials & Equipment

Part of the pleasure of embroidery lies in selecting the proper tools and choosing lovely materials to enhance your work.

Today embroiderers have an enormous range of high-quality fabrics and threads from which to choose, as well as a great variety of tools and accessories – some essential, some optional – which will help to make your work enjoyable.

FABRICS

The fabrics normally used for counted thread embroidery are called **evenweave**. This means they have the same number of threads per inch/centimetre in both directions, vertical (warp) and horizontal (weft).

Plain weave, or tabby weave, refers to the most basic weaving method, in which each thread is passed over and under a single thread each time. Sometimes groups of threads are woven in this way, but the basic weave is the same. All evenweave fabrics are plain weaves but, not all plain weaves are evenweave.

Evenweave fabrics are woven from natural fibres (such as linen, cotton, and wool), synthetic fibres, and also from natural-synthetic blends. The degree of fineness or coarseness of the fabric is called its count and is measured by the number of threads per 1 in (2.5 cm). For example, 18-count fabric has 18 threads to 1 in (2.5 cm); 32-count has 32 threads per 1 in (2.5 cm). These fabrics come in a wide variety of widths and in a variety of different colours (except for fine linen, which comes in white or cream only). These can be adapted to suit your particular project. The

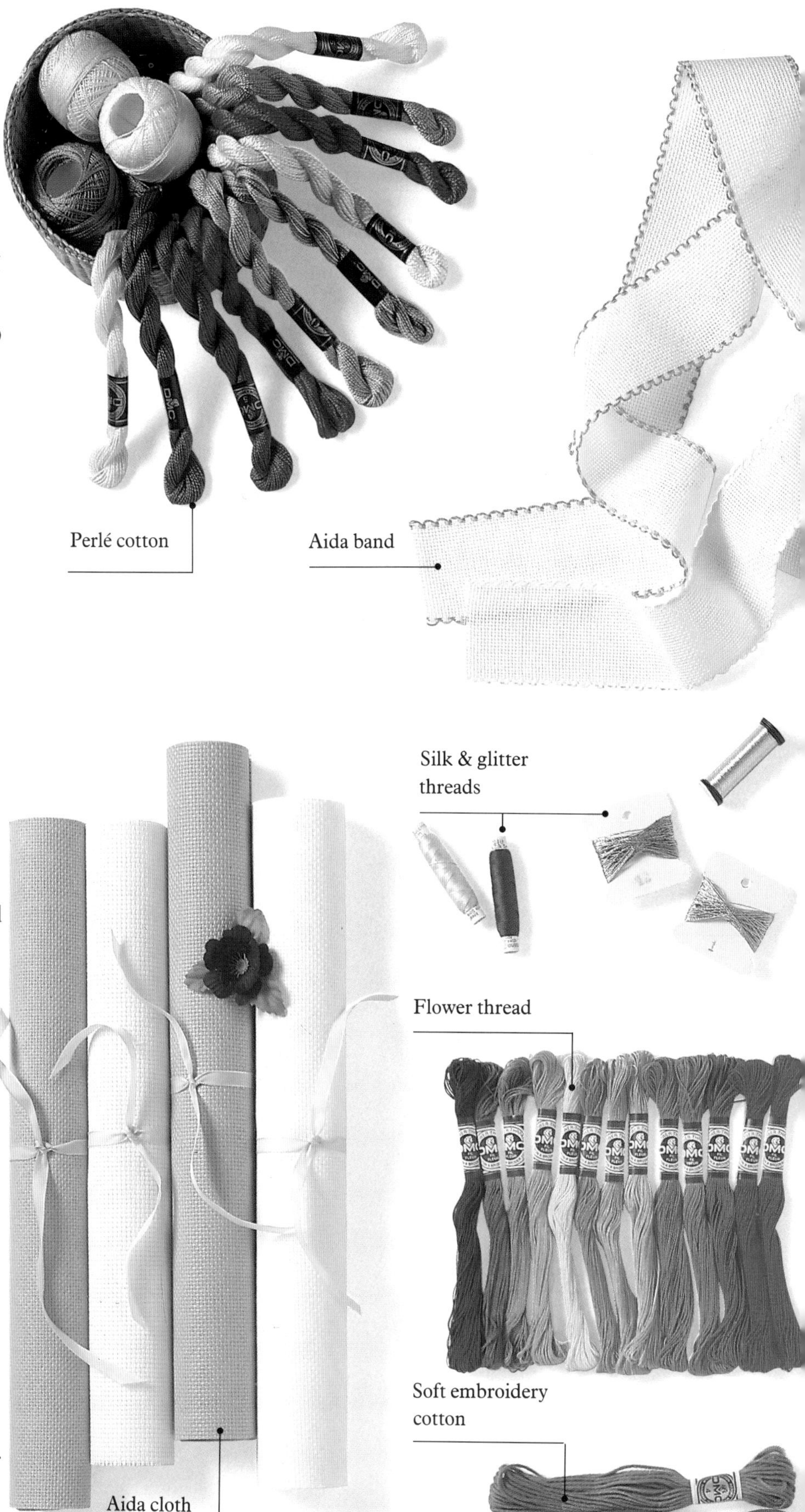

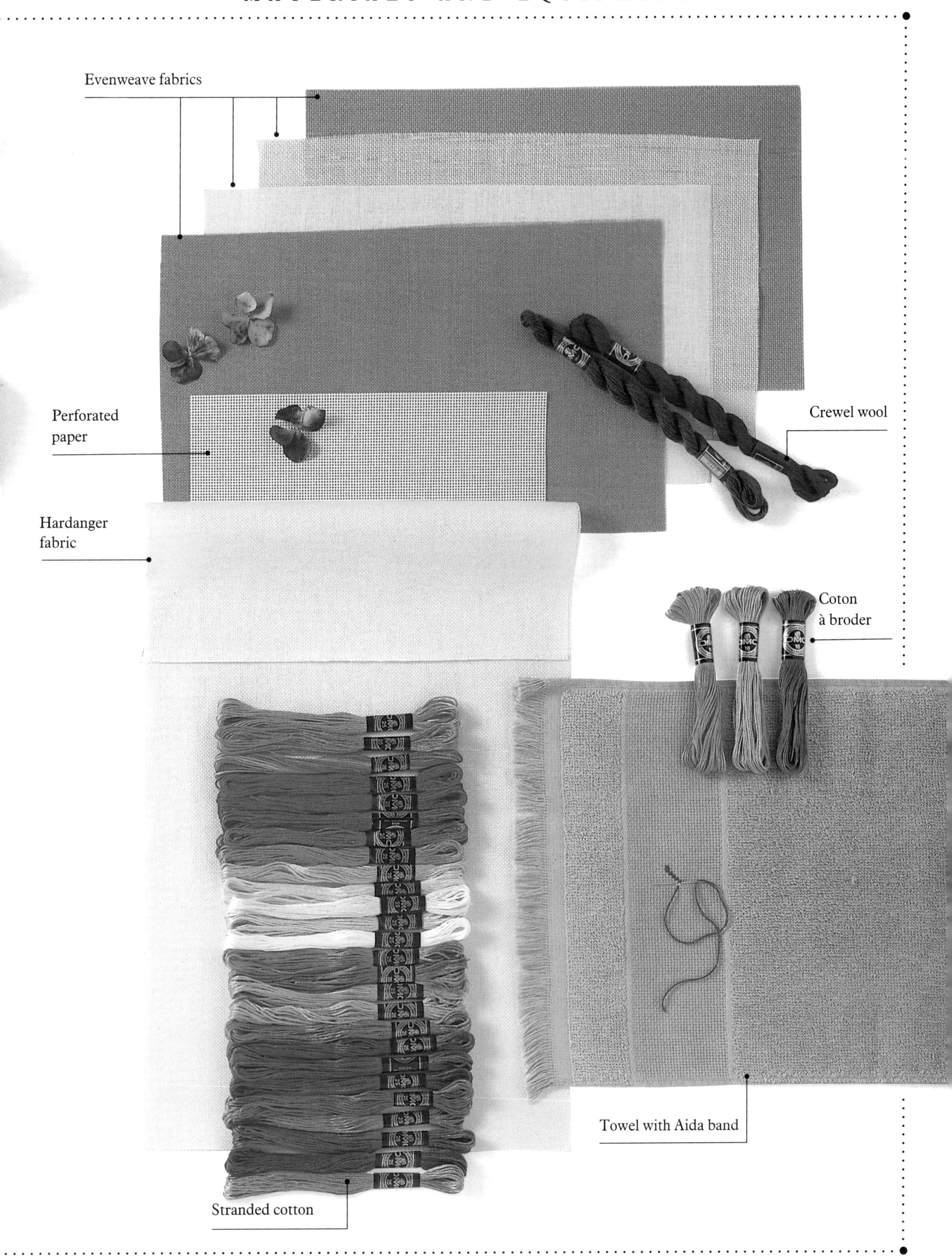
Evenweave fabrics
Perforated paper
Hardanger fabric
Crewel wool
Coton à broder
Towel with Aida band
Stranded cotton

most suitable materials for other counted thread techniques are described in more detail in the appropriate technique sections.

Single-thread evenweave Practical and popular, this fabric is used for projects from handkerchiefs to tablecloths. It is woven from single threads; the degree of fineness ranges from 14- to 36-count. Stitches are normally worked over two or more threads or thread intersections. Some of these evenweave fabrics have a relatively loose weave, which makes them especially suitable for pulled work. Others are woven with slightly irregular threads, which produces a pleasingly natural texture. This also distorts the stitches very slightly, which enhances the handcrafted quality of the work.

Hardanger fabric This fabric is woven with pairs of threads. The normal count is 22 *pairs* of threads per 1 in (2.5 cm). Although it is traditionally used for Hardanger work (*see pages 128-141*), it can be used for all other counted thread techniques as well.

Aida cloth This cloth is woven from blocks of four threads; the holes between threads are clearly visible. It is most often used for cross stitch, with each stitch worked over a single intersection. Some Aida is woven with a removable grid of contrasting threads placed at 10-thread intervals to make counting easier. Aida cloth ranges from coarse 6-count to a fine 18-count. Most Aida has a matt finish, but it may have a damask finish with shiny warp threads.

Special products Many fabrics have been created especially for counted thread projects. These include evenweave fabrics divided into squares with satin or contrast-coloured weave lines; the squares are filled with a variety of embroidered motifs. There are also damask fabrics with circular evenweave inserts for embroidery, tea towels and guest towels with bands for cross stitch motifs, and strips of Aida cloth with decorative edging to use for bookmarks or headbands. Perforated paper requires no hemming and is often used for cards and for tree ornaments.

Other suitable fabrics The following method will help you to determine whether a fabric is a true evenweave. Work a line of basting at

VARIETIES OF FABRICS

The range of fabrics now available for embroidery is one of its most attractive features. In selecting a fabric, you should consider not only the final use of the project, but also your choice of thread and style of embroidery. Most fabric or needlecraft shops will help you achieve the best possible results. Some different fabrics are shown here for quick reference. Single-thread evenweave, featured in the top two pictures, is an extremely popular choice.

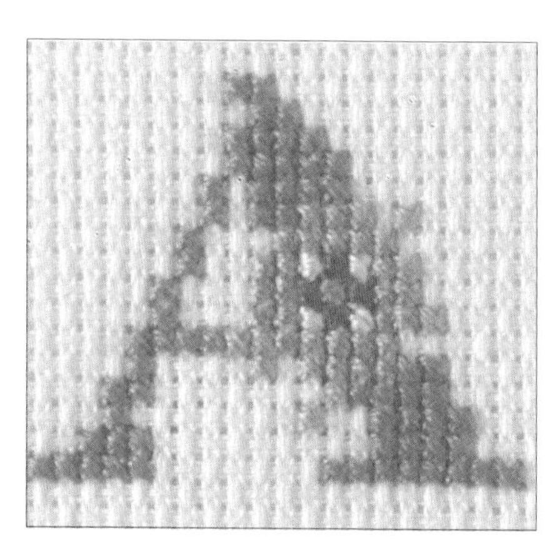

18-count cotton

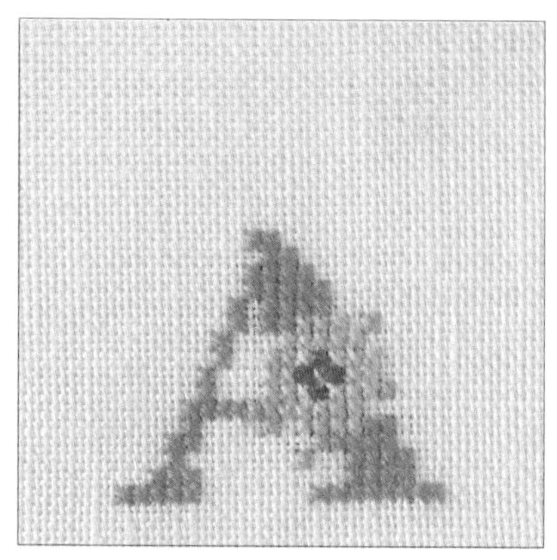

32-count cotton

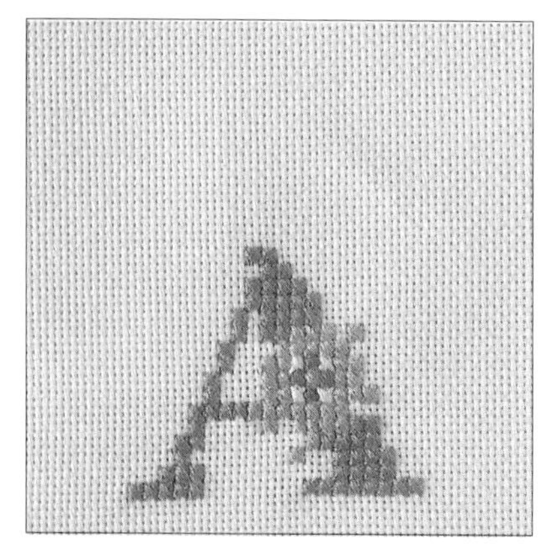

16-count Aida

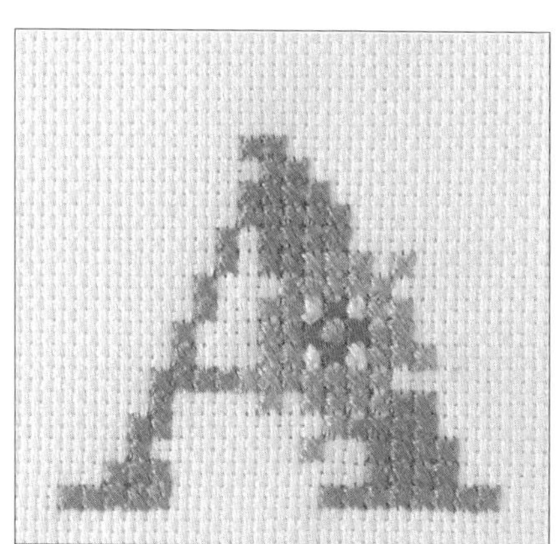

22-count Hardanger

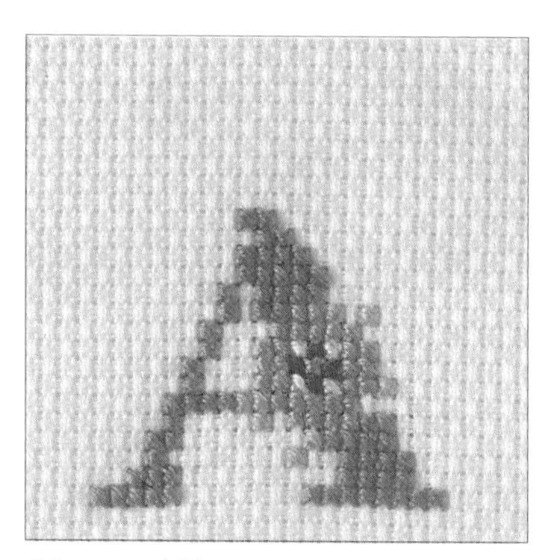

14-count Aida

least 2 in (5 cm) long in a contrasting colour along one horizontal thread. At one end of this line work another line, but follow a vertical thread. Complete the square, making sure that you follow the fabric threads exactly so that the basting forms a perfect 2 in (5 cm) square.

Count the threads in both directions. If the number is the same, the fabric is evenweave. If there is a slight difference, this means the fabric is an uneven weave. However, it may still be used as long as the motifs are positioned either horizontally or vertically, but not both ways. Where motifs are worked at right angles, the uneven weave will produce a distortion – motifs aligned in one direction will be wider and shorter than those aligned in the other.

Fabric that is not a true evenweave or is too fine for the threads to be counted can still be used for cross stitch if the stitches are worked over a canvas grid (*see page 28*).

THREADS

Many different threads are used for counted work. As a general rule, the thread used for the stitching should be comparable in thickness to the fabric threads. The best threads have a fairly smooth texture which enhances the crisp character of the embroidery. Wool is not usually a good choice, although fine crewel yarn lends itself to pattern darning. For large-scale stitching, a thicker wool thread might be used.

Please note that all the projects in this book have been worked in DMC threads. The particular colour of thread has been specified where it is important, but you may wish to adapt these to match your own colour schemes.

Stranded cotton or floss This is a lustrous thread made of six easy-to-separate strands. A single strand can be used for very fine work; more for bolder effects. It comes in hundreds of colours and is extremely versatile.

Perlé cotton This thread is spun from two plies, which are twisted to produce a beaded or "pearl" effect. It is usually used as a single strand. Perlé cotton comes in several thicknesses from no. 3 (thick) to no. 12 (very thin); no. 5 is most often used and is available in the greatest range of colours. Its high lustre and strength make perlé cotton suitable for many different counted thread techniques, from cross stitch to pulled work.

Coton à broder Slightly less glossy than stranded or perlé cotton, this is a smooth thread used by itself. It gives stitches a firm definition with a soft sheen and is especially well suited to blackwork. The colour range is somewhat more limited than for stranded or perlé cotton.

Flower thread This cotton thread has a matt finish and a soft texture. It gives cross stitch work a lovely subtle effect. It is available in a broad range of colours.

Soft embroidery cotton This relatively thick thread has a matt finish and is used on coarse fabric, always in a single strand.

Linen thread This thread has a firm texture and considerable strength, which makes it especially suitable for pulled work. It is not as widely available as cotton threads and comes in a more limited range of colours.

Silk and rayon threads Silk threads give a luxurious quality to the stitching, but are more expensive than cotton threads. Glossy rayon floss gives a similar effect.

Other threads Many kinds of threads can be used in counted thread work. Fine lace and crochet cottons are often used in open work; metallic threads can be used to embellish cross stitch and blackwork. Sewing threads are needed to finish projects.

TOOLS

It is important to choose the right tools for your particular embroidery project. Embroidery and sewing needles come in a wide range of sizes; the correct scissors, pins, and marking pens are also important. Counted thread embroidery is best worked in a hoop, which makes counting fabric threads easier. A stand for the hoop will free both your hands for stitching.

Tapestry needles Virtually all counted thread work is done with a tapestry needle, which has a large eye and a blunt point. It slips easily between the fabric threads without piercing them. Tapestry needles range in size from 13 (large) to 26 (small). The size of needle required is specified in the list of equipment for each individual project. For very large-scale work, a knitter's needle (essentially an extra large tapestry needle) may be required. Make sure that the needle is large enough for the thread; the eye end should separate the fabric threads so that the embroidery thread passes through smoothly.

Hand-sewing needles Sharps, darners, and betweens are used in basting and finishing. Sharps are general-purpose needles for hand-sewing. Darners are useful for basting because their length makes it easy to take several large stitches at a time. Betweens are short and easy to manipulate.

Beading needles These are extremely fine and long needles, used for adding beads to embroidery.

Bodkins These are particularly useful when threading cord, yarn, or ribbon through casings.

Crewel and chenille needles These sharp-pointed embroidery needles have large eyes. Chenille needles are thicker and made in the same range of sizes as tapestry needles. Use either crewel or chenille needles to add surface stitchery or when working cross stitch over a piece of canvas.

Curved needles These are useful for many aspects of finishing work, especially in upholstery.

Scissors It is important to have the correct scissors for your purpose, as several different types are available. Buy good quality scissors; use them only for their intended purpose and they will stay sharp for a longer period of time. Dressmaking shears are used for cutting large pieces of fabric and so have long blades. They are an efficient way of cutting large areas. Embroidery scissors are small with sharp points. They are used for precise cutting of small threads. The points of these scissors should meet smoothly and precisely.

Hoops These come in a wide range of sizes and are used to hold small projects or sections of a larger design. They hold the fabric taut, so that stitches will lie smoothly, even when the work is released from the frame. Most embroidery hoops have a screw on the outside ring to adjust tension; spring hoops have an inner tension ring that easily lifts in or out.

Slate or scroll frames These rectangular frames come in many sizes and allow large sections to be worked on at the same time. Stands are available to clamp onto tables or chair arms. The maximum width is determined by the webbing or tape attached to the rollers at the top and bottom; excess length is wound around rollers at top and bottom.

Stretcher frames These are cheaper alternatives to scroll frames. They are made of wooden stretcher bars slotted together at the corners. The bars can be combined to make different sizes of frame. Remember that the working area of a stretcher frame is the space *inside* the frame.

Iron A steam iron is recommended for pressing embroidery.

Pins Fine, long, glass-headed pins are easy to handle. The glass heads can withstand the heat of an iron.

Tape measure and ruler Use a tape measure for measuring fabric; use the ruler for counting threads.

Thimble Most embroiderers use a thimble for efficient and painless hand-sewing.

Set square This tool is used to measure 90° angles accurately.

Fabric markers Ink may be permanent or temporary, fading with water or light. Test on fabric first.

Magnifying glasses These come in all sizes and may attach to a frame or hang on a cord around the stitcher's neck. Line magnifiers make it easier to read complicated charts.

Masking tape or woven tape Bind fabric edges with tape to prevent fraying. Masking tape has an adhesive backing; woven tape must be sewn on.

Thread organizer Use this to keep the threads for each project neat and easily accessible.

Design tools Other useful tools include tracing and graph paper, coloured pencils, and a stitch converter. This last can be used to calculate the finished size of a design when worked on a given fabric.

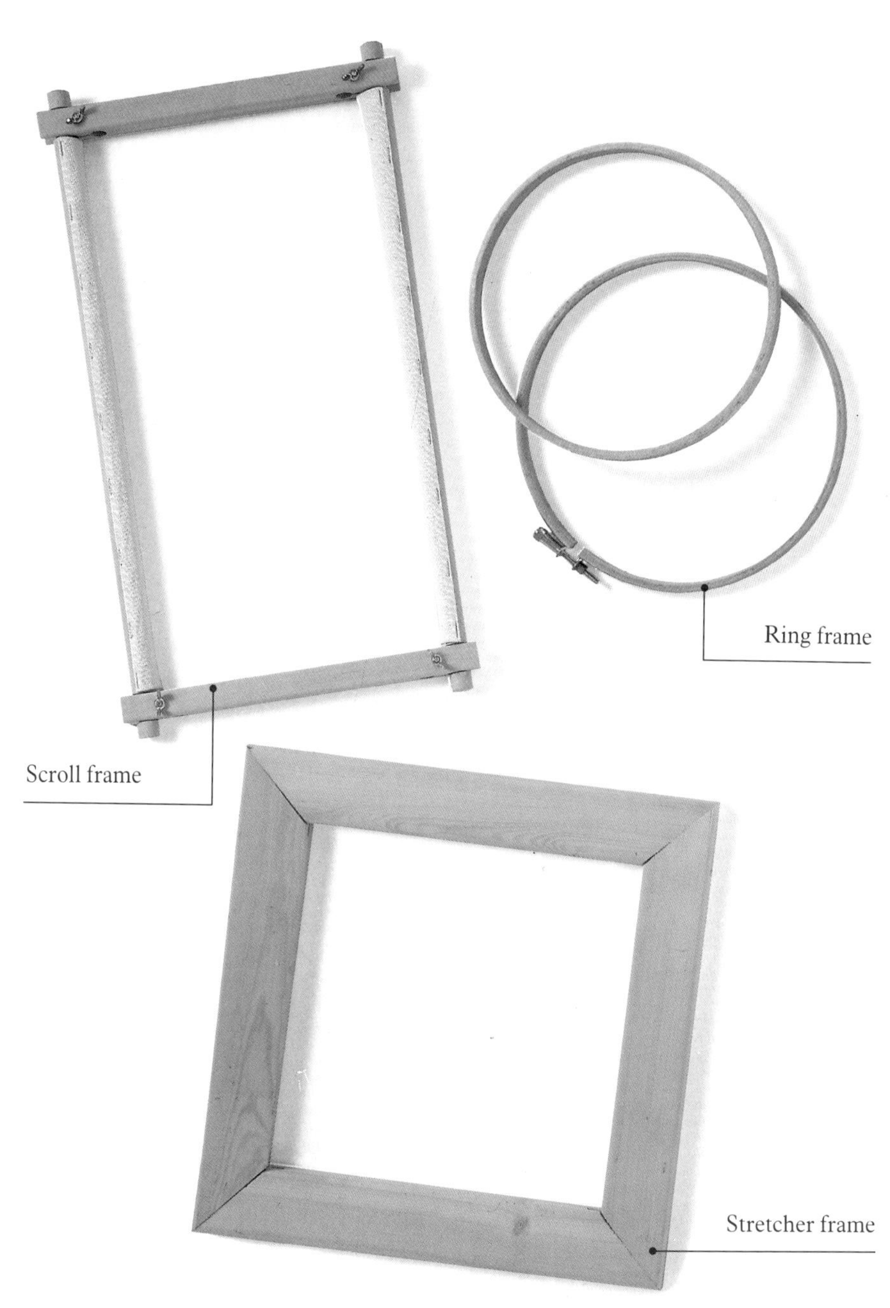

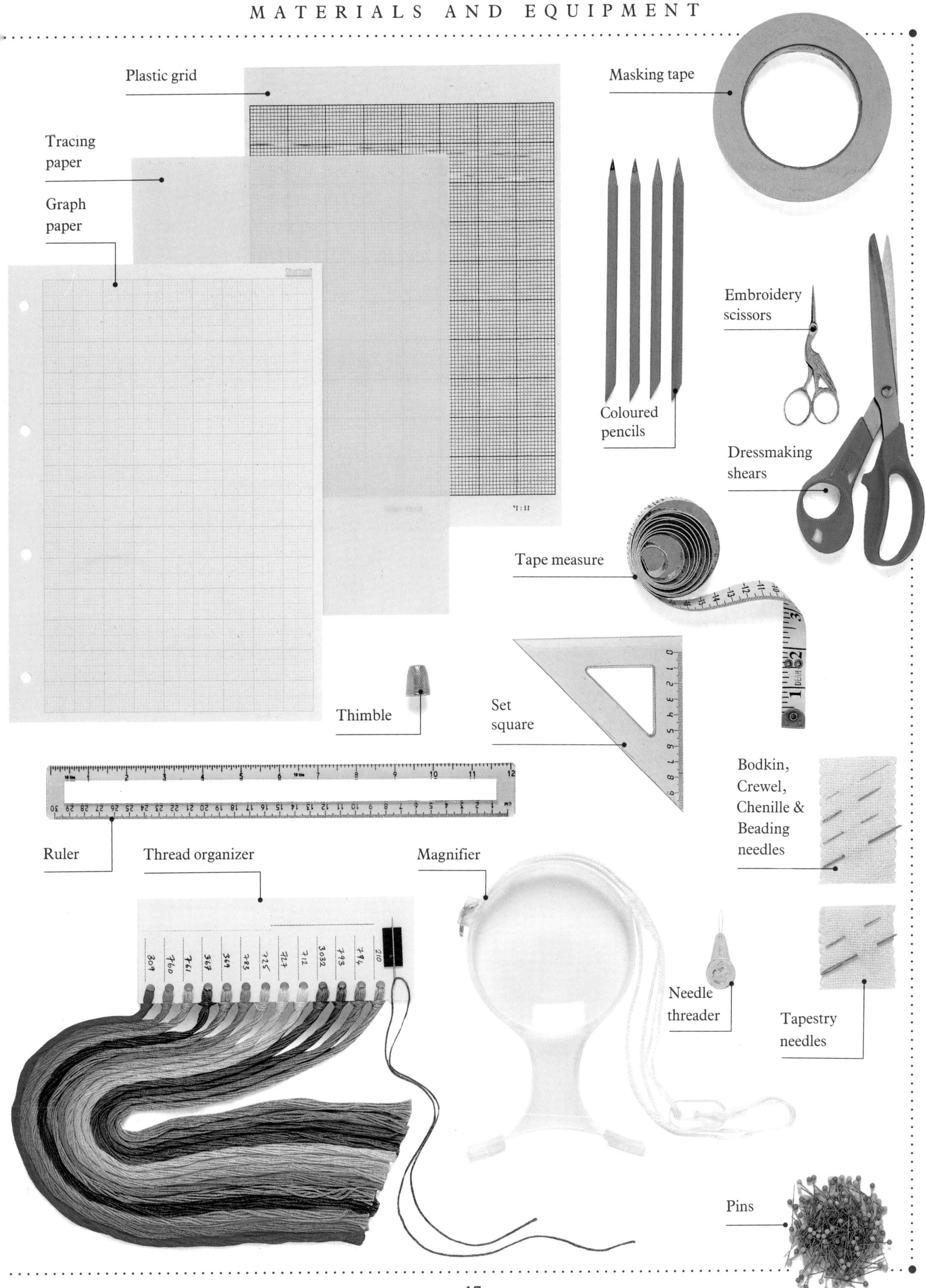
Plastic grid
Tracing paper
Graph paper
Masking tape
Coloured pencils
Embroidery scissors
Dressmaking shears
Tape measure
Thimble
Set square
Ruler
Thread organizer
Magnifier
Bodkin, Crewel, Chenille & Beading needles
Needle threader
Tapestry needles
Pins

Basic Techniques

There are some basic methods and techniques that apply to nearly all forms of counted thread embroidery. It is important to understand and be able to use the methods described in the following pages before starting to work on the projects in this book.

PREPARING THE FABRIC

Some simple and basic preparation is usually required before evenweave fabric is ready to be embroidered. First, it should be preshrunk (if necessary), pressed, and cut to the desired size. Then the raw edges should be bound and the centre clearly marked.

Preshrinking and pressing

If the finished embroidery will ever be washed, it is important to test the fabric in advance for possible shrinkage.

- Cut a small piece of the fabric about 2 in (5 cm) square. Carefully draw around it on a sheet of paper.
- Immerse the square in hand-hot water for about 10 minutes. Allow it to dry, then press it. Place it on the drawn square. If it has shrunk, place the entire piece of fabric in hot water, let it dry, and press it.
- Before stitching on any fabric (whether or not you have preshrunk it), press it to remove any creases. Work on a well-padded ironing board, using either a steam iron or a dry iron and damp cloth.

Cutting the fabric

The fabric should be cut several inches/centimetres larger than the area to be embroidered. Project instructions will normally specify the size, but you may wish to increase the margin of the fabric to allow for a particular size of embroidery frame.

- Cut the fabric along a thread to ensure a straight edge. With most evenweave fabrics, this is easy to do, since the weave of these fabrics is relatively coarse. When working on a very fine evenweave, you should pull out a single thread; that will leave a space which you can use as a cutting guideline (*see illustration below*).

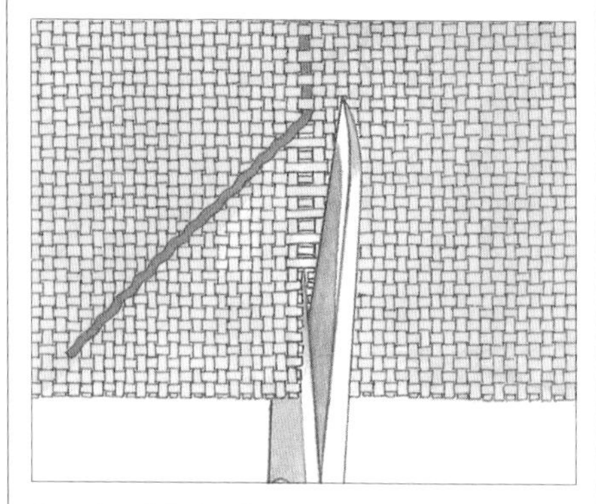

Cutting fabric along a pulled thread

Do not attempt to tear your fabric, as this is likely to distort it.

Binding the fabric edges

It is usually advisable to bind the edges of the fabric before beginning to stitch, to prevent fraying. This can be done by working a line of machine zigzag close to the raw edge or by working overcast stitches by hand (*see illustration below*).

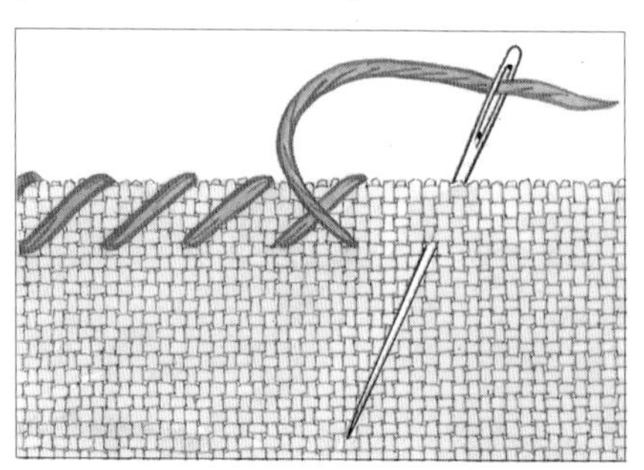

Overcasting edge to prevent fraying

Another way to secure the raw edges is simply to bind them with masking tape, which can be easily removed without damaging the threads.

Straightening the fabric

In counted thread embroidery, it is essential that the fabric be straight — that is, the vertical (*warp*) and horizontal (*weft*) threads must cross each other at right angles. Otherwise the stitching will be distorted.

- To check that the fabric is straight, lay the cut piece on a flat surface, and place a set square (*see pages 16–17*) at each corner in turn. The edges of the fabric should follow those of the set square. If they do not, pull the fabric gently at a 45° angle to the weave (that is, on the bias) until the piece is straight. A little steam from an iron may help with this in difficult cases.

Marking the centre of the fabric

For most counted thread work, you will need to mark the centre of the fabric. This will serve as a guide to positioning the embroidery (*see the starting point on page 21*).

If the complete design is given in the chart and the design is worked in the centre of the fabric, it is usually sufficient to mark the centre point of the fabric only. To do so simply fold the fabric in half horizontally and vertically, finger pressing after each fold. Your stitching can then begin at the point where the lines intersect.

If only part of the design is given on the chart (*for examples see cushion cover chart on page 72*), mark the centre of the design accurately with basting stitches as follows:

- Measure along two adjacent edges of the fabric and then mark the centre carefully with a pin.
- Use a tapestry needle to work a line of basting (long running stitch)

between the fabric threads and through the centre both horizontally and vertically (*see illustration below*).

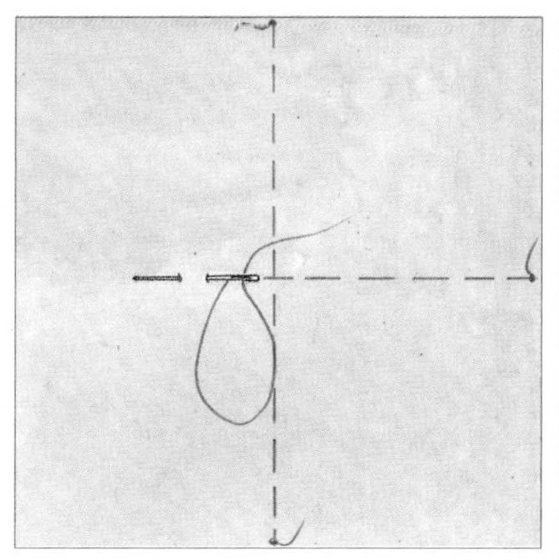

Marking centre with basting

A tapestry needle must be used so that the basting does not interfere with the counted thread stitches and so that it can be easily removed when no longer needed. It is also best to use a contrasting colour for the basting thread. This will help to ensure that the basting is not inadvertently caught up in the embroidery.

FRAMING FABRIC

Once the fabric has been prepared, it can be framed, or mounted, in an embroidery frame (see page 16 for types of frame).

Ideally the frame used should be large enough for the entire area that is to be stitched to be visible. Depending on the size of the embroidery, the fabric can be mounted in either a ring frame or a rectangular frame.

If the embroidery covers a fairly large area, it will not be possible to have the entire stitching area visible. In this case, the fabric will require repositioning, and a ring frame that is large enough for one or more motifs is most suitable.

It is best to avoid repositioning the frame if an embroidered picture is being worked. Unless the picture is very small, a rectangular frame is preferable for this type of project.

Mounting in a ring frame

- Before mounting the fabric, adjust the screw on the outer ring so that the two rings fit together easily but not too tightly.
- Separate the two rings of the frame, and place the inner ring on a flat, firm surface. Place the fabric, face up, on top of it.
- Press the outer ring down over the fabric evenly (*see illustration below*).

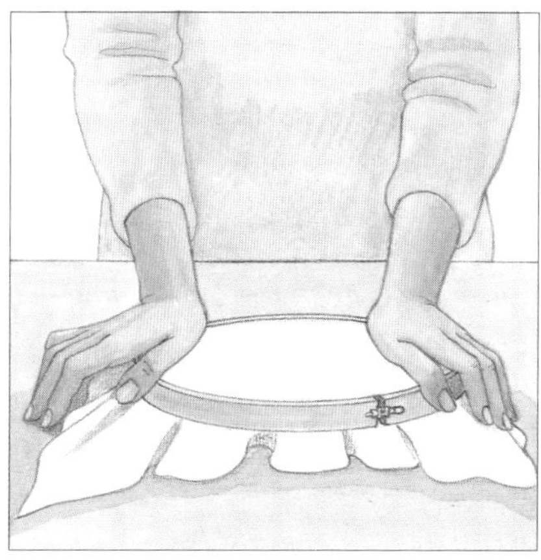

Pressing down the outer ring

Pressing the rings together should require pressure. If the outer ring slips on too easily, retighten it slightly and try again. The fabric should be as taut as a drumhead. Check that the fabric threads are straight.

WORKING WITH A FRAME

Working counted thread embroidery on evenweave fabric mounted in a frame has several advantages. It helps to produce even embroidery stitches, leaves both of your hands free (thereby speeding up your work), and makes counting the fabric threads easier.

Take the time to choose the type of frame most suitable to the size and type of your work (*see framing fabric above*). For a stretcher frame you will need to buy four stretchers, two matching the required width of your fabric and two matching the required length (*see ring and scroll embroidery frames on page 16*).

If previously worked stitching must go between the rings of a ring frame, protect it by placing a sheet of tissue paper over the work before positioning the outer ring; then tear away the tissue from the working area (*see photograph*). The colours not in use in this piece of embroidery are "parked" outside the design area (*see multicoloured embroidery on page 22*).

When you put work in a ring frame aside and will not be working on it for a few days, or even a few hours, loosen the rings. This helps to prevent flattening the stitches caught between the rings. Alternatively, wrap the inner ring with cloth tape before positioning the fabric and outer ring.

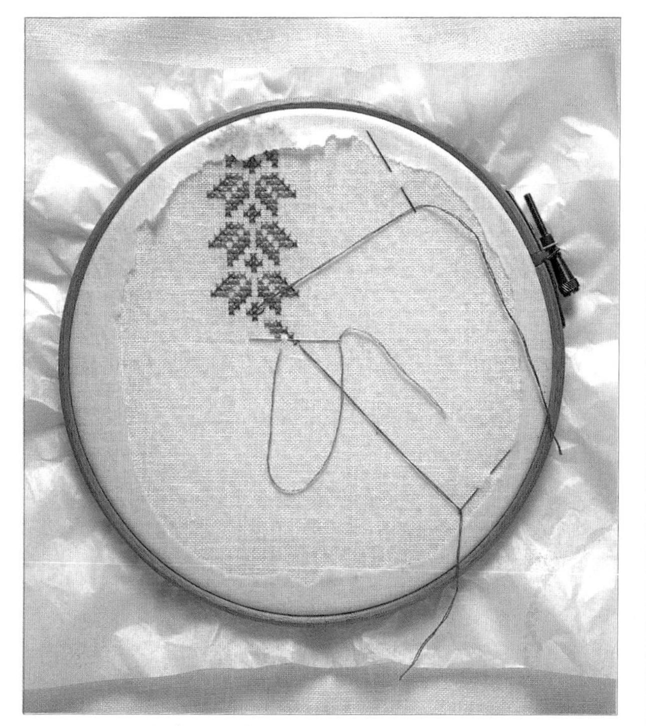

Protecting stitches with tissue paper

Mounting in a stretcher frame

- To mount fabric in a stretcher frame, begin by marking the inner edge of each stretcher at the centre.
- Next mark the centre of each edge of the fabric.
- Match one centre point on the fabric with the corresponding point on the frame and pin the fabric in place at this point.
- Fix the opposite point to the frame in the same way, pulling the fabric taut (*see illustration below*).

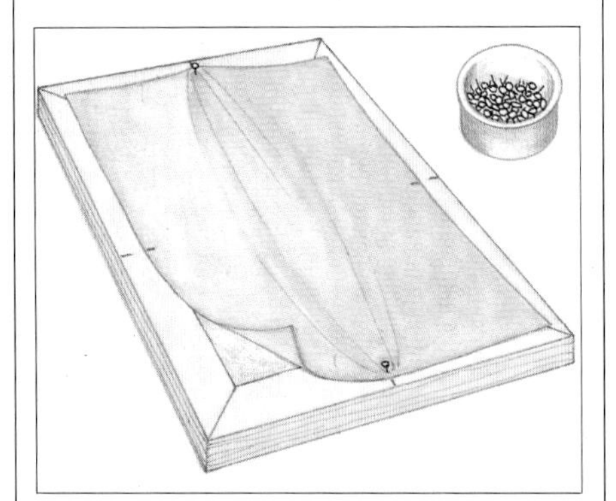

Fixing first two centre points

- Repeat this process in the other direction, so that all four centre points are attached.
- Work outward from these points, along alternating sides, placing pins at intervals of about ¾ in (2 cm) (*see illustration below*).

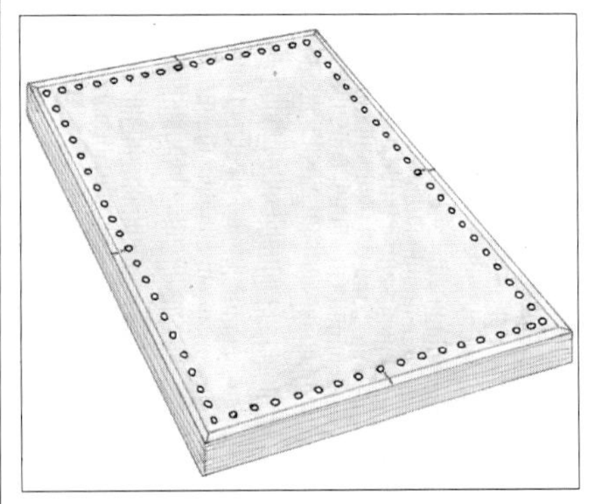

Fabric mounted in a stretcher frame

While mounting, remember to pull the fabric taut and take care to keep the weave straight.

Mounting in a scroll frame

The following basic method of mounting fabric in a scroll frame is suitable for most counted thread work. There are slight variations in the method, depending on the construction of the frame.

- Mark the centre point of the webbing attached to the top and bottom rollers. Bind the side edges of the fabric with a woven cloth tape, using hand or machine stitching.
- Turn under and then carefully press a narrow hem along the top and bottom edges of the fabric.
- Mark the centre points on all sides.
- Starting from the centre, overcast the fabric to the webbing, using strong thread (*see illustration below*).

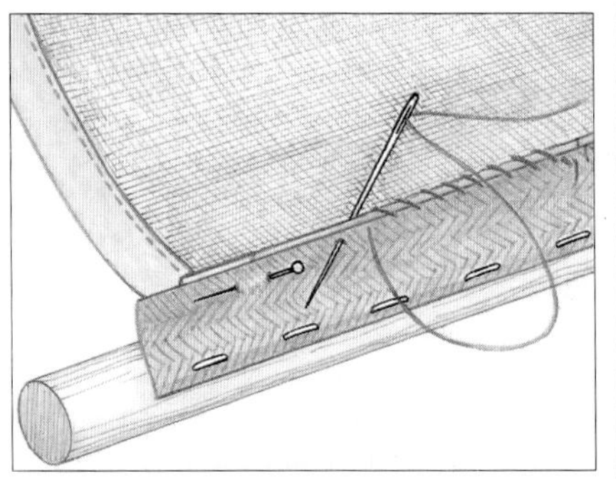

Overcasting the fabric to the webbing

- Attach the battens, or side rollers, to the ends of the top and bottom rollers; fasten them so that the fabric is held fairly taut. (If the fabric is too long, you should roll up the excess at the bottom, the top, or both.)
- Thread a large sharp-pointed needle with string, leaving the string on the ball. Lace the fabric to the batten, stitching through the tape with stitches about 1½ in (4 cm) apart (*see illustration below*).

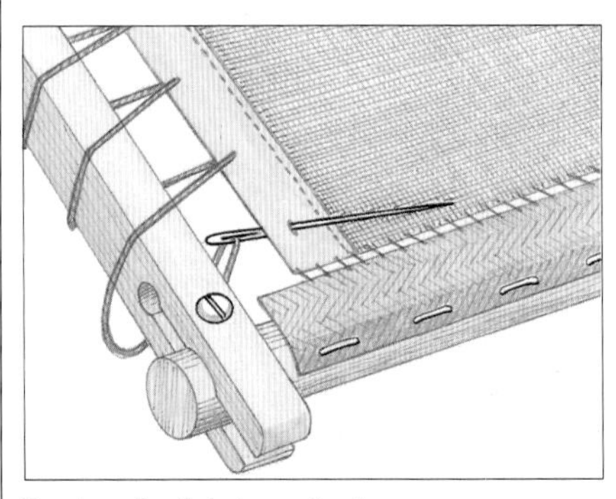

Lacing the fabric to the batten

- Cut the string off, and tie it securely at both ends of the batten.
- Lace the other side of the fabric to the other batten in the same way, pulling the fabric taut.

CHARTS AND DIAGRAMS

Designs for counted thread work are normally given in the form of charts, on which each stitch is indicated.

After reading the project instructions for working a specific embroidery, you can then transfer the design directly onto the fabric by following the chart. Step-by-step stitch diagrams are given for a wide variety of embroidery stitches.

In this book you will find two types of charts: box and line charts. The following section explains these types of chart in detail and gives tips on how to use them in the projects. It also shows how to follow stitch diagrams.

Working from box and line charts

On a cross stitch chart, each square or "box" of the grid represents a stitch, or a space on the fabric, equal to the size of a stitch (*see illustration below*).

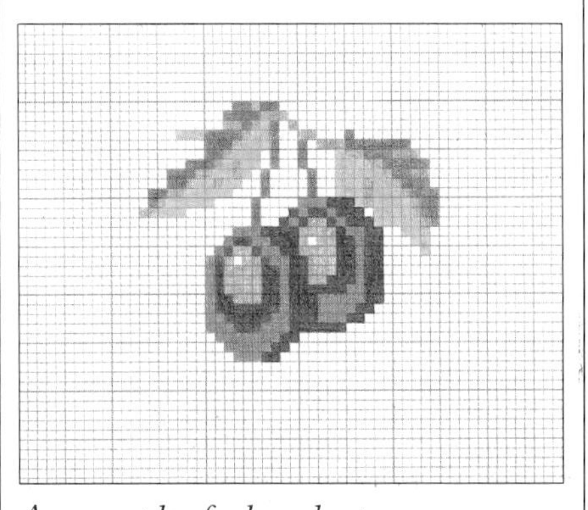

An example of a box chart

Different types of evenweave fabric can be used for counted thread embroidery (*see page 14*). Depending on the evenweave fabric used, each stitch could cover the intersection of two threads (as in Aida cloth) or could be worked over more threads. Thus the lines on the grid of a box chart do *not* represent fabric threads.

When several colours of thread are used, each one is marked on the chart with a colour or symbol. The chart key in the Materials list explains what colour each symbol represents.

On a line chart, the grid lines *do* represent fabric threads, and the stitches are represented by lines drawn on this grid (*see illustration next column*). This type of chart is normally used for stitch diagrams or techniques other than cross stitch.

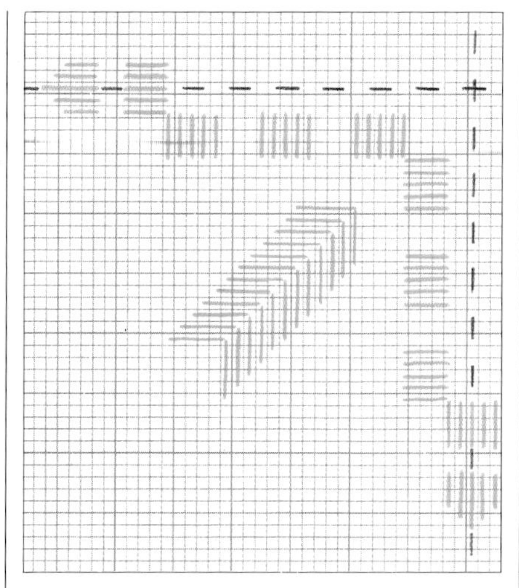

An example of a line chart

These distinctions between box and line charts are not rigid. Different stitches can be given on a box chart (*see blackwork chart on page 105*).

In some charts the stitches are not shown individually; instead, the chart will simply show areas to be filled with certain stitches (*see pulled work chart on page 121*).

Establishing the starting point
When working cross stitch designs, normally start in the centre. Otherwise, you might position the design incorrectly and run out of space. This is the reason for marking the centre of the fabric. In this book the centre of each cross stitch design is marked on the chart with a cross.

For a repeating design (*see the Bulgarian cushion cover on page 72*), only part of the design (that is, one repeat) is charted. After working the section shown, you must either rotate or reverse the chart. The chart will show the centre lines of the design and sometimes a few stitches beyond those lines to get you started on adjoining sections. Where a chart shows only a part of the design, the best starting point is marked with an arrow. The instructions and annotation with the chart will tell you how to complete the design.

Before beginning any counted thread project, study the chart, the colour key, and any annotation to make sure that you understand how to position the design.

Counting chart squares
When counting squares on a chart, it is easier to count across and down, or across and up, rather than to count diagonally.

Reading stitch diagrams
In this book, arrows are sometimes used on stitch diagrams to clarify working instructions. The large, bold arrows indicate where the threaded needle first comes up through the fabric to begin the stitch (*see the pulled work example on page 113*).

Other arrows (smaller ones) are used to show where the needle last went down and where it next comes up (*see illustration below*).

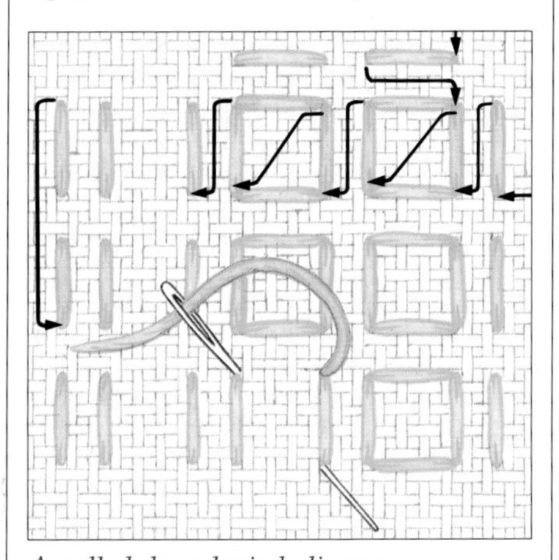

A pulled thread stitch diagram

If the thread must be fastened off for a new starting point, the starting position for the next stitch is indicated on the diagram.

In stitch diagrams, needles are shown as though worked with a sewing motion, flat against the fabric. However, on framed fabric, most stitchers insert needles straight up and down.

Diagrams and left-handed readers
Some of the stitch diagrams will be equally easy to follow for right- and left-handed people, especially if the vertical method of stitching is used. However, a few of the techniques, notably hemstitching, are worked without a frame and shown as worked by right-handed people. In such cases, you may find it useful to prop the book up in front of a mirror and follow the mirror image.

TRANSFERRING DESIGNS

There are various ways of transferring the outline of a counted thread embroidery design onto the fabric. For cross stitch this is usually unnecessary, as the design is worked from a chart. However, some of the other counted thread techniques are worked within outlines, and you will need to transfer these onto the fabric. For this, either of the following methods is suitable.

Tracing
- For this simple method, tape the design to a flat surface.
- Lay the fabric on top, holding it in place with tape or weights, and trace the design directly onto it. Use a water-soluble marking pen, if the work will be washed, or a sharp pencil if it will not.

It may help to darken the design outlines on the paper with a felt-tip pen before you begin. Alternatively, tape the design to a window, then tape the fabric over it; the daylight will make the design outlines visible.

Tracing and basting
This method has the advantage of leaving no mark on the fabric.
- First trace the design carefully and clearly onto tissue paper.
- Frame up the evenweave fabric and baste the tracing over it around all four edges.
- Work small running stitches through both layers around all the design outlines (*see illustration below*).

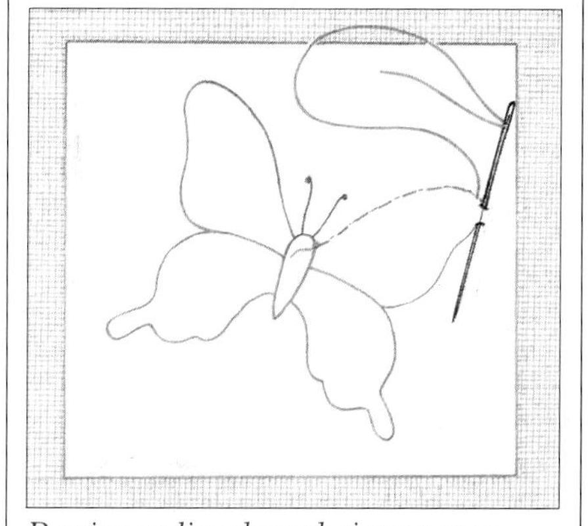

Basting outline through tissue paper

- Finally, gently tear away the tissue, leaving the basted outline on the evenweave fabric.

STITCHING

Every embroiderer has favourite ways of working. Here are some of the most useful techniques. They include tips for preparing your threads, for starting and finishing thread ends, and for working the embroidery stitches.

Preparing the thread

- Cut the thread about 18 in (45 cm) long, shorter if it tends to fray. Threads that are too long will slow down your work considerably.
- To separate stranded cotton floss, gently pull the strands apart. For a smooth effect, especially in cross stitch, it is a good idea to separate the strands first, then rejoin those required for the stitching.
- To thread a needle, flatten the strand(s) between finger and thumb and slip the end through the eye of the needle. Or use a needle threader (*see illustration below*).

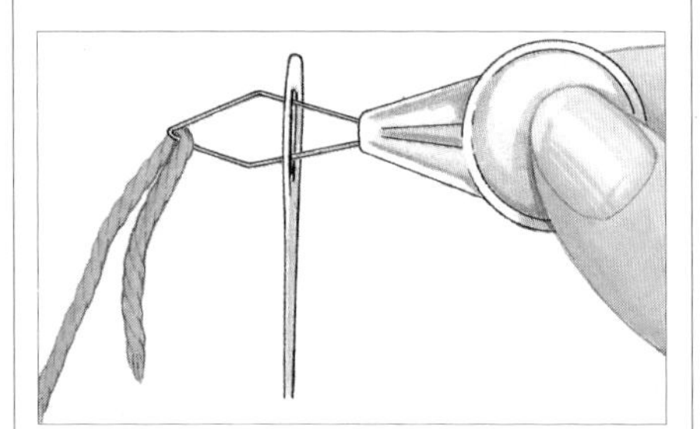

Using a needle threader

- An alternative method of threading the needle without a needle threader is to loop the thread around the end of the needle, hold this tightly, and then press the needle eye firmly down over the loop.

Starting and finishing the thread

Do not begin work with a knot on the wrong side of the fabric. It either will make a bump (visible on the right side) or will pull through the work after you have started stitching. Instead, it is better to use one of the following methods:

Beginning with a waste knot:

- Knot the end of the thread and insert the needle from front to back, a few inches/centimetres ahead of the line of stitching.
- Bring the needle up at the starting point (indicated on the charts by an arrow) and work your first stitches over the thread on the underside (*see illustration below*).

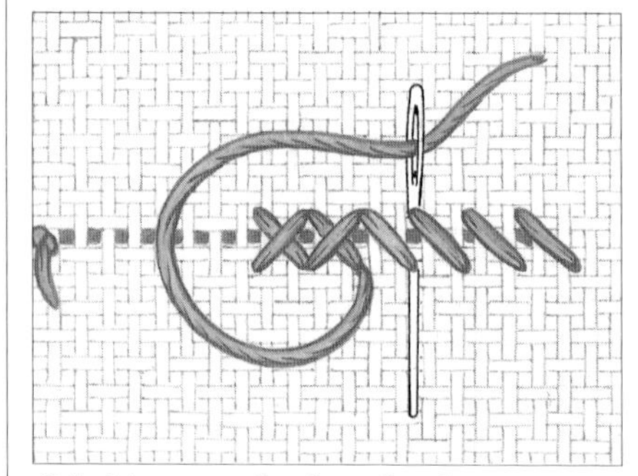

Stitching over the thread end

After the thread end has been secured in this way, cut off the knot close to the surface.

Beginning with backstitches:

- Work one or two backstitches just before the starting point to anchor the thread securely.
- Stitch until you have covered the backstitches (*see illustration below*).

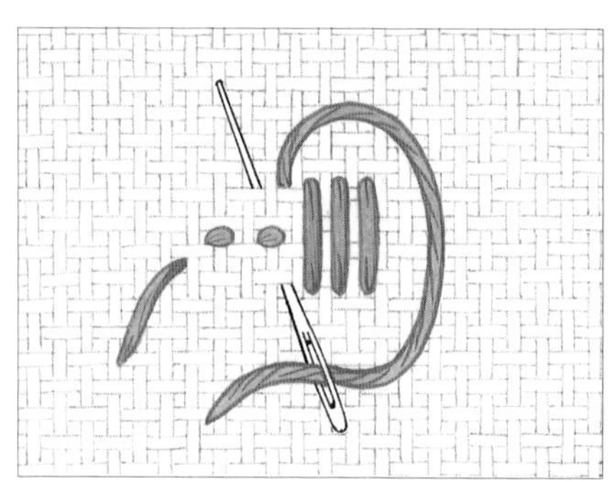

Stitching over a backstitch fastening

- Cut off the thread end carefully so that it is close to the surface.

Beginning by fastening the thread to existing stitches:

- If some stitches have already been worked in the area, you can fasten the new thread on the wrong side by taking it through the underside of the existing stitches and anchoring it with one or two backstitches.
- A new thread can also be fastened in this way by leaving a long end on the right side, away from the work, fastened with a couple of backstitches; later it can be undone and threaded into a needle and secured on the wrong side. For tightly worked stitches, you may prefer to use a crewel needle, which has a sharp point, to fasten threads this way.

Finishing thread ends:

- To finish a thread, simply run it through the stitches below.

Do not carry threads across long distances on the wrong side. Depending on the weight of the fabric and the colour of the thread, such jumps may be visible. As a general rule, avoid jumps longer than ½ in (1.25 cm).

Working the stitches

If your work is in a frame, work the stitches straight up and down with a stabbing motion. Ideally, the frame should be supported on a stand or propped against a table so that you can use both hands for stitching to speed up work. If you are right-handed, keep your left hand on top.

Wherever possible, bring the needle up through a "clean" hole (one with no stitches) and take it down through a "dirty" hole (one already containing one or more stitches). This produces a smoother effect.

Multicoloured embroidery

In a multicoloured design you may find it convenient to use several colours simultaneously rather than fastening off small amounts. One way to do this is to "park" needles when not in use (*see page 19*). Simply take the needle out of the way of the stitching on the right side and insert it in the fabric temporarily.

Another fastening off method is to use only one needle, remove it from the discontinued thread, and pin this thread securely out of the way on the right side of the fabric.

Stitching tension

Stitching with a consistent tension produces beautiful work in which the stitches are even and smooth, and neither too tight nor too loose. Using an embroidery frame will also help improve your tension.

Practice helps too! Before beginning a project, work a small sample to familiarize yourself with the stitches, fabric, and thread.

DESIGN TECHNIQUES

After you have worked some of the projects in this book, you may wish to try your hand at adapting designs or creating original designs. Here are a few practical techniques to get you started.

Adapting charted designs

It is relatively easy to enlarge or reduce the scale of a charted cross stitch design. You can use a different count of fabric or work the stitches over a different number of threads. For example, a design that is worked over two threads of evenweave fabric can easily be made 50 percent larger simply by working the stitches over three fabric threads.

To change the fabric, use the following procedure:

- Divide the number of stitches across the design by the desired size in inches (inches must be used because the thread count is based on this unit) of the finished work. This will give you the number of stitches per inch in the enlarged design.

For example, if the original design is worked on 16-count Aida and has 128 stitches across and thus measures 8 in (20 cm) and you wish it to be 12 in (30 cm) across, divide 128 by 12 to get 10.67 stitches per inch. To obtain your desired size, you could use either 11-count Aida fabric or a 22-count single thread evenweave fabric.

- Check the finished size by dividing the number of stitches by the stitch count. In this case, 128 divided by 11 equals 11.64 in (29.5 cm), only a little less than the desired size. Check the length measurement in the same way.

Adapting drawn designs

The quickest way to enlarge or reduce the scale of a design that is drawn, rather than charted, is to take it to a photocopier and have it done mechanically.

You can also scale it up or down using a grid as follows:

- If the design is not printed with a grid, draw one on top, making all the squares the same size.
- Draw another grid containing the same number of squares, but making each square larger or smaller as required. For example, if the original grid has 1 in (2.5 cm) squares, and you wish to increase the design by 50 percent, draw a new grid with 1½ in (3.8 cm) squares.
- Copy the design square by square onto the grid (*see illustration below*).

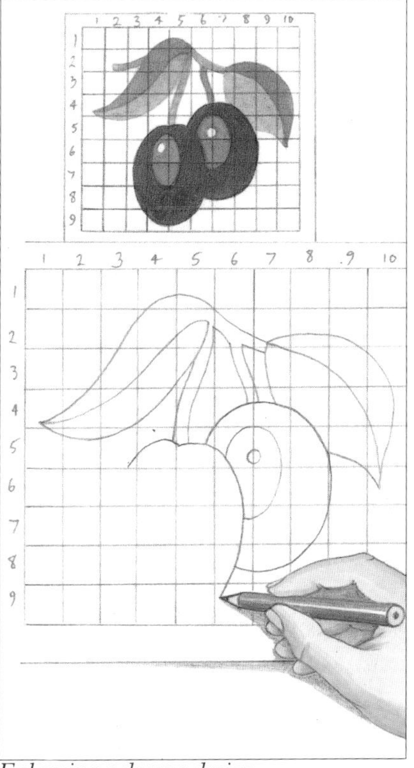

Enlarging a drawn design

MAKING YOUR OWN CROSS STITCH CHART

As you become more confident in using cross stitch charts, you may wish to create your own from a photograph or drawing. To do this, you need to place a grid over your chosen picture.

Sheets of acetate printed with grids of various sizes are available in needlecraft shops. When the acetate grid is in place, your picture is instantly converted to a chart; squares containing two colours are assigned to one colour or the other. You can stitch directly from this, provided that the acetate grid is fixed securely to the source picture. Or copy the image onto graph paper, square by square, using coloured pencils (*see photograph right*).

Tracing paper printed with a squared grid is also available in shops that sell artists' supplies. Fix the paper over the picture, then colour in the squares.

You can change the size of the original image by selecting a grid smaller or larger than the stitch count used for your cross stitch chart. For example, place a 14-count grid (14 stitches to the inch) over the source, but stitch it on 11-count Aida cloth (11 stitches to the inch) to make it about 25 percent larger.

Charting a cross stitch design

Cross Stitch

With the exception of running stitch, cross stitch is probably the most widely used of all stitches. It is used to embellish clothing and furnishings in countries as diverse as Russia, Iran, Bulgaria, Thailand, Mexico, and Denmark. In Western Europe and North America it is today more popular than ever and is used in a wide range of styles, from naïve to subtle and intricate. Cross stitch is ideal both for decorating practical objects and also for creating more sophisticated pictorial embroideries. Its regular square shape and smooth, appealing texture can be used successfully for outlines, fillings, Assisi work, borders and motifs.

Cross Stitch Techniques

The popularity of cross stitch is easily explained: it is extremely simple to work, and it lends itself beautifully to solid blocks of colour as well as fine detail. Here are the methods for working basic cross stitch and five interesting and useful cross stitch variations.

BASIC CROSS STITCH

The basic cross stitch is simply a diagonal cross worked between the four corners of a square. When worked on evenweave fabric it is normally worked over two vertical (warp) *and two horizontal* (weft) *threads (or pairs of threads on Hardanger fabric). On Aida cloth the cross stitch is worked over one or two intersections of the grouped threads* (see two-sided cross stitch).

To reduce or enlarge the size of the stitches, choose finer or coarser fabric and embroidery thread, or work the stitches over a different number of threads. Cross stitches should cover the fabric fairly densely, though not solidly.

Working an individual stitch

- To work one cross stitch at a time, bring the needle up at the lower right-hand corner, down at the upper left-hand corner, and up at the lower left-hand corner (*see illustration below:* **1**).
- Cross the first diagonal formed with another worked from lower left to upper right to complete the stitch (**2**).

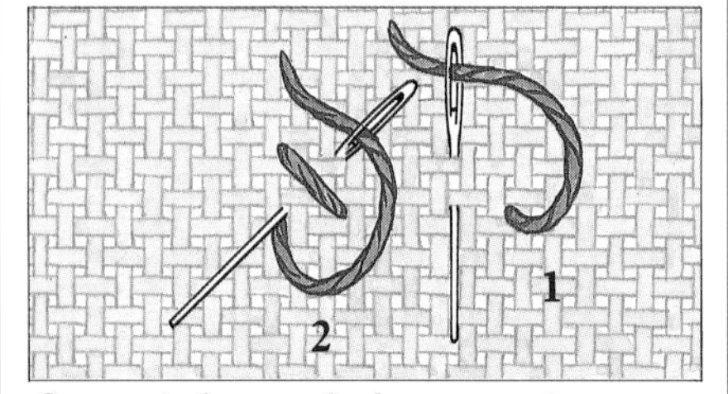

Cross stitches worked one at a time

- To work the stitches in a row from right to left, bring the needle up at the lower left-hand corner to begin the next stitch. The needle is shown in position to work the next stitch (*see illustration next column*).

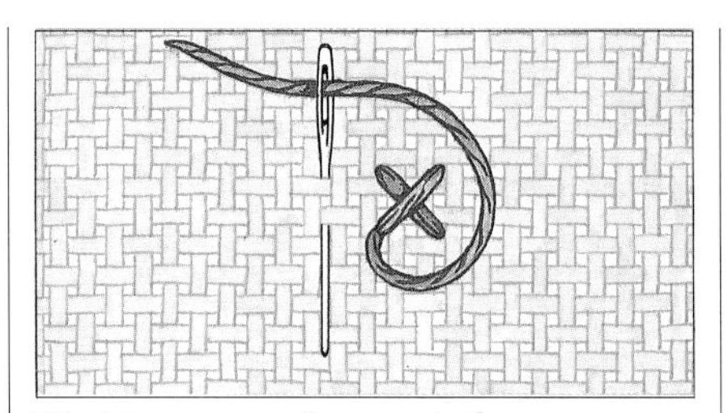

Working a row of cross stitch

The cross stitch can be reversed so that the top half slants from lower right to upper left; many left-handed embroiderers find this easier. It is important only to be consistent; be sure all stitches are crossed in the same direction.

Working the stitch in two journeys

Working one cross stitch at a time produces the most even effect, but working the stitches in two journeys is quicker for covering large areas. This method also uses slightly less thread and helps to ensure that all the stitches slant the same way.

- To work cross stitch rows in two journeys, first work all of the lower stitches in the row (*see starting arrow on illustration below*). Then cross these stitches on the return journey.

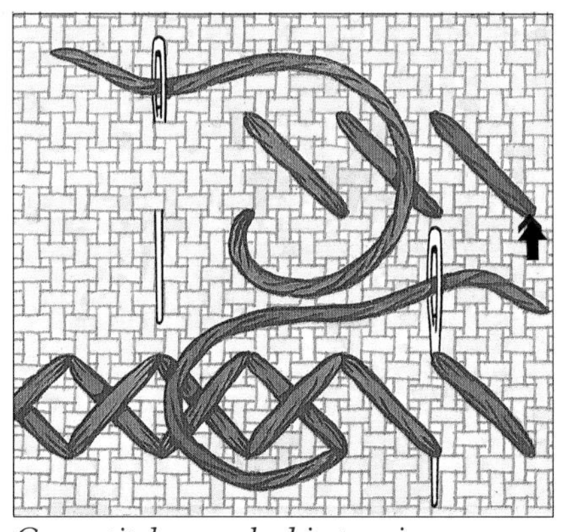

Cross stitches worked in two journeys

OBLONG CROSS STITCH

This stitch is the simplest variation of the basic cross stitch. It is typically worked over two warp threads and four weft threads (or vice versa) and forms a long and narrow cross stitch.

As it is worked below, the resulting stitches appear tall and thin. However, if the drawing is turned sideways and the stitch is then worked over four weft threads and two warp threads, the result will be a short, wide stitch.

Working the stitch

- To work oblong cross stitch, work the first half of the stitch from right to left. Cross these diagonals on the return journey (*see illustration below*).

Even rows of oblong cross stitch

Staggering the rows of oblong cross stitches creates an interesting texture (*see illustration below*).

Staggered rows of oblong cross stitch

SMYRNA STITCH

Also called leviathan or double cross stitch, this variation combines well with basic cross stitch and can be used as an "accent". For example, it could be used to suggest the single blossom of a flower. Other possibilities are shown on page 31. Smyrna stitch can also be worked in rows as well.

Interesting two-colour effects can be created by working the upright cross in a contrasting colour. Stranded cotton is the most versatile embroidery thread for cross stitch (see page 15).

Working the stitch

Smyrna stitch is shown here worked over four warp and four weft threads, but on Aida cloth the stitch can be worked over two groups of threads.

- To begin the stitch, you should first make a basic cross stitch (*see illustration below:* **1**, **2**, **3**, **4**).
- Make a vertical stitch by bringing the needle up at the centre of the base of the cross stitch (**5**) and down at the centre top (**6**).

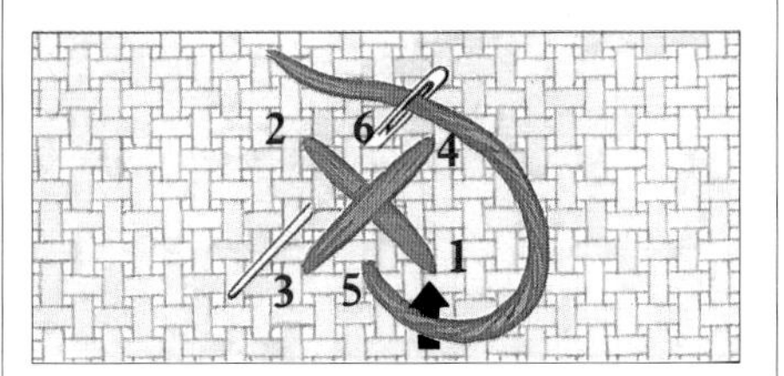

Beginning the Smyrna stitch

- Make a final horizontal stitch by bringing the needle up at centre left (*see illustration below:* **7**) and down at centre right (**8**), thus forming an upright cross over the basic cross stitch base. The needle is shown in position to begin the next stitch.

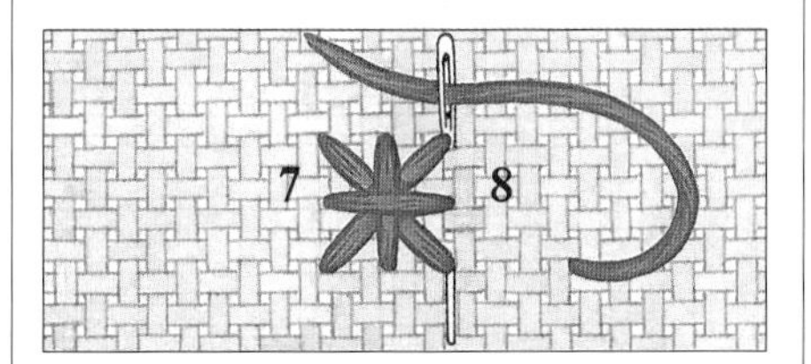

Completed stitch and start of next stitch

- To work Smyrna stitch in rows, begin at the upper left-hand corner of your embroidery and work from left to right. Work back from right to left on the row below.

TWO-SIDED CROSS STITCH

Because it produces cross stitches on both sides of the fabric, this method of working cross stitch is useful for items such as handkerchiefs, where both sides of the fabric will be visible.

Two-sided cross stitch is worked in four journeys across a single row of stitches. The four journeys and the half stitches made at one end of the row are necessary in order to form a double-sided stitch.

Working the stitch

Before you begin, secure the thread on the right-hand side. This leaves a long loose end to fasten off later (*see page 22*).

- Work a row of diagonal stitches from right to left as for basic cross stitch, but omit every other stitch.
- At the end of the row, bring the needle up in the centre, under the last diagonal stitch. Then take the needle out to the left of the stitch.
- Take the needle down at the lower left-hand corner, then bring it up in the centre again, but to the right of the stitch. This now forms a half stitch (*see illustration below*).

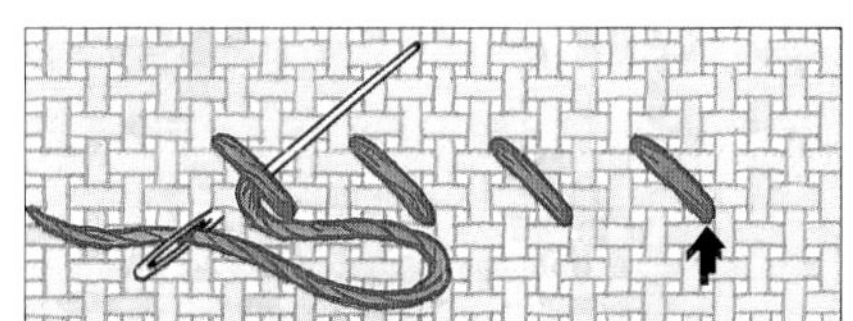
Starting the second journey

- Take the needle down at the upper right-hand corner of the end stitch and up at the lower left-hand corner of the next (*see illustration below*).

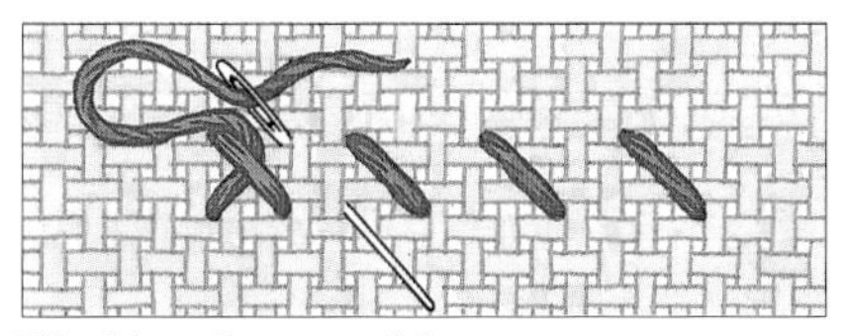
Working the second journey

- Work back across the row to complete the cross stitches.
- At the end of the row, take the needle down at the upper right-hand corner of the last stitch to complete the last stitch.
- To begin the third journey, you should bring the needle up at the lower left-hand corner of the end stitch (*see illustration below*).
- Work back across the row, filling in the spaces with diagonal stitches.

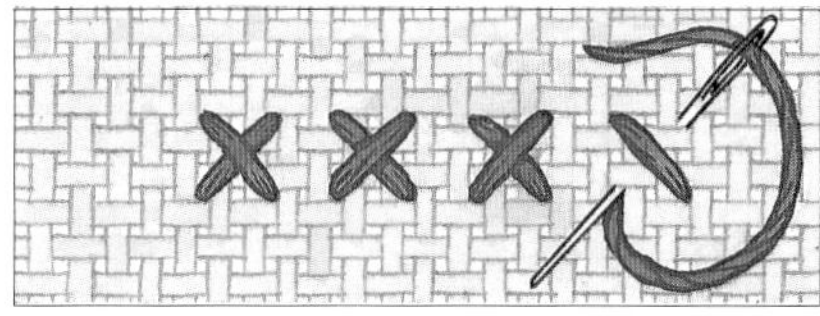
Starting the third journey

- At the end of the row, bring the needle up again at the lower left-hand corner of the last stitch.
- Take it down in the centre of the stitch, thus covering the half-stitch made at the end of the first pass.
- Bring the needle up at the lower left-hand corner of the next stitch (*see illustration below*).

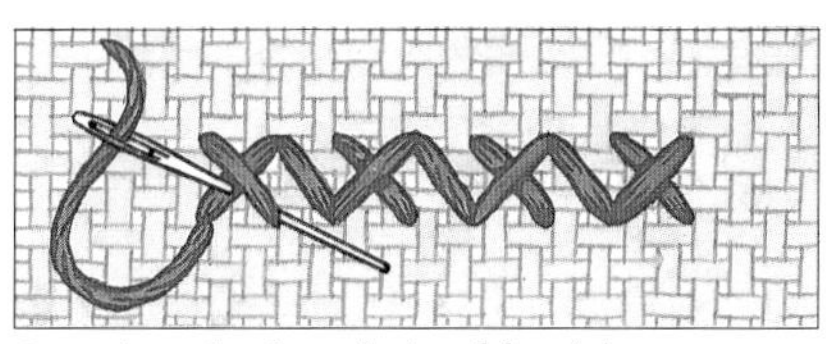
Starting the fourth (and last) journey

- Work across the row, completing the stitches. Note that the last stitch to the left will have a different slant; this is unavoidable.
- When the work is complete, secure the thread neatly under the last stitch. Now unfasten the beginning thread end, thread it into a needle, and fasten it securely.

ITALIAN CROSS STITCH

This cross stitch variation should be worked in a relatively thin thread in order to display its structure – a cross enclosed in a square. Using a thin thread also reduces bulk at the four corners of each stitch where the needle must be brought through several times.

Italian cross stitch looks the same on both sides of the fabric and can be used for the background stitching in Assisi work (see page 29).

Each successive row of stitches is worked on top of the previous one.

Working the stitch

- Starting at the lower left-hand corner of your embroidery, make a straight stitch from left to right over the chosen number of fabric threads.
- Bring the needle up at the chosen starting point.
- Make a diagonal stitch to the upper right-hand corner, again bringing the needle up at the starting point (*see illustration next column*).

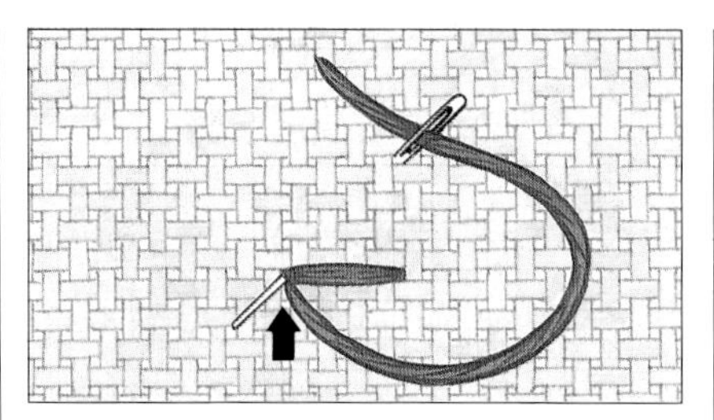

Making first side of square and first diagonal

- Make a vertical stitch to the upper left-hand corner, bringing the needle out at the lower right-hand corner (*see illustration below*). The needle is in position to begin the next stitch.

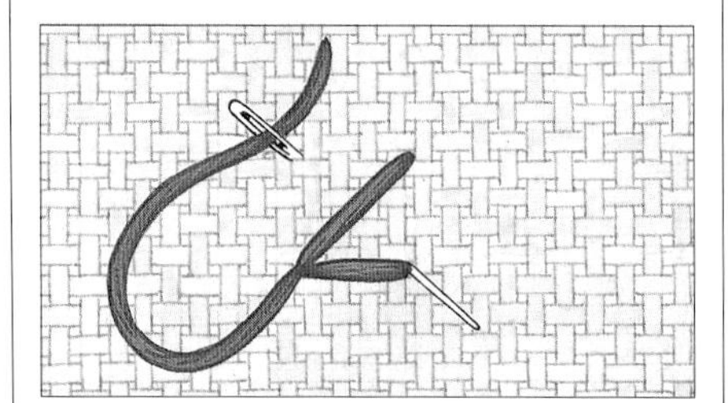

Making second side of square and bringing needle up to begin next stitch

- Continue in this way to the end of the row. Then at the end of the row, work a single vertical stitch as shown (*see illustration below*).

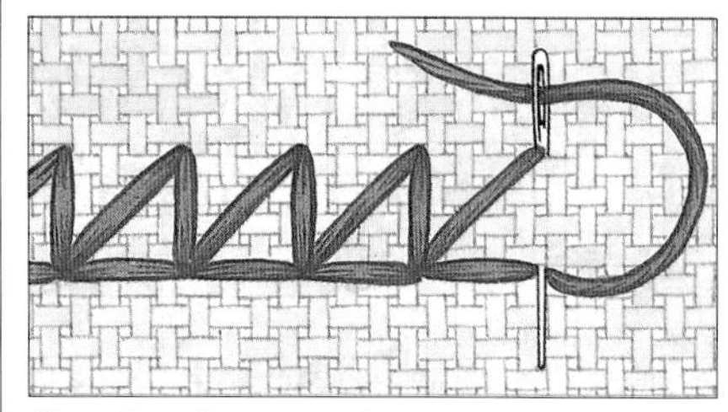

Starting the return journey

Work back across the row, crossing the first diagonal stitches as you go (*see illustration below*).

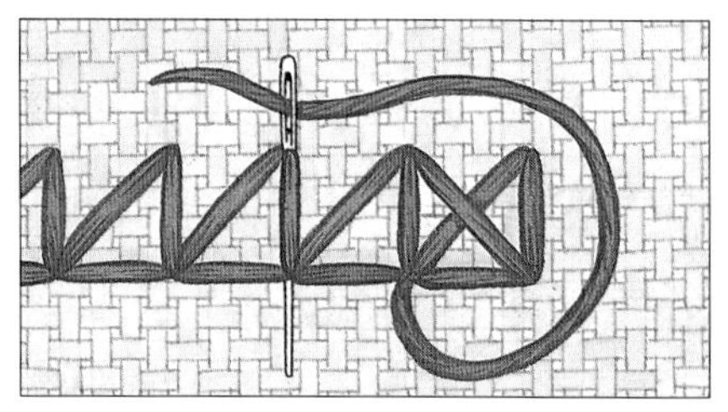

Working the return journey

CROSS STITCH ON NON-EVENWEAVE FABRIC

To work basic cross stitch on non-evenweave fabric, such as sweatshirt material, cut a piece of needlepoint canvas slightly larger than the design area. It can be either single- or double-thread, but not interlock.

Allow two canvas threads for each stitch. For example, if the scale is 14 stitches to 1 in (2.5 cm), use either 28-gauge single-thread canvas or 14-gauge double-thread canvas. For very fine work allow a single thread intersection for each stitch.

Using a canvas grid

Baste the piece of canvas to the background fabric outside the area to be stitched (*see photograph lower left*), aligning the canvas grid with the warp and weft of the fabric as closely as possible.

Using a crewel or chenille needle, fasten the thread by working the first stitches over the end (*see page 22*). Work the cross stitches with a firm tension to compensate for the thickness of the canvas. When the embroidery is complete, remove the basting and unravel any canvas threads that are not covered by cross stitches (*see photograph lower right*). Then carefully remove the other canvas threads, one at a time. (This is why the canvas should not be interlock.) It may also help to dampen the work slightly to allow the individual threads to be removed more easily.

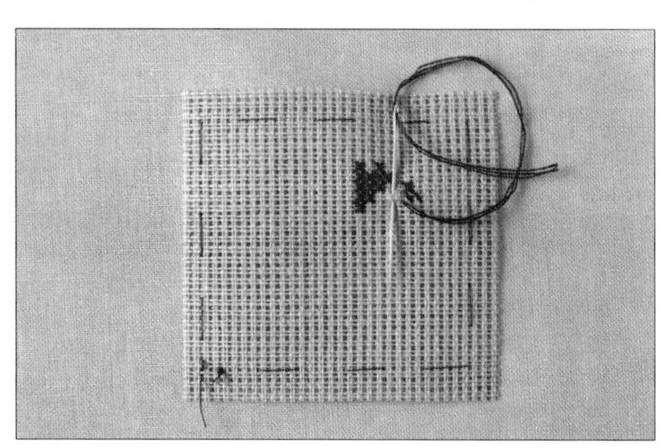

Working cross stitches over a canvas grid

Removing the canvas threads

LONG-ARMED CROSS STITCH

Also known as long-legged cross stitch, this stitch consists of crossed stitches that overlap each other, producing an attractive braided effect.

For a clearly defined effect, use a relatively thin embroidery thread.

Working the stitch

The longer arm of the stitch is shown below worked over eight vertical threads and four horizontal threads. However, it can be worked over more or fewer threads as long as it is twice as wide as it is tall.

- Bring the needle up at the lower left-hand corner (*see illustration below:* **1**) and down eight threads to the right, four threads up (**2**). Bring the needle up again four threads below (**3**).

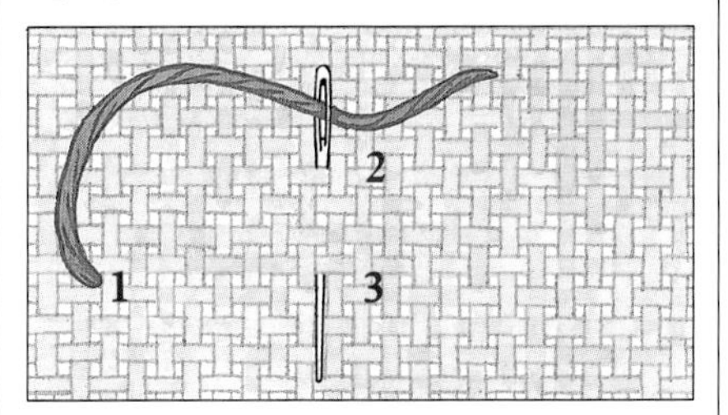

Working the longer arm of the stitch

- Take the needle down at the upper left-hand corner, four threads to the left (*see illustration below:* **4**), and bring it up four threads below.
- Working from left to right, make the adjoining cross stitches in the same way.

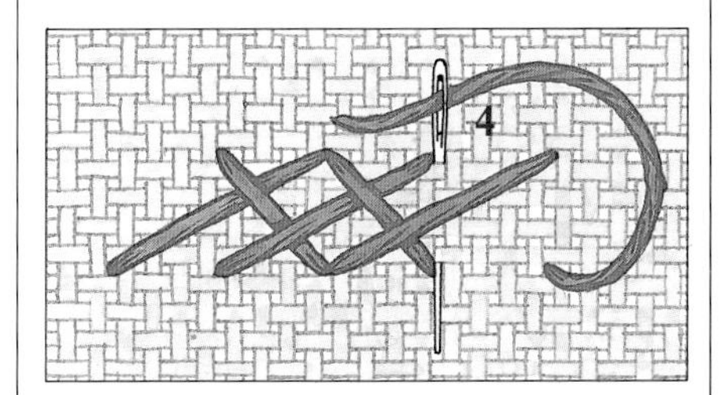

Completing the long-armed cross stitch

Work each row under the previous one. An interestingly varied texture can be created by reversing the direction of working on each row.

ASSISI EMBROIDERY

As its name suggests, Assisi work is of Italian origin. It is a type of cross stitch embroidery in which the background is filled with stitching and the motifs are left mainly unstitched, forming a reversed or negative image. This design technique is called voiding. The outlines of the motifs are worked in double running stitch, as also are any details within the motif. This stitch is also known as Holbein stitch, because of its frequent appearance in the costumes of 16th-century aristocrats painted by Hans Holbein.

Assisi work flourished chiefly in the 17th century, although the term dates only from the beginning of the 20th century when this style of embroidery was revived in and around Assisi. Traditional Assisi work is wonderfully complex, filled with mythical creatures, such as dragons, and complex, swirling, interlaced vines and foliage. Borders of delicate scrollwork in double running stitch help to soften the outline of the rectangular stitched areas and sometimes link one motif with another.

Choosing colours and threads

Assisi work is well suited to household linens and other furnishings, and can also be used to decorate clothing and accessories – for example, a belt or the cuffs of a blouse. It is not essential to stick to the traditional dark red cross stitch filling, black outlines and cream fabric, but a good contrast of light and dark colour should be used in order to preserve the distinctive character of the work. Dark blue or green shows up well against white or cream fabric, but you could also try black thread on pale blue or wine red on pearl grey.

Various types of embroidery thread can be used, but a smooth single thread such as perlé cotton or coton à broder is ideal, as it gives the stitching a crisp effect.

Working the outlines

- First work around the outlines (following a chart or a line of basting stitches) with even running stitches. In the sample the stitches are worked over two fabric threads. Go back over the single running stitches, filling in the spaces (*see illustration below*).

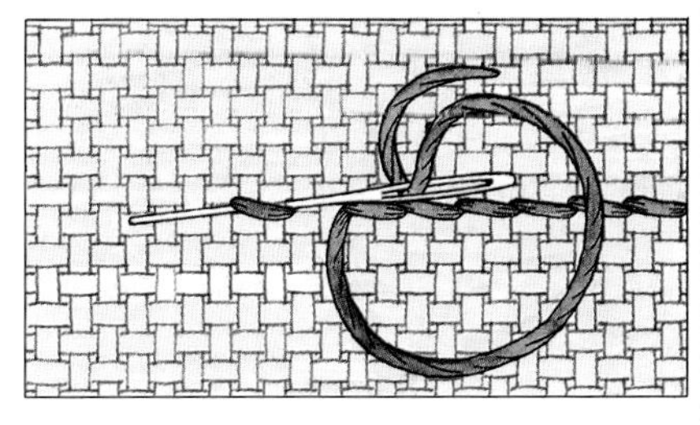

Working double running stitch

- To keep the second journey straight, always insert the needle above the stitch and bring it up below the stitch as shown above.

Filling in the background

When the outlining is complete, fill in the background with cross stitch (*see illustration below*) or, if you prefer, Italian, two-sided, or long-armed cross stitch.

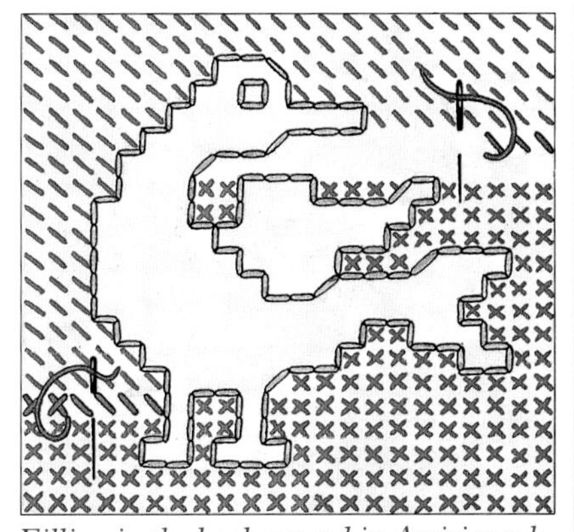

Filling in the background in Assisi work

- In some Assisi work the running stitches may need to go diagonally over the fabric in places for a smoother outline. If this is the case in your embroidery, you will need to fill the half square of background with a single diagonal stitch.

Working the motif

- Finally, add any details within the motif, using double running stitch.

Cross Stitch Project Variations

Simple basic cross stitch is the most versatile of all of the many embroidery techniques that are worked by forming crossed stitches in various configurations. With the exception of the Peacock Placemat (*see page 82*), all of the projects with instructions in this chapter are worked in simple basic cross stitch. Here are some suggestions for how to use the other cross stitch techniques given on pages 26 to 29.

In Assisi work the background is filled with stitching and the motifs are left mainly unstitched. This attractive bird and leaf design shows how creative the voiding technique can be.

OBLONG CROSS STITCH

Oblong cross stitch produces a texture fairly similar to basic cross stitch's, but because the stitch has an oblong rather than a square shape, it does not produce such a smooth and regular surface. It is best suited to large motifs in solid colours. It can also be used to create interesting colour effects in staggered rows *(see page 26)*.

Sample of oblong cross stitch

SMYRNA STITCH

Smyrna stitch produces a striking and distinctive texture that is very hard wearing. Try using it for the snowflake Christmas Tree Sachet design *(see page 66)*, working each individual Smyrna stitch over four fabric threads. If you choose a 28-count fabric, this will make the embroidered motif twice as large as on the sachet.

This size of embroidery in Smyrna stitch would also make an attractive pin cushion or brooch cushion. Experiments with different threads and background fabrics.

Sample of Smyrna stitch

TWO-SIDED CROSS STITCH

Two-sided cross stitch *(see page 27)* is suitable for items where both sides of the fabric will be visible *(see Clematis Napkins on page 59 and Peacock Napkins on page 82)*. The Greetings Card motifs *(see page 68)* adapt easily to a handkerchief. For an extra-neat finish on the wrong side, use two-sided cross stitch. Bookmarks *(see page 85)* would also be attractive.

Sample of two-sided cross stitch

ITALIAN CROSS STITCH

Italian cross stitch is identical on both sides of the fabric and is slightly more durable than two-sided cross stitch. The Eagle motif on the Tote Bag *(see page 53)* could be used for an attractive cushion design.

To vary the texture, work the design in Italian cross stitch *(see page 28)*, either using a thinner thread or working the stitches over four fabric threads, rather than three. This will then make the motif 25 percent larger. This stitch could also be used on napkins *(see page 82)*.

Sample of Italian cross stitch

CROSS STITCH ON NON-EVENWEAVE

Several of the cross stitch projects in this chapter could be worked on a non-evenweave if desired. You will need to work the basic stitch over a canvas grid *(see page 28)*.

LONG-ARMED CROSS STITCH

The long arms of this stitch create a very attractive braided texture. Long-armed cross stitch is well worth experimenting with and will give a very different look to a simple basic cross stitch motif worked in a solid colour. This stitch can also be used as the background filling stitch in Assisi embroidery *(see page 82)* – as shown in the photograph opposite.

Sample of long-armed cross stitch

ASSISI EMBROIDERY

The Peacock Placemat *(see page 82)* and the samples below and opposite illustrate the type of motifs used in creating a voided design. Some of the motifs on pages 33–49 could also be used for Assissi work.

Sample of Assisi work

Cross Stitch Motifs

The following pages contain a wide variety of motifs to make using the basic techniques described in the previous section. They include flowers and fruit, birds and animals, alphabets and numerals, traditional motifs, and a selection of borders. These inspirational designs can be used in many different ways on your own original cross stitch projects. For example, the alphabets can form monograms on linens, clothing or accessories. Use a border to embellish the hem of a skirt or the lower edge of a curtain. Embroider a bird or animal on a child's T-shirt or add a festive Christmas motif to a Christmas stocking.

If the material is not evenweave, work the motif over canvas (*see page 28*). To turn a corner on a border, place a small mirror diagonally across the corner square and copy the reflection. If the border is asymmetrical, like the Greek key, the design must be reversed at the centre.

FLORAL ALPHABET

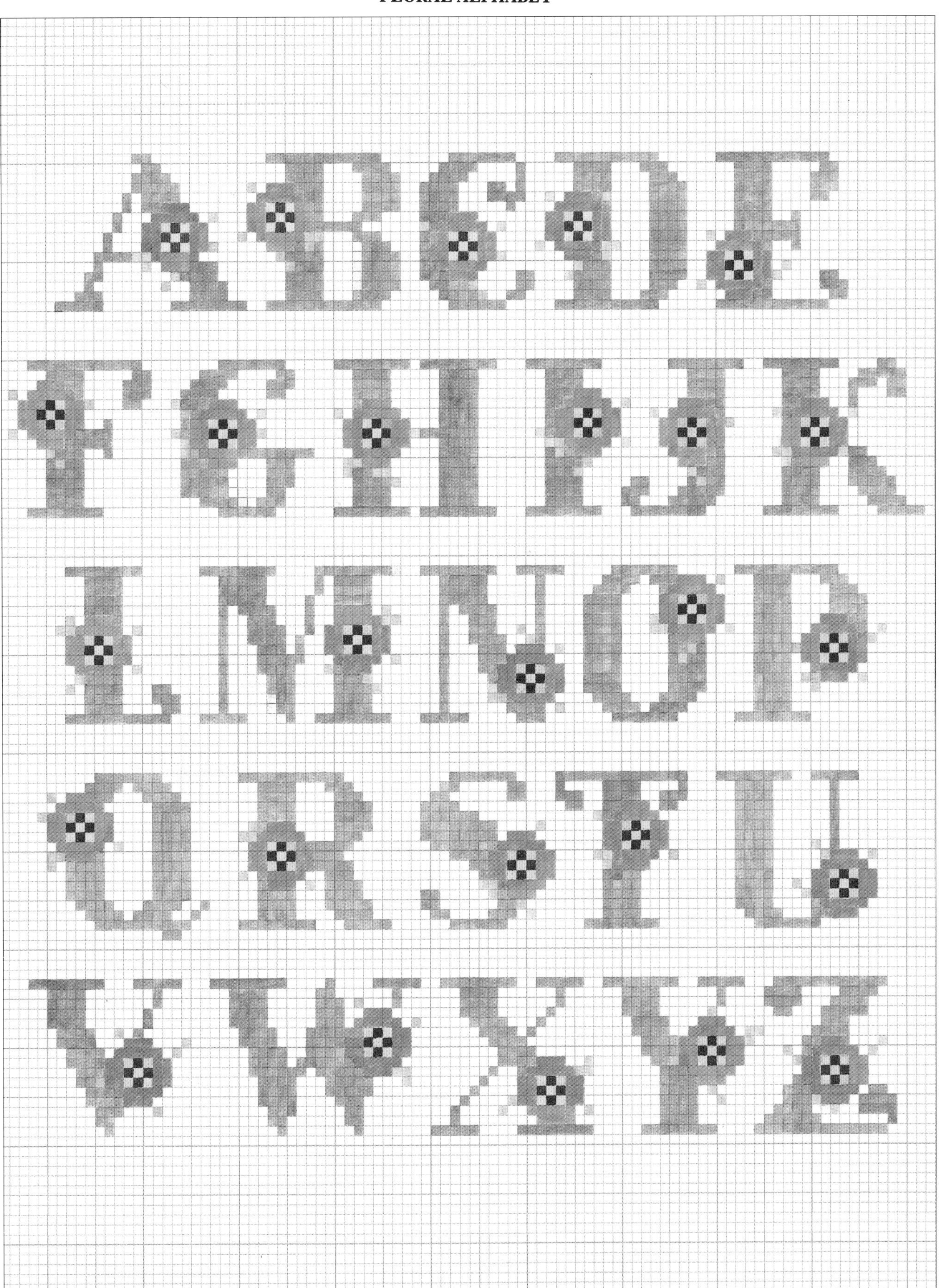

SCRIPT ALPHABET

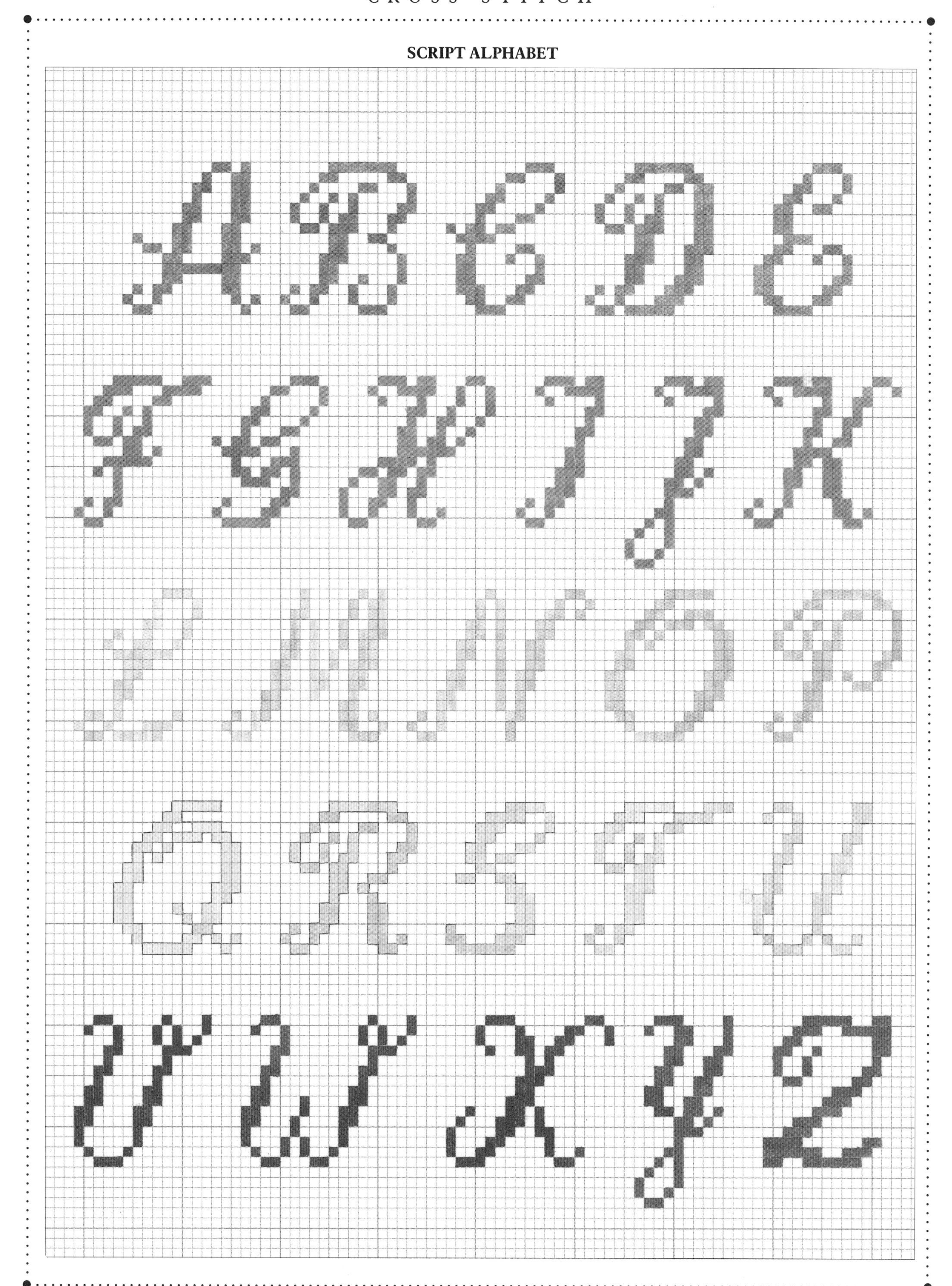

BLOCK ALPHABET

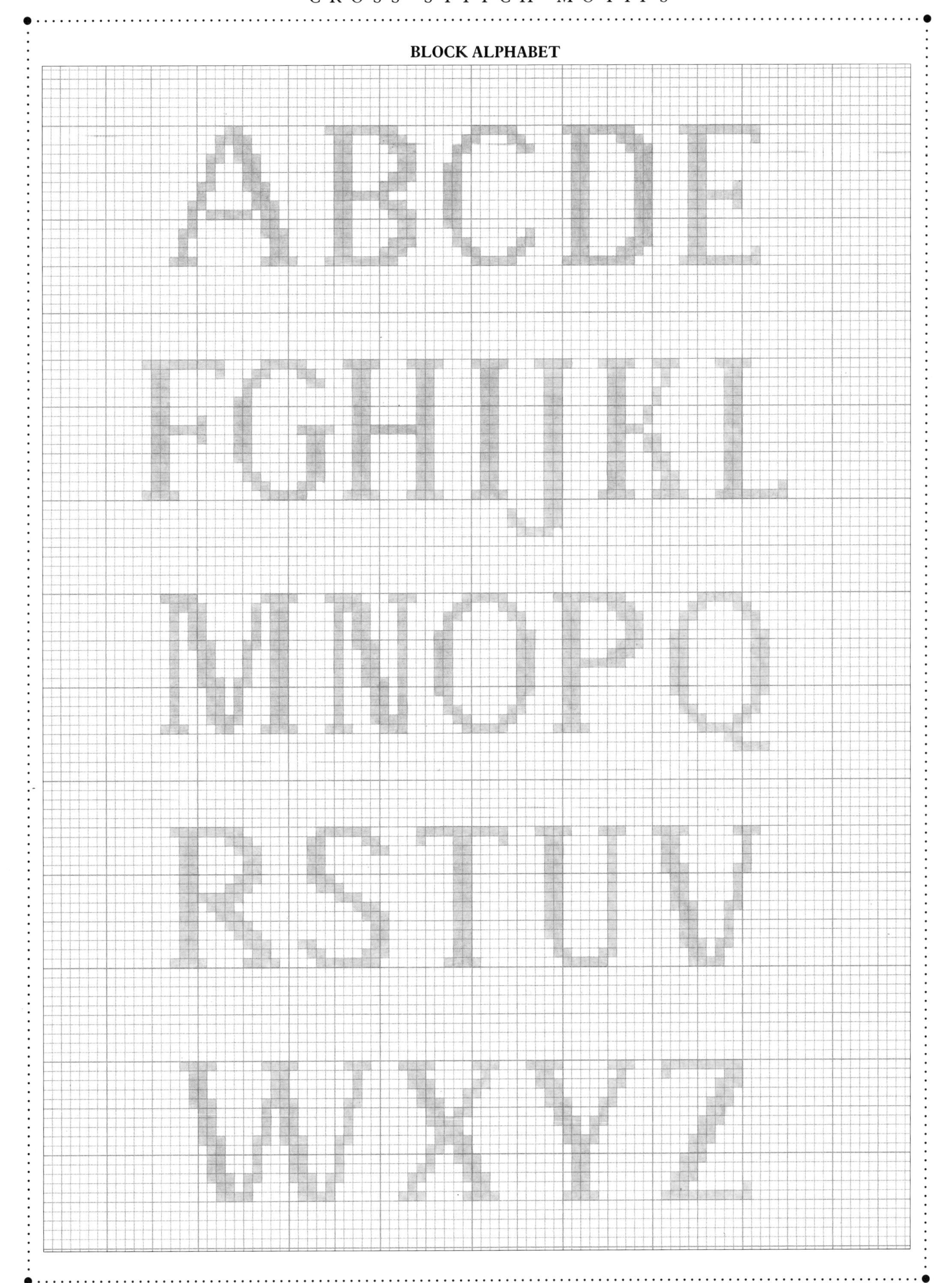

NUMERALS

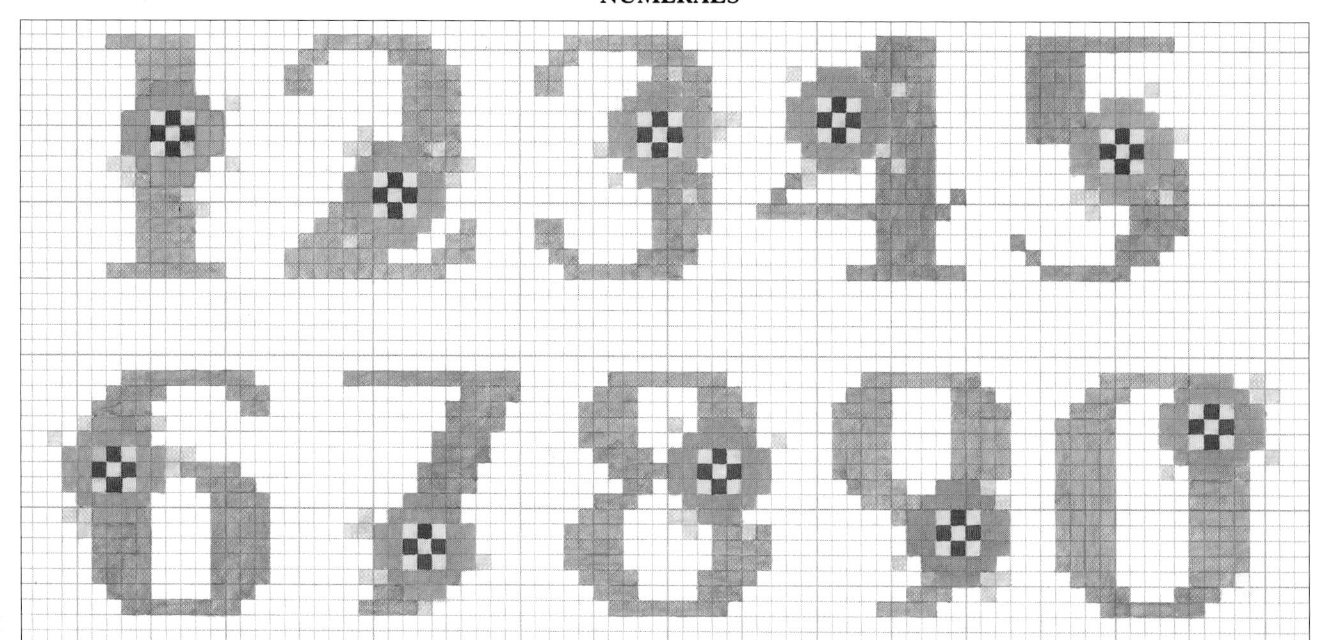

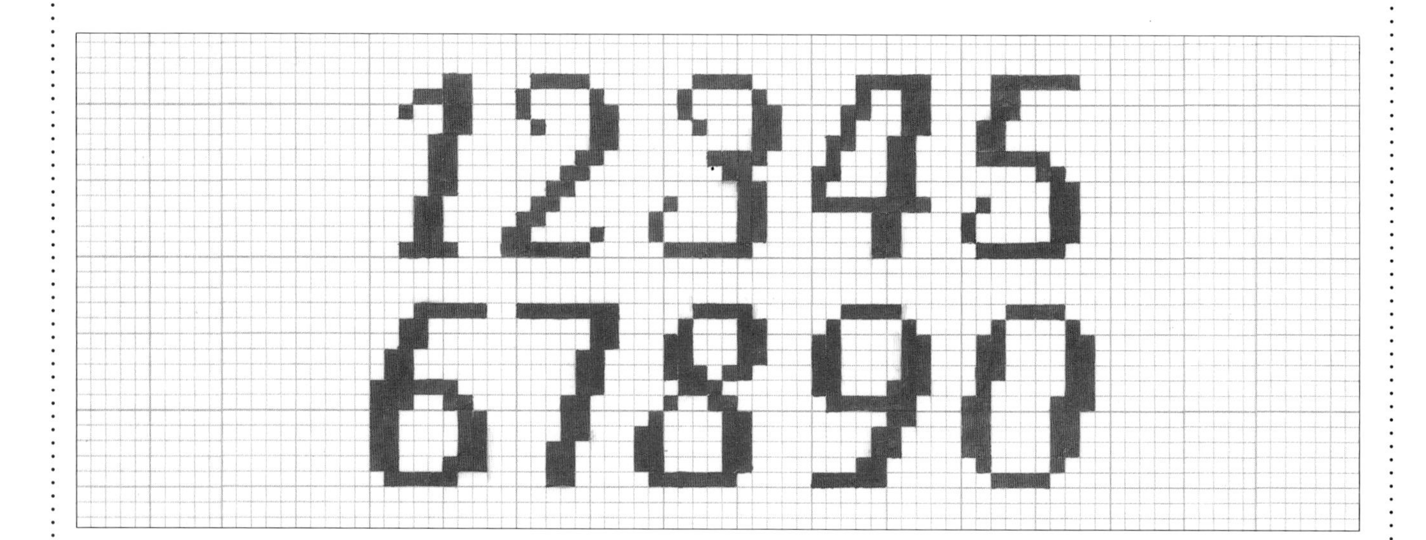

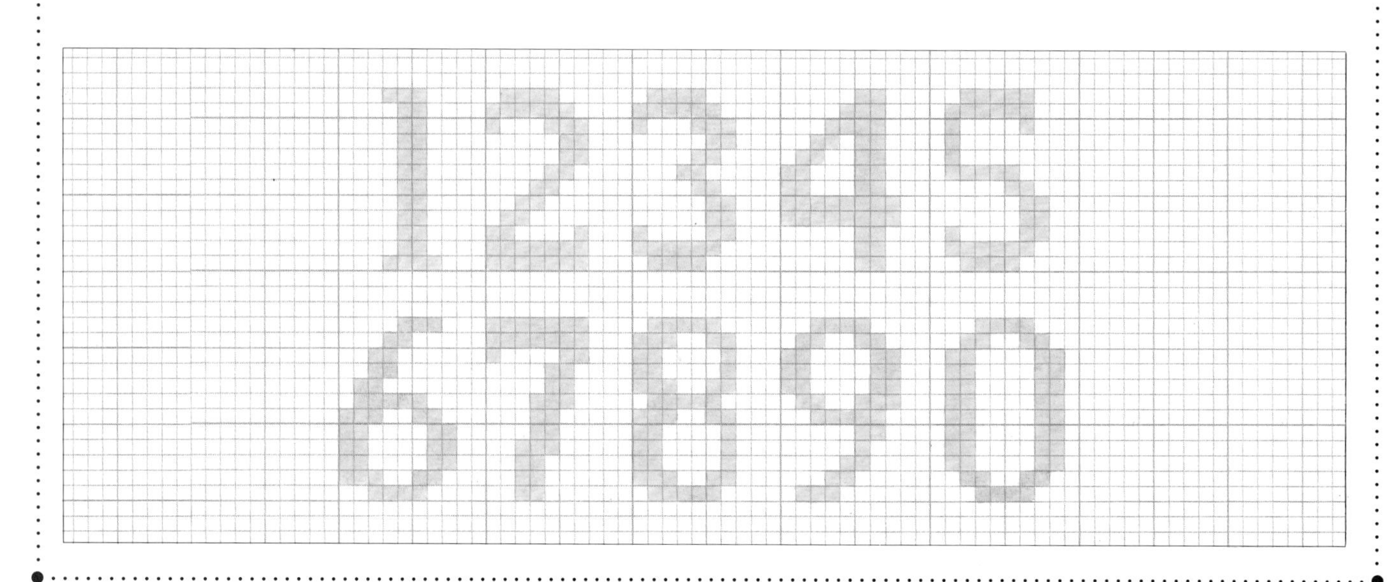

FRUIT MOTIFS

CHRISTMAS MOTIFS

BIRDS

BUTTERFLIES

FLOWERS

FLOWERS

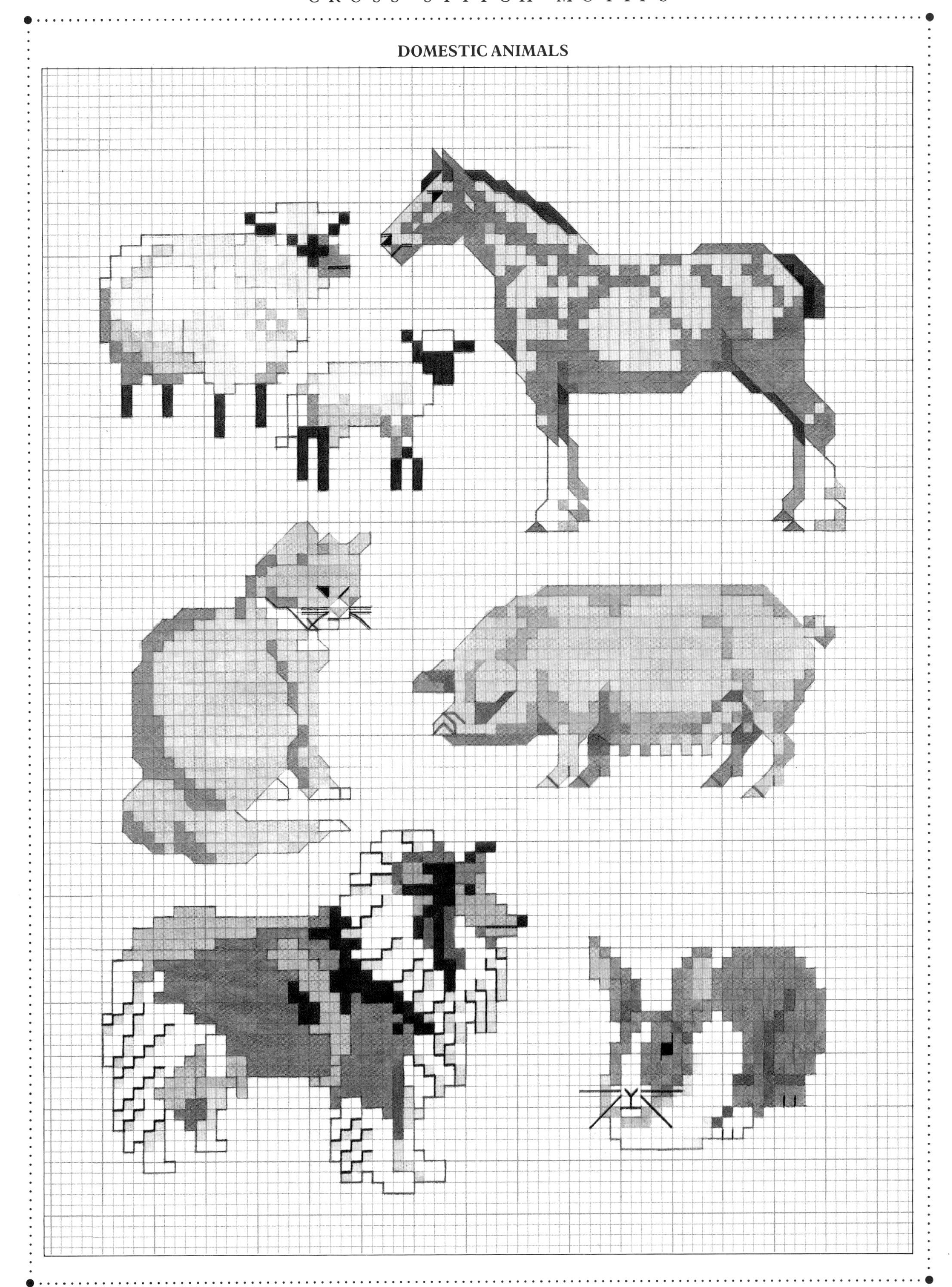

DOMESTIC ANIMALS

WILD ANIMALS

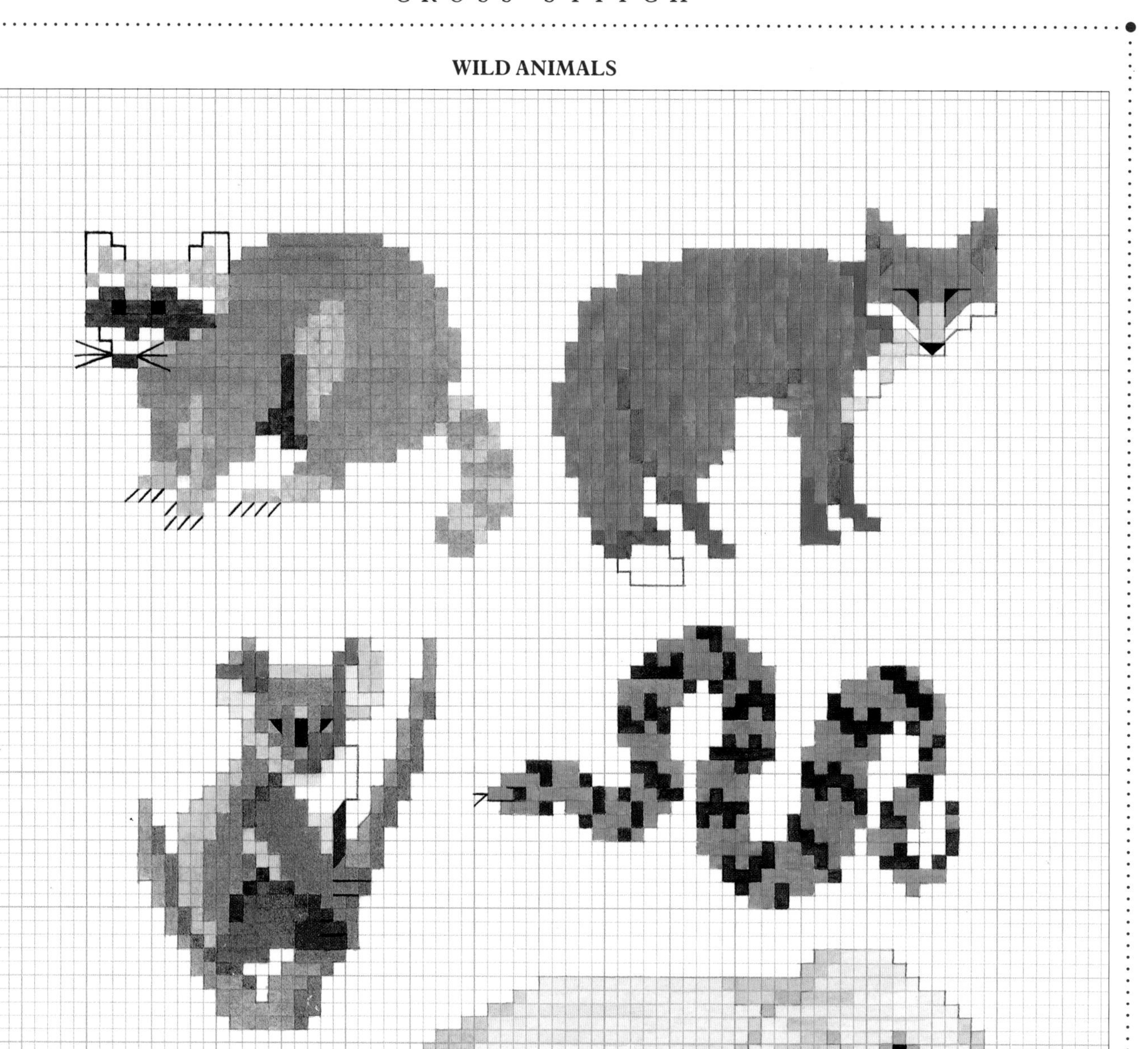

SEASHORE MOTIFS

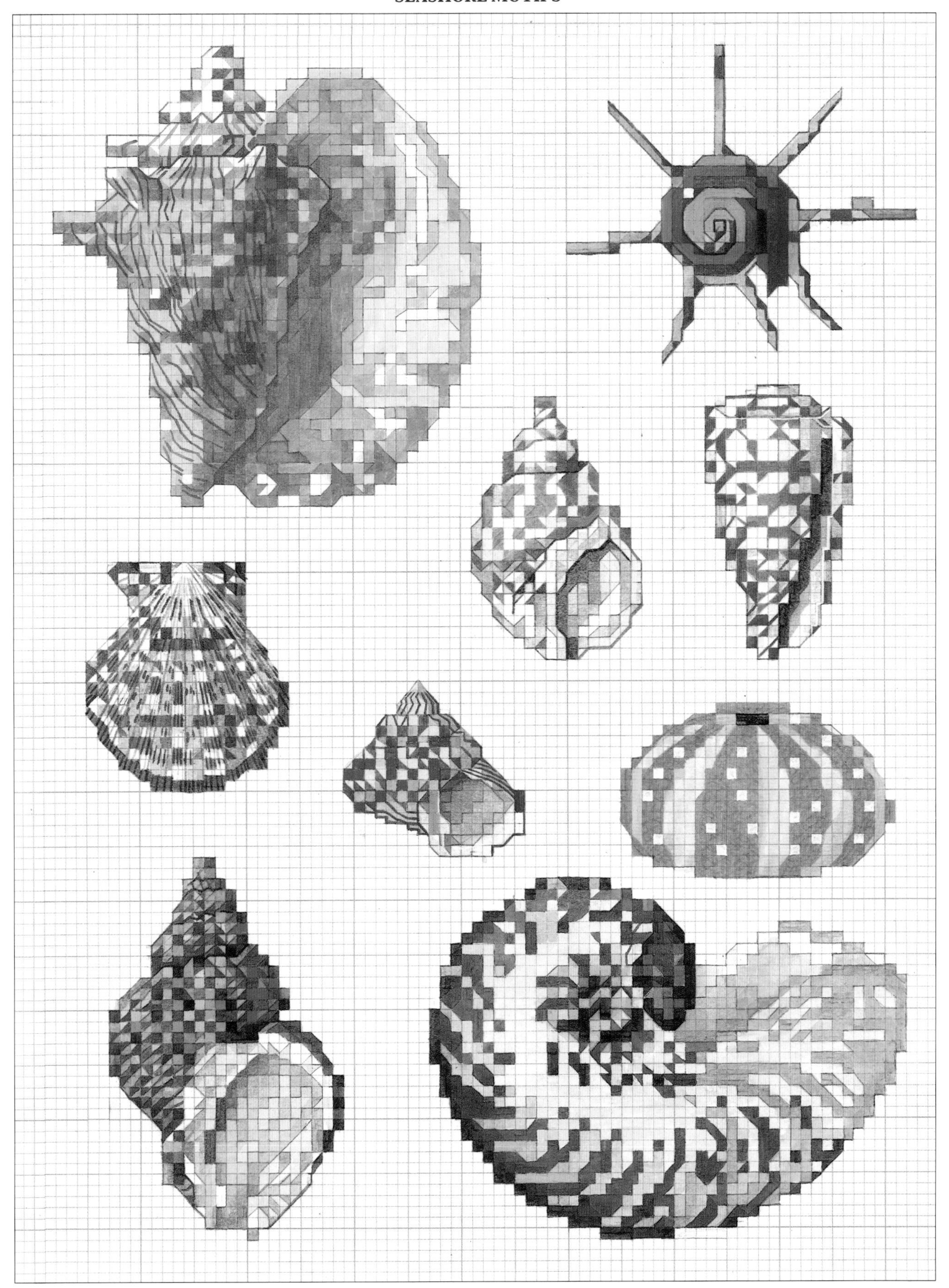

BORDERS

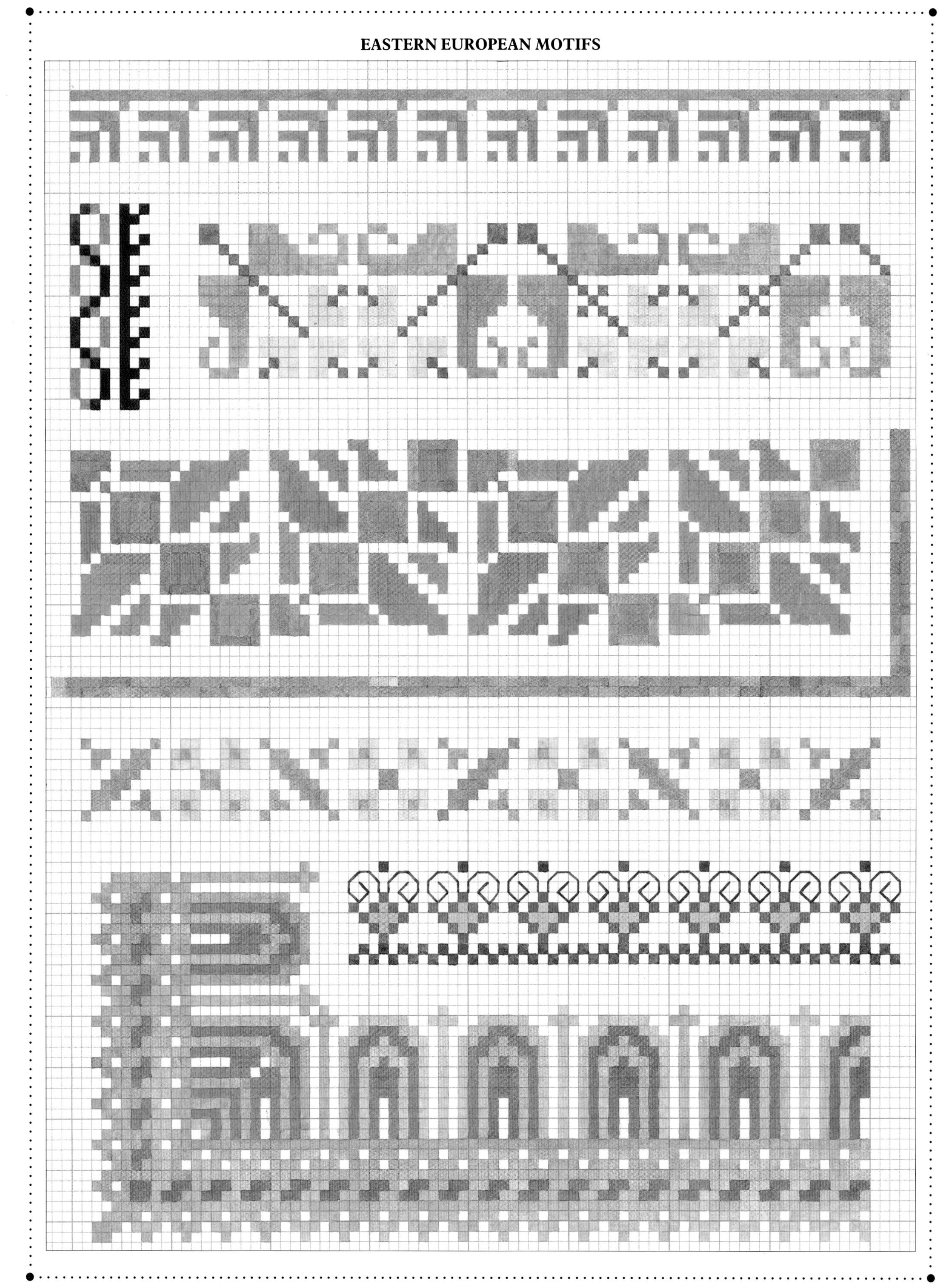
EASTERN EUROPEAN MOTIFS

AMERICAN INDIAN MOTIFS

Georgian-Style Pictures

Two well-known examples of Georgian architecture – Robert Adam's Pulteney Bridge in Bath, and the Governor's Palace in Williamsburg, Virginia, United States – are the subjects of these two pictures. Soft, matt-finish flower thread has been used for the embroidery.

SIZE

Picture: 6¾ × 8 in (17 × 20.5 cm)

MATERIALS

For each picture: 28-count white evenweave, 14 × 16 in (35 × 41 cm)
Fabric used: Zweigart "Glasgow," shade 100
Poster board, 9½ × 11 in (24 × 28 cm)
Thin wadding or flannel, 9½ × 11 in (24 × 28 cm)
Strong thread for lacing
Sewing needle
Tapestry needle, size 24

For Pulteney Bridge picture:
DMC flower thread, 1 skein:

	2800		ecru
	2358		2318
	2798		2734
	2415		2732
	2644		2730
	2579		2833
	2673		2609
	2640		2413

CHART FOR PULTENEY BRIDGE PICTURE

For Governor's Palace picture:

2800	2758
2415	2839
2642	2833
2644	2732
ecru	2734
2579	2673
2609	2400
2640	2730
2414	2766
2318	2632
2415	2918
2413	2950
2407	2922

Backstitch:

2609	2644
2414	ecru

Working the embroidery

1 Bind the edges of the fabric with tape or overcasting. Mark centre of fabric with a row of basting or running stitches (*see page 90*).

2 Mount work securely in an embroidery frame.

3 Work embroidery in cross stitch, using a single strand of thread in needle and following the appropriate chart. Each square on the chart represents a single stitch.

4 Embroider the details on the work in backstitch as indicated on chart.

Completing the pictures

1 Press work wrong side up on a well-padded ironing board, or block the work carefully (*see page 151*).

2 Lace embroidered picture over the poster board backing (*see page 152*). The picture is now ready to frame.

CHART FOR GOVERNOR'S PALACE PICTURE

Eagle Tote Bag

An American Indian design depicting a majestic eagle flying over a pine wood enlivens both sides of this sturdy tote bag. It is ideal for shopping, books, or needlework.

SIZE

Finished bag: 16 × 12½ × 4 in (40 × 32 × 10 cm)

MATERIALS

Outside: ⅝ yard (57 cm) 18-count evenweave cotton at least 47 in (120 cm) wide

Fabric shown: Zweigart "Davosa," shade 307

Lining: ⅝ yard (57 cm) closely woven, medium weight fabric.

DMC coton à broder, 2 skeins each colour:

335 ecru

DMC coton à broder, 5 skeins, colour as desired

Poster board, 12½ × 4 in (32 × 10 cm)

Tapestry needle, size 20

CHART FOR EAGLE TOTE BAG

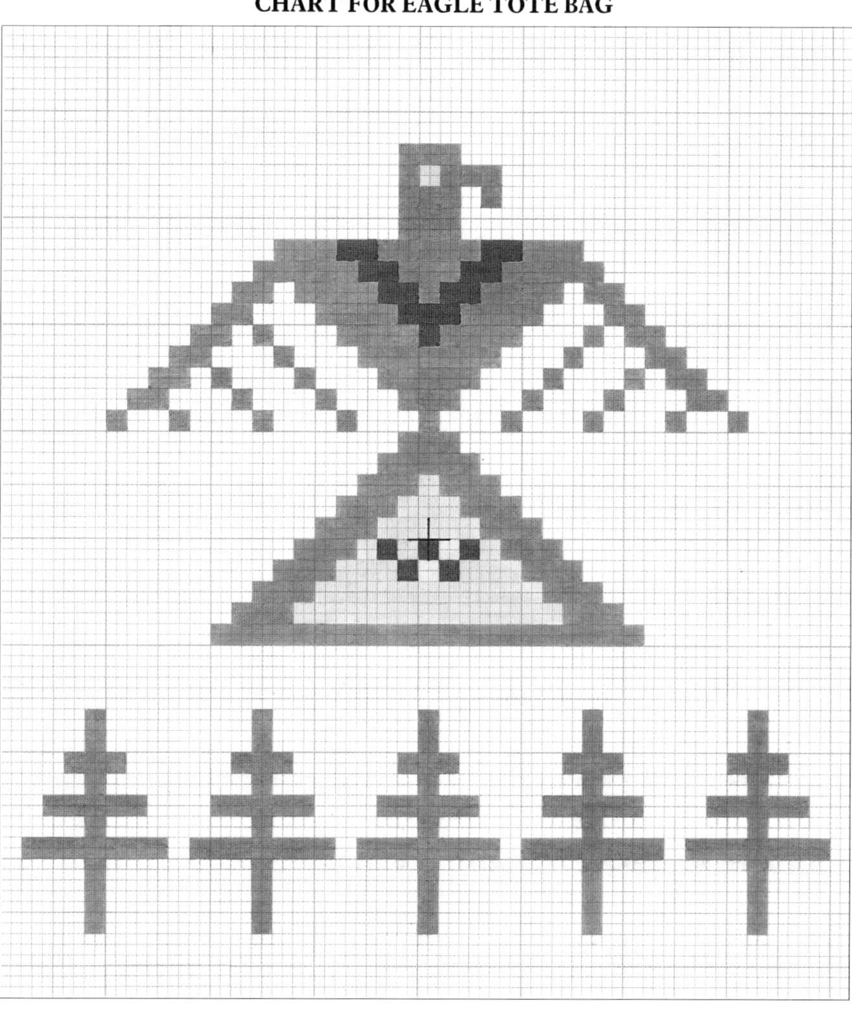

Working the embroidery

1 Cut a piece of outside fabric 37½ × 17½ in (95 × 45 cm). Overcast raw edges to prevent fraying. Baste centre lines (*see illustration below*).

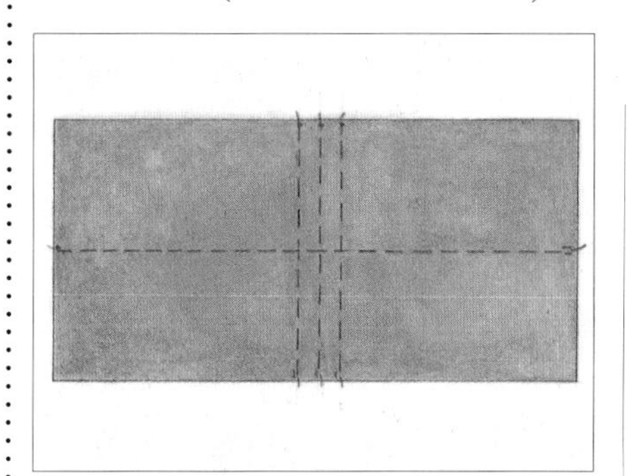

Marking the vertical and horizontal centre lines with basting or running stitch

2 Work two more lines of basting stitch 2 in (5 cm) on either side of horizontal centre line. These mark lower edges of front and back of bag.

3 Begin the embroidery where the vertical basting line crosses one of the outer horizontal lines. Start with lower left-hand stitch of centre pine tree and follow the chart. Each square represents one stitch, worked over three fabric threads. Use a single strand of embroidery thread.

4 Work the second side of bag.

Making up the bag

1 Press the completed embroidery carefully from the wrong side on a well-padded ironing board.

2 Fold the bag in half, right sides together, along the centre horizontal line of basting (leave basting thread in place). Machine stitch the two side seams; use ⅝ in (1.5 cm) seam allowance. Press seams open.

3 Square the bottom as follows: On a flat surface fold one side down so that seam is aligned with the basting line; this makes a right-angled triangle (*see illustration below*).

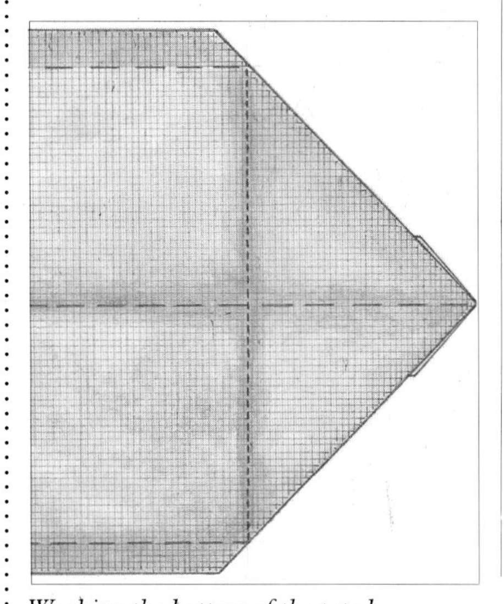

Working the bottom of the tote bag

Pin corner in place. Measure 2 in (5 cm) from the point along the basting line, then lightly mark a line perpendicular to the basting thread. Machine stitch along this line. Pin, measure, and stitch at the other corner. Press the seams flat.

4 Turn bag right side out and push out the bottom corners. Press side seams 2 in (5 cm) from the seam to make them square.

5 From the lining fabric, cut one piece 37½ × 17 in (95 × 44 cm); one piece 14 × 9½ in (36 × 24 cm); one strip 47 × 2 in (120 × 5 cm). Cut same size strip from outside fabric.

6 Stitch main fabric strip to lining strip along the long edges; use ⅜ in (1 cm) seam allowance. Turn strip right side out; press edges flat. This strip will form the handle of the completed tote bag. It should be made of a strong, flexible material.

7 Cut ends diagonally, overlapping by ¾ in (2 cm). Machine stitch the ends securely together.

8 Place lining fabric on a flat surface. Pin strip to lining 6 in (15 cm) from side edges. Baste the strip, then topstitch around all edges, ending the stitching 2 in (5 cm) from the top edges (*see illustration below*).

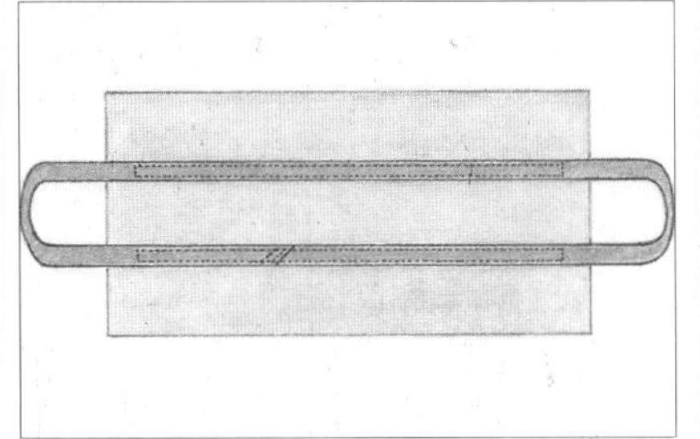

Attaching the handle strip to the lining

9 Fold the lining in half, as for the outer bag, so that the the short (top) edges are aligned and the handles are on the outside. Stitch the side seams; use ⅝ in (1.5 cm) seam allowance. Square the bottom following the instructions in step 3.

10 Insert the lining into outer bag. Match side seams and pin together; turn under both top edges about ¾ in (2 cm). Pin and baste, then topstitch or slipstitch edges together.

11 Fold the remaining lining piece lengthwise and stitch the long edges together; use ⅝ in (1.5 cm) seam allowance. Press seam open, then centre it and stitch across one end (*see illustration below*).

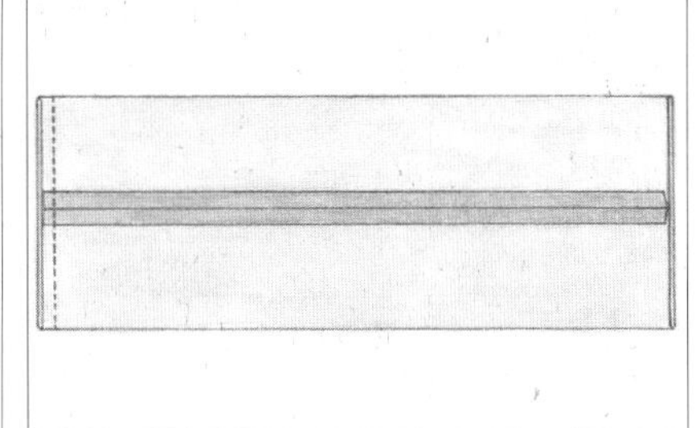

Stiching three sides of the fabric cover

12 Ensure the cover is right side out. Then insert the card carefully. Tuck in the raw edges of the cover and slipstitch them. Place poster board in bottom of tote bag.

Detail of the eagle tote bag

Teddy Bear Pictures

A windmill and yo-yo provide amusement for these cheerful teddies. The pictures will brighten a child's bedroom or playroom and make delightful presents. They are easy to stitch on Aida cloth and are designed to fit ready-made oval frames.

SIZE

Each picture (without frame):
7 × 5 in (18 × 13 cm)

MATERIALS

For windmill teddy: DMC stranded cotton, 1 skein each colour:

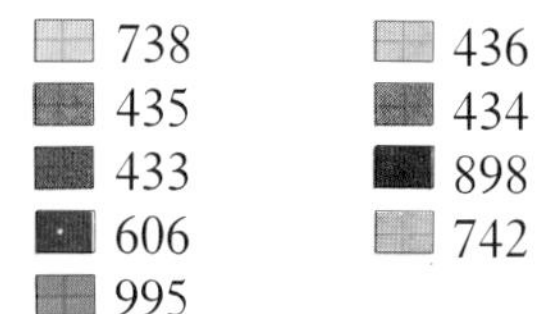

For yo-yo teddy: DMC stranded cotton, 1 skein each colour:

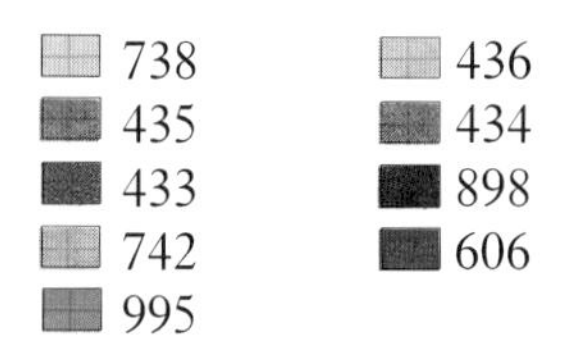

For each teddy: 16-count cream Aida cloth, 8 in/20 cm square
Fabric shown: Zweigart, shade 264
Iron-on interfacing, medium weight, 7 × 5 in (18 × 13 cm)
Backing: cotton fabric, 7 × 5 in (18 × 13 cm)
Sewing needle and strong thread
Tapestry needle, size 24
Oval embroidery frame, 7 × 5 in (18 × 13 cm)

CHART FOR WINDMILL TEDDY

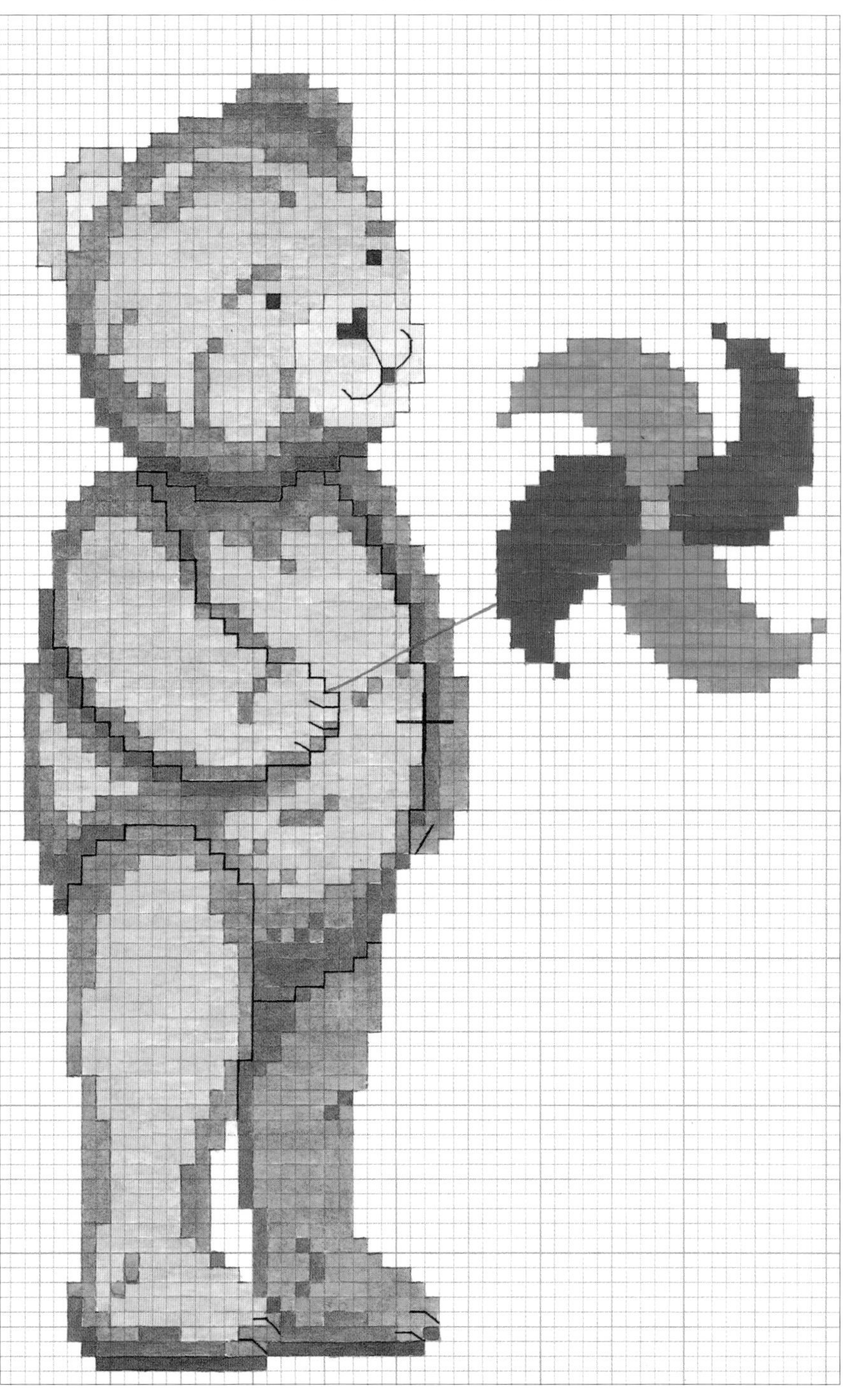

Working the embroidery

1 Bind the edge of the fabric with tape or overcast stitches. Mark the centre with a few basting or running stitches (*see page 18*). Mount fabric in embroidery hoop.

CHART FOR YO-YO TEDDY

2 For each teddy, work the cross stitch embroidery with two strands of thread, following the appropriate chart. Start in the centre of the design each time (indicated by a cross). Each square represents one stitch.

3 Work the body outlines in shade 898, using backstitch (*see page 98*) and two strands of thread.

Windmill toy

The teddies are embroidered in the same way, but different techniques are needed to work the toys.

For the rod holding the windmill, make a single long stitch from the paw to the windmill, using two strands of 995. Keep the strands parallel, not twisted. Fasten ends securely on the wrong side.

Yo-yo toy

Using two strands of shade 318, backstitch curved lines (*see page 98*) to indicate a moving yo-yo. Make a single long stitch from the paw to the yo-yo, using two strands of shade 995. Keep the strands parallel. Tie the threads into a bow and secure.

Completing the pictures

1 For each picture, place inner ring of hoop on iron-on interfacing; draw around it. Cut out shape and iron it to wrong side of embroidery. Be careful that the fabric threads are vertical and the design is centred.

2 Trim the excess fabric to within 1¼ in (3 cm) of the interfacing edge. Make small gathering stitches ⅜ in (1 cm) from the fabric edge. It is helpful to leave a long end.

3 Place the embroidery face down on a flat, smooth surface, and lay the inner hoop on top. Pull up the gathering stitches, distribute evenly, and fasten off.

4 Lace the fabric edges together and secure (*see illustration below*).

5 Cut the backing fabric to fit the hoop. Sew or glue in place to cover the lacing stitches. Fit the outer ring of the hoop in place.

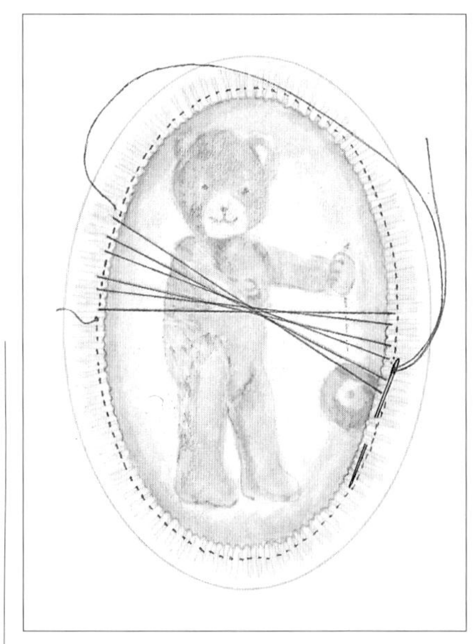

Lacing the fabric edges

Ring of Clematis

Richly hued blossoms of clematis make a pretty design for the centre of a tablecloth and its four corners and also adorn the matching napkins. The centre motif is suitable for a round or square table.

SIZE
Tablecloth: 52 in (132 cm) square; napkins: 14 in (36 cm) square

MATERIALS
For a tablecloth and up to 6 napkins:
28-count evenweave linen or cotton, 2½ yd/2.3 metres, 55 in/140 cm wide
Fabric shown: Zweigart "Linda," shade 264
DMC stranded cotton, amount per colour as shown:

1 skein

2 skeins

209
210
367
368

DMC no. 8 perlé cotton, 1 ball, colour to match fabric
Tapestry needle, size 24

CHART FOR CENTRAL MOTIF

Working the embroidery

1 Preshrink fabric if necessary and mark vertical and horizontal centres of cloth (*see page 18*) with lines of basting or running stitch.

2 Work tablecloth centre motif in cross stitch; work details in backstitch (*see page 98*) where indicated on chart (*see above*). Use two strands of cotton; work all stitches over two fabric threads, starting by arrow. Note that chart gives only one quarter of design. Rotate chart 90° to complete the remaining three sections.

3 Work the small motifs in each corner of tablecloth, positioning in each corner as shown on the single motif chart (*see page 60*).

4 Press embroidery from the wrong side on a well-padded surface.

Making up the tablecloth

1 Straighten the end of the fabric, and carefully trim off selvedges.

2 Cut a piece of fabric 54 in (137 cm) long for the tablecloth; remainder will be used for napkins. Prepare hem: pull out the eighth and the ninth threads from the edge to form the folds. Then carefully pull out the 31st and 32nd threads to work the hemstitching (*see page 153*).

3 Work hemstitching (*see page 153*) using perlé cotton. Include three vertical threads with each stitch.

Making up the napkins

1 On the remaining fabric, baste between fabric threads to mark 16 in (41 cm) square for each napkin. Where four corners meet, mark the 32nd thread inward in both directions with a line of basting (*see photograph below*); this marks the inner edge of the hemstitching. Mark corners of any additional napkins in the same way.

2 Without cutting out napkins, frame entire piece of fabric and work the small single motifs, positioning as shown on the motif chart.

3 Cut napkins along main lines of basting in step 1. Turn up hems as for tablecloth; complete with hemstitching. Press.

Detail of the central design

CHART FOR THE SINGLE MOTIF

POSITIONING MOTIFS FOR THE NAPKINS

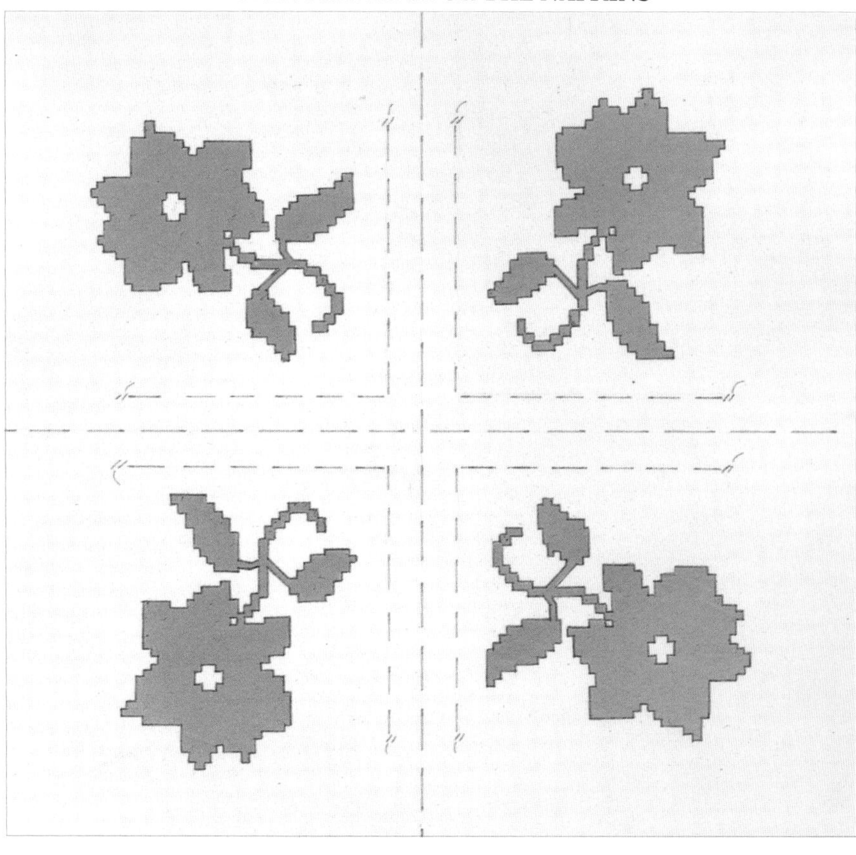

Traditional American Sampler

This charming sampler with its profusion of plants and animals evokes an idyllic picture of colonial America. Use the alphabet and numerals to include your own name and date of completion.

SIZE

Sampler (without frame): 11½ × 14½ in (29 × 36.5 cm)

MATERIALS

25-count evenweave linen 14 × 17 in (36 × 43 cm)

Fabric shown: Zweigart "Dublin," shade 101

DMC stranded cotton, 1 skein each colour:

3363	520
422	3045
420	869
898	758
347	891
930	931
746	3371

Tapestry needle, size 24

Graph paper

Cardboard, 11½ × 14½ in (29 × 36.5 cm)

Polyester wadding, 11½ × 14½ in (29 × 36.5 cm)

Detail from the American sampler

Working the embroidery

1 On graph paper, mark an area 111 squares wide × 9 squares deep. The 56th square is the centre.

2 Using the alphabet provided, or one of the designs in the Motif Library (*see pages 33–35*), chart your name, working outward from the centre square. If your name is long, abbreviate to just your initials.

3 Mark in pencil the vertical and horizontal centres of the fabric; mark the crossing point with basting or running stitches (*see page 90*). Bind the edges (*see page 18*), and mount the fabric in a frame or embroidery hoop (*see page 19*).

4 Position the centre of the design at the marked centre of the fabric. Using two strands of thread in the needle, work the embroidery in cross stitch, backstitch and straight stitch. Work all stitches over two fabric threads. Note that the half-cross stitch is sometimes used.

Making up the sampler

1 Carefully press or block the work as required (*see page 151*).

2 Lace the work over the board and wadding, using heavy thread (*see page 152*). It is now ready to frame.

The chart for the complete American sampler is shown on the opposite page. The completed project is shown on page 64.

CHART FOR AMERICAN SAMPLER

1234567890
1993
MARIA BURROUGHS

Christmas Tree Sachets

These little sachets make charming tree ornaments or party decorations. They look attractive and will provide a refreshing fragrance for the room. Keep a few extra ones in hand for last-minute presents!

SIZE

Bag (unfilled): 5 × 3½ in (13 × 9 cm) (approx)

MATERIALS

For robin sachet: 14-count Aida cloth, 5½ × 7½ in (14 × 19 cm)
Fabric shown: Zweigart, shade 101
DMC stranded cotton,
1 skein each colour:

924	927
610	349
898	310

blanc neige

For Christmas rose sachet: 14-count green Aida cloth, 5½ × 7½ in (14 × 19 cm)
Fabric shown: Zweigart, shade 670
DMC stranded cotton,
1 skein each colour:

452	352
453	819
3078	700

blanc neige

For snowflake sachet: 14-count red Aida cloth, 5½ × 7½ in (14 × 19 cm)
Fabric shown: Zweigart, shade 954
DMC stranded cotton,
1 skein:

blanc neige

For all sachets: Narrow ribbon to match fabric or main embroidery colour, ¾ yd (69 cm)
Narrow lace to match fabric or main embroidery colour, 7½ in (19 cm)
Potpourri, *c.* 1 oz (25 g)
Tapestry needle, size 24

CHART FOR ROBIN DESIGN

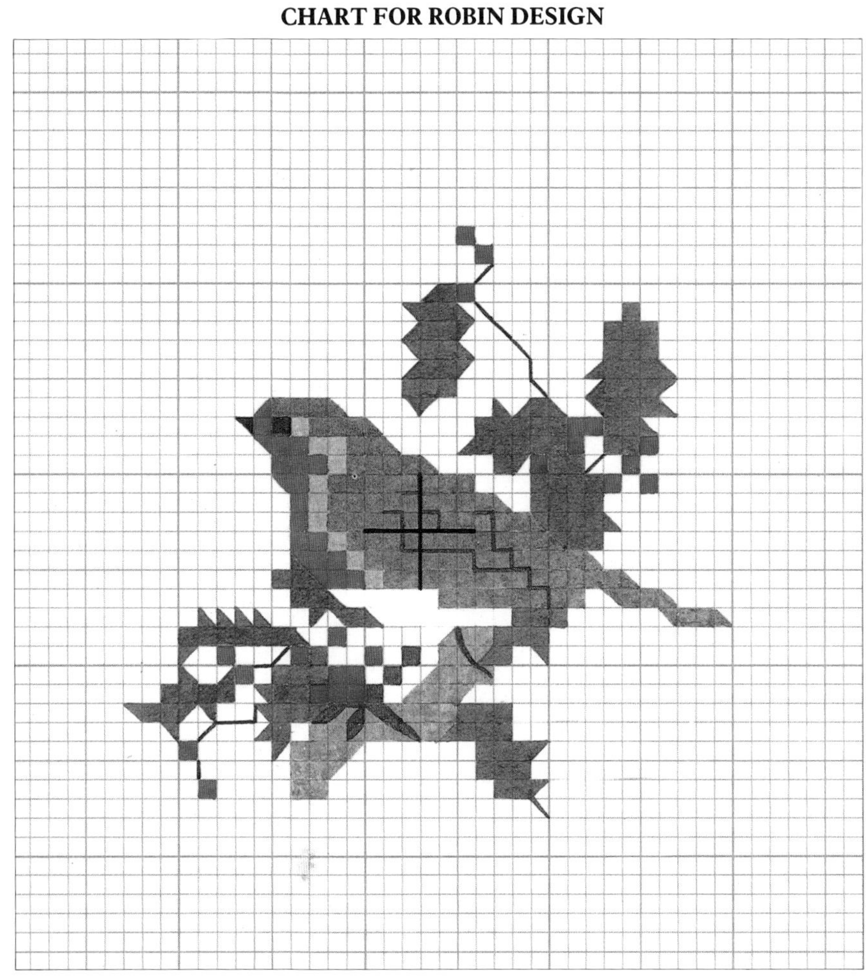

Working the embroidery

1 Overcast the edges of the fabric to prevent fraying. Using matching sewing thread, work a line of gathering stitches 1 in (2.5 cm) in from one long edge. The completed stitches should be about ¼ in (6 mm) in length.

2 Fold the other long edge to meet the line of basting. Finger press along fold. Refold fabric in opposite direction; finger press. The two creases cross at the centre of the working area.

3 Starting at the centre, work design in cross stitch using two strands of thread (*see the charts on pages 65 and 66*). The centre of each of the three designs is marked on each chart with a cross. Each square on the charts represents one stitch.

Making up the sachet

1 Press completed work carefully on the wrong side.

2 Turn under and press ¼ in (6 mm) along the edge with the gathering thread. Stitch lace over this edge, either by hand or with a machine using zigzag stitching.

3 With right sides together, join the two short edges. You should allow ¼ in (6 mm) seam allowance.

4 Fold the bag with the seam centred. Stitch across lower edge, using ¼ in (6 mm) seam allowance (*see illustration below*).

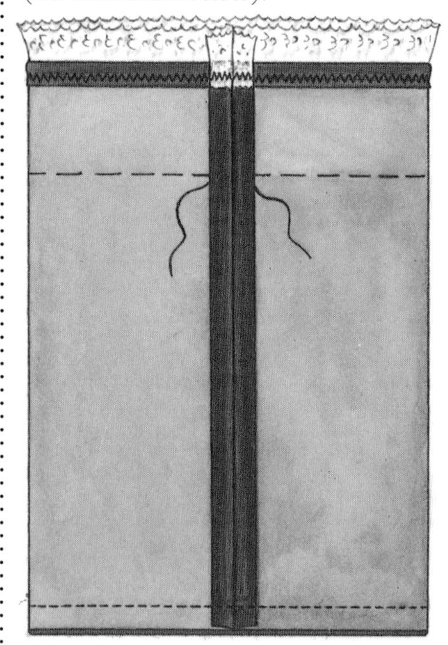

Fold the sachet so that the seam goes in the centre.

5 Cut 8 in (20 cm) ribbon. Loop ribbon and sew to inside edge near vertical seam. Place the ends near the gathering stitches.

6 Turn bag right side out and fill with potpourri. Pull up gathers, and tie threads securely.

7 Wrap rest of ribbon around gathers and tie a bow, securing with a few stitches.

You could also use them to hold sweets at Christmas parties!

CHART FOR CHRISTMAS ROSE DESIGN

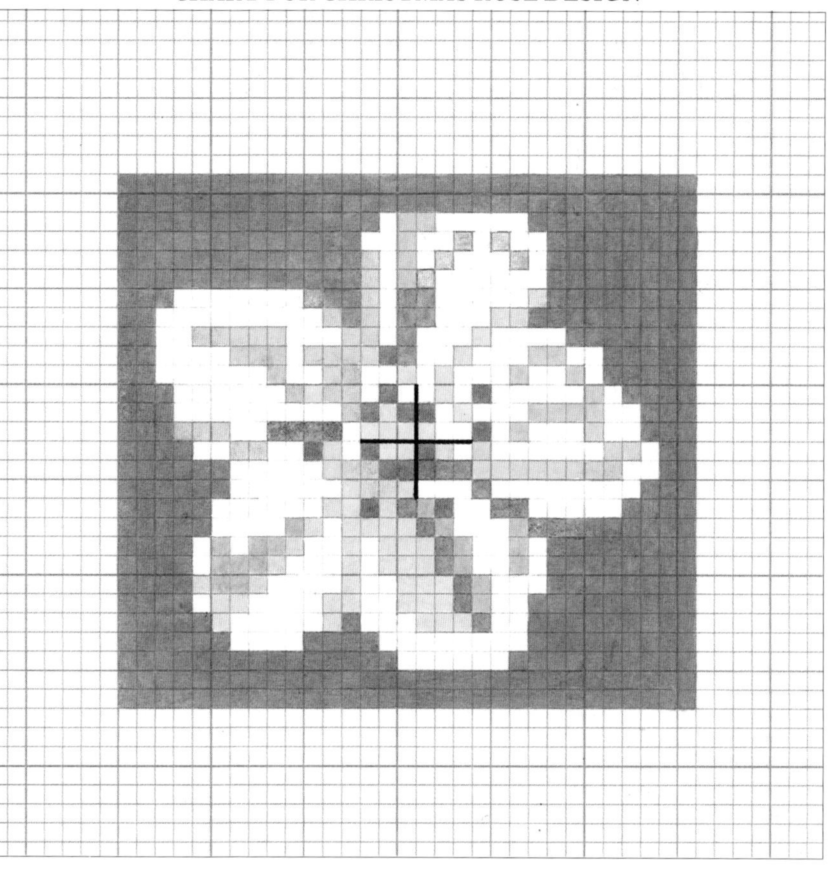

CHART FOR SNOWFLAKE DESIGN

Greetings Cards

An embroidered greetings card will be kept and treasured. Here is a bouquet for any appropriate event and two designs for special occasions: a St Valentine's Day Cupid, and bunnies for a child's birthday.

BOUQUET CARD

SIZE

Stitched area: 1½ × 2½ in (4 × 6.5 cm)

MATERIALS

White 16-count Aida cloth, large enough to fit embroidery hoop

DMC stranded cotton, 1 skein each colour:

520	989
335	3766
798	3041
3752	743
333	818

Tapestry needle, size 24
Greetings card for embroidery, 4½ × 3½ in (11.5 × 9 cm) with rectangular opening 3 × 2½ in (8 × 5.5 cm)
Glue stick

Detail of Bouquet card

CHART FOR BOUQUET CARD DESIGN

Working the embroidery

1 Mark the centre of the fabric with basting or running stitch (*see page 90*). Mount the fabric in a frame or hoop (*see page 16*).

2 Embroider the design in cross stitch, following the above chart and using two strands of thread.

Making up the card

1 Remove the basting carefully. Then lightly steam press the completed embroidery on the wrong side, making sure that it is completely flat. This will remove any creases in the final framed picture and should be followed for any of the designs. Use a well-padded ironing board.

2 Open card and place it face down. Place embroidery over opening, centring it carefully. With a pencil, lightly mark the worked fabric so that it fits just inside top edge, bottom edge, and centre fold of card.

3 Remove the fabric and trim away the excess; cut between the fabric threads. The trimmed fabric should lie flat when the card is folded.

4 Glue the embroidery to the centre section of the card. Reposition, if necessary, before the glue sets.

5 Spread glue on the right-hand flap. Press it over the centre section to frame the embroidery.

CHART FOR VALENTINE'S CARD DESIGN

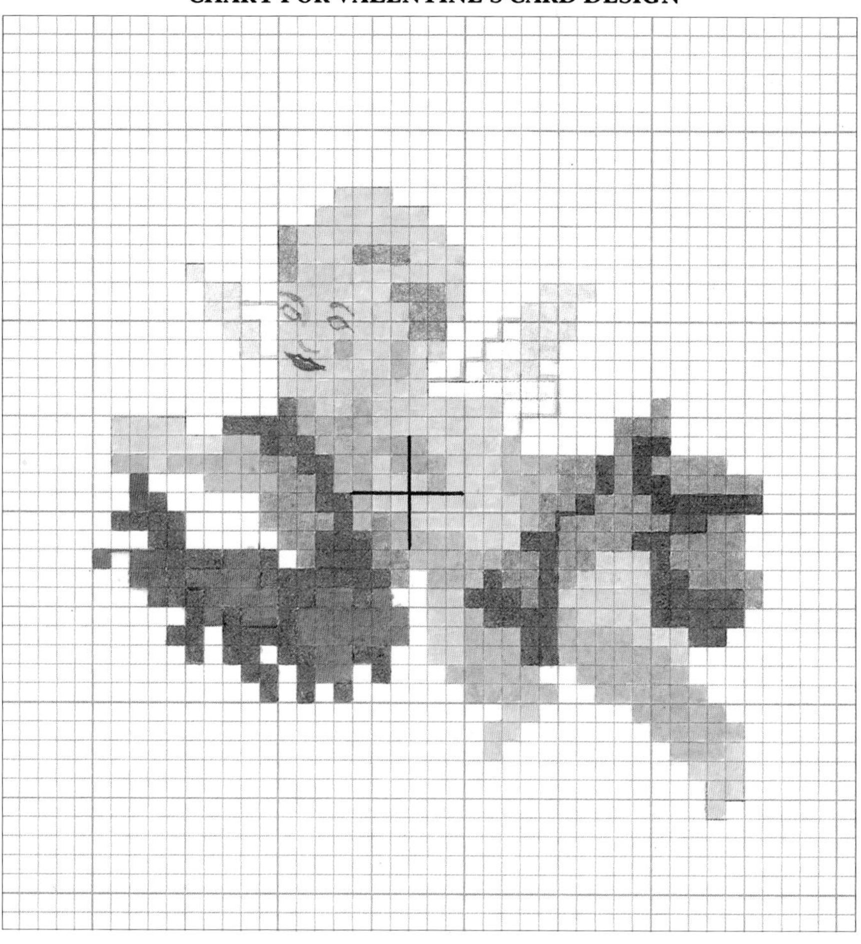

VALENTINE'S CARD

SIZE

Stitched area: 2 × 2¼ in (5 × 5.5 cm)

MATERIALS

Cream 16-count Aida cloth, large enough to fit embroidery hoop

DMC stranded cotton, 1 skein each colour

3712	501
522	928
3770	3774
3046	372

blanc neige

Tapestry needle, size 24
Greetings card for embroidery, 4½ × 3½ in (11.5 × 9 cm) with circular opening 2½ in (6.5 cm) in diameter
Glue stick

Working the embroidery

1 Mark the centre of the fabric with basting or running stitches (*see page 90*) and mount in a frame or hoop.

2 Embroider the design in cross stitch with two strands of thread, following the above chart. Embroider facial features of the cupid in tiny backstitches with a single strand of colours shown.

Making up the card

1 Remove the basting and steam press embroidery on the wrong side.

2 Open the card and place face down. Place the embroidery over the opening, centring it carefully. With a pencil, lightly mark the worked fabric so that it fits just inside the card's top edge, bottom edge and centre fold.

3 Remove the fabric and trim away the excess; cut between the fabric threads. The trimmed fabric should lie flat when the card is folded.

4 Glue the embroidery to the centre section of the card. Spread glue on the right-hand flap; press it over the centre. Allow to dry.

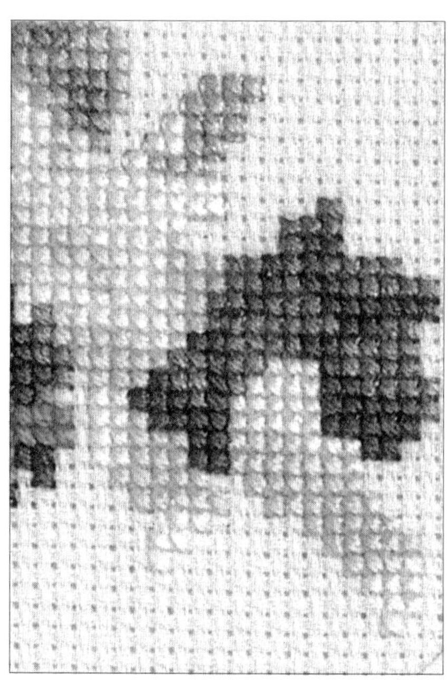

Detail of Valentine's card

BUNNIES CARD

SIZE

Stitched area: 2 in (5 cm) square

MATERIALS

White 16-count Aida cloth, large enough to fit embroidery hoop

DMC stranded cotton, 1 skein each colour:

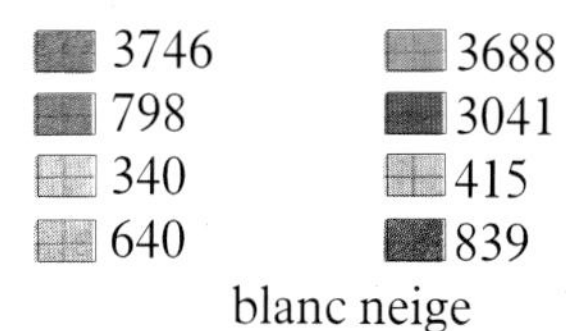

blanc neige

Tapestry needle, size 24
Greetings card for embroidery, 4½ × 3½ in (11.5 × 9 cm) with circular opening 2½ in (6.5 cm) in diameter
Glue stick

CHART FOR BUNNIES CARD DESIGN

Working the embroidery

1 Mark the centre of the fabric with basting or running stitches (*see page 90*). Mount the fabric in a frame or hoop (*see page 18*).

2 Embroider the design in cross stitch with two strands of thread, following the above chart. Then embroider the facial features onto the bunnies in tiny backstitches using a single strand of colour 839; add whiskers in straight stitch. Follow the chart carefully as you work details on the faces.

Making up the card

1 Remove the basting. Lightly steam press the embroidery on the wrong side. It is helpful to use a well-padded ironing board.

2 Open the card and place it face down. Place the embroidery over the opening, centring it carefully. With a pencil, lightly mark the fabric so it will fit just inside the card's top edge, bottom edge, and centre fold.

3 Remove the fabric and trim away the excess; cut between the fabric threads. The trimmed fabric should lie flat when the card is folded.

4 Glue the embroidery to the centre section of the card. Reposition, if necessary, before the glue sets.

5 Spread glue on the right-hand flap. Press it over the centre section to frame the embroidery.

Detail of Bunnies card

Bulgarian Cushion

Traditional Bulgarian motifs give a crisp yet lively character to this handsome cushion. The embroidery is worked in deep red stranded cotton on coarsely woven ecru linen.

SIZE

Cushion: 16 in (40 cm) square. (If the fabric is not an exact evenweave, the finished work will not be a true square.)

MATERIALS

19-count evenweave linen, ½ yd (46 cm), at least 36 in (91 cm) wide
Fabric shown: Zweigart "Cork," shade 23
DMC stranded cotton, 6 skeins: 347

Tapestry needle, size 18
Cushion pad, 16 in (40 cm) square
Sewing thread to match

CHART FOR ONE-QUARTER OF CUSHION DESIGN

Working the embroidery

1 Iron fabric to remove any creases. Cut two pieces, each 18 in (46 cm) square. Straighten raw edges and overcast to prevent fraying. Set one piece aside for cushion back.

2 Mark vertical and horizontal centres of cushion top with basting or running stitches (*see page 18*). Mount fabric in embroidery frame (*see page 19*).

3 Embroider motif in cross stitch. Use four strands of embroidery thread; work all stitches over two fabric threads.

Note that the cushion chart shown above right gives only one-quarter of design. To work the full design for the cushion, rotate chart 90° and repeat design on the chart for the remaining three sections.

Making up the cushion

1 Remove basting threads. Steam press embroidery on wrong side on a well-padded surface.

2 Run a line of basting around all four sides of the embroidery between the 12th and 13th threads from the outer edge. The 13th thread is the seam line. When you have completed the basting on four sides, trim fabric to within ½ in (1.25 cm) of seam line.

3 Pin cushion top and back pieces together around seam line, right sides facing. Trim back piece to match front. Machine stitch around edges, leaving a 10 in (25 cm) opening.

4 Overcast raw edges of the opening of the cushion. Trim diagonally across the corners, and carefully turn the cushion right side out. Press the cushion lightly. Insert cushion pad. Pin the opening edges securely together, then slipstitch them closed by hand.

Golden Frame

A glint of gold thread gives added richness to the elegant Greek key and rosette design on this picture frame. The frame can be used either vertically or horizontally to provide the ideal setting for your favourite photograph.

SIZE

Frame: 9½ × 8 in (24 × 20 cm)
Opening: 6¾ × 5⅛ in (17 × 13 cm)

MATERIALS

25-count evenweave linen, ⅜ yd (30 cm), at least 44 in (110 cm) wide
Fabric shown: Zweigart "Dublin," shade 326
DMC stranded cotton, amount per colour as shown:

- 918, 2 skeins
- 921, 1 skein
- 729, 1 skein
- ☒ 921, 1 skein

DMC Fil d'Or à Broder or other fine gold thread, 1 spool
Tapestry needle, size 20
Foam padding, 9½ × 8 × ⅜ in (24 × 20 × 1 cm)
Cardboard for mounting, 16½ × 12 in (42 × 30 cm)
Scissors or craft knife
Ruler and set square
Tracing paper
White glue
Double-sided adhesive tape
Sewing needle or curved upholstery needle; thread to match fabric
Optional: Thin, clear plastic sheet, 6¼ × 8 in (16 × 20 cm)

CHART FOR A PORTION OF GOLDEN FRAME

Working the embroidery

1 Mark a rectangle 12 × 10¼ in (30 × 26 cm) on fabric. Cut fabric large enough to fit embroidery frame or hoop. Overcast edges and mount.

2 Measure in 1⅜ in (3.5 cm) along adjacent sides of a corner.

3 Use three strands of 729 and one strand of gold thread in needle. Work a line of cross stitch along two adjacent sides for 4 in (10 cm) in each direction over two threads.

4 Position main motif four fabric threads inside the outer line, following the chart. Note that some stitches are worked over four fabric threads. Complete main motif, then work the line of gold cross stitches.

Completing the frame

1 Photocopy or scale up template A (*see page* 77) by 200 per cent. Trace around outside edge and cut out.

2 Photocopy or scale up template B by 200 per cent as above. Trace around outside edge (X) and inside edge (Y) onto cardboard. Cut out the centre to make window for picture area.

3 Photocopy or scale up template C and D by 200 per cent. Trace and cut out one each from cardboard. These two pieces form the stand.

4 Use the scaled-up templates A, B, and C illustrated on page 77 to cut the following shapes from the card-board: A: one piece same size, one piece with ¾ in (2 cm) all around; B: one piece with ¾ in (2 cm) extra all around; C: one piece same size but extended 2 in (5 cm) for hinge, one piece ¾ in (2 cm) larger than template but with same extension as before (*see illustration below*).

Cutting templates A, B and C

5 Apply thin layer of glue to card-board frame; press onto foam padding. Allow glue to dry, then cut away foam from inside opening.

6 Place embroidery face down with frame on top. Fold edges over frame and hold in place with pins, folding the corners (*see illustration below*).

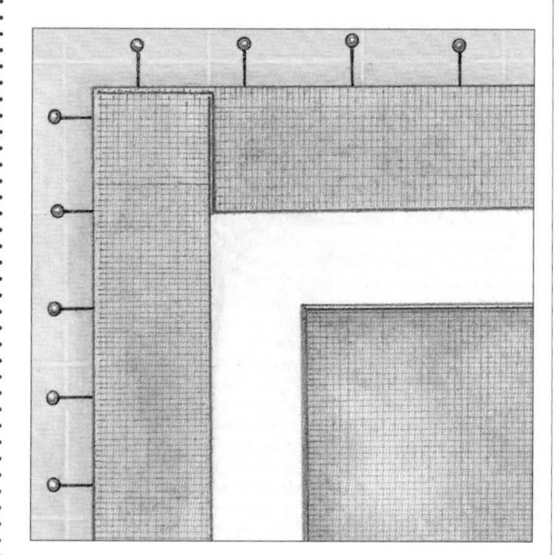

Pinning the edges in place

7 Check that the design is properly positioned. Glue seam allowances in place, making sure folded corners do not extend beyond edges. Then allow to stand until dry.

8 Cut out fabric in centre, leaving a ¾ in (2 cm) seam allowance. Clip into corners, then glue edges to the cardboard (*see illustration below*).

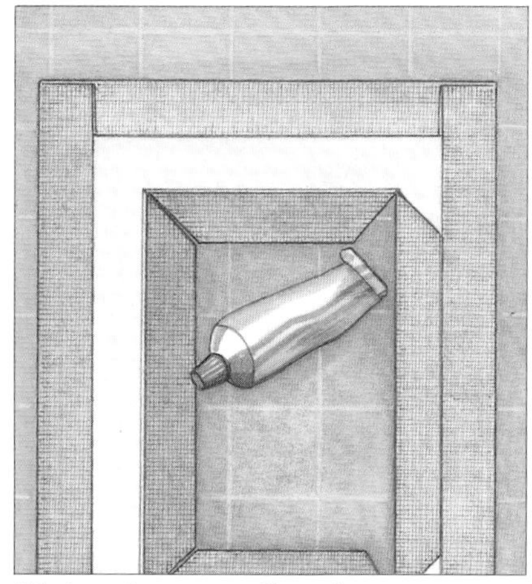

Gluing edges to cardboard

To strengthen corner, paint wrong side with diluted white glue. Allow to dry under a weight, such as a book.

9 Apply glue to one side of backing board. Cover with the smaller fabric piece. Glue larger piece to other side, centring it with even edges. Cut the corners diagonally and glue edges in place (*see illustration below*).

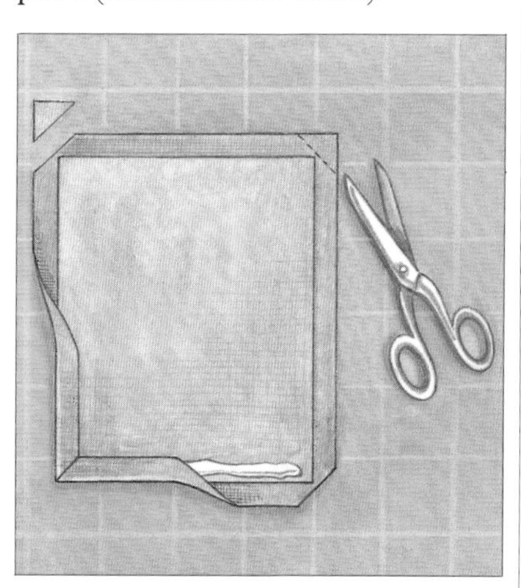

Finishing the corners

10 Apply thin layer of glue to the fabric and board shapes C. Stick the smaller one centrally on top of the larger and glue. Fold extra fabric over all edges and glue on back (*see illustration below*).

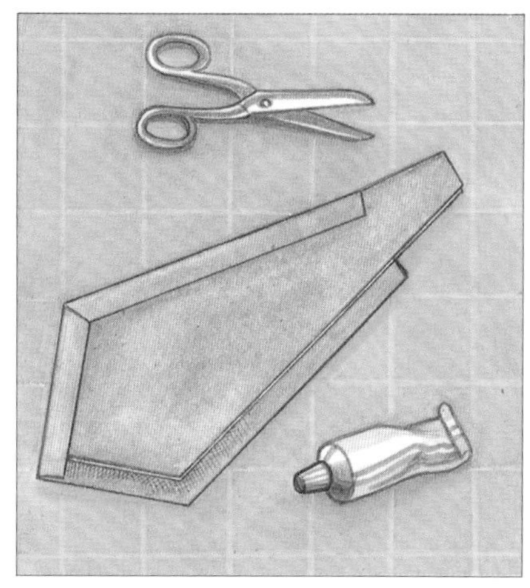

Positioning the two shapes C

11 Glue the two extensions of shape C together to form a flap. Allow all pieces to dry under a weight.

12 Place covered backing board on a flat surface, the side with the folded edges underneath. Position shape C on top, aligning edges with lower left-hand corner. Position shape D over flap, aligning edges with upper right-hand corner (*see illustration below*).

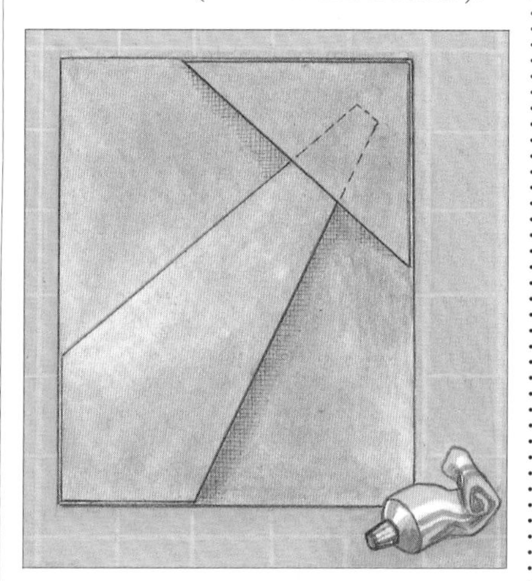

Placing shape D in position

13 To join front and back of frame, apply double-sided adhesive tape to inner side of frame back, just inside top and side edges. Position front of frame on top, making sure that the edges are aligned, then press together firmly. Slipstitch top and side edges together, making stitches small and inconspicuous. Insert photograph.

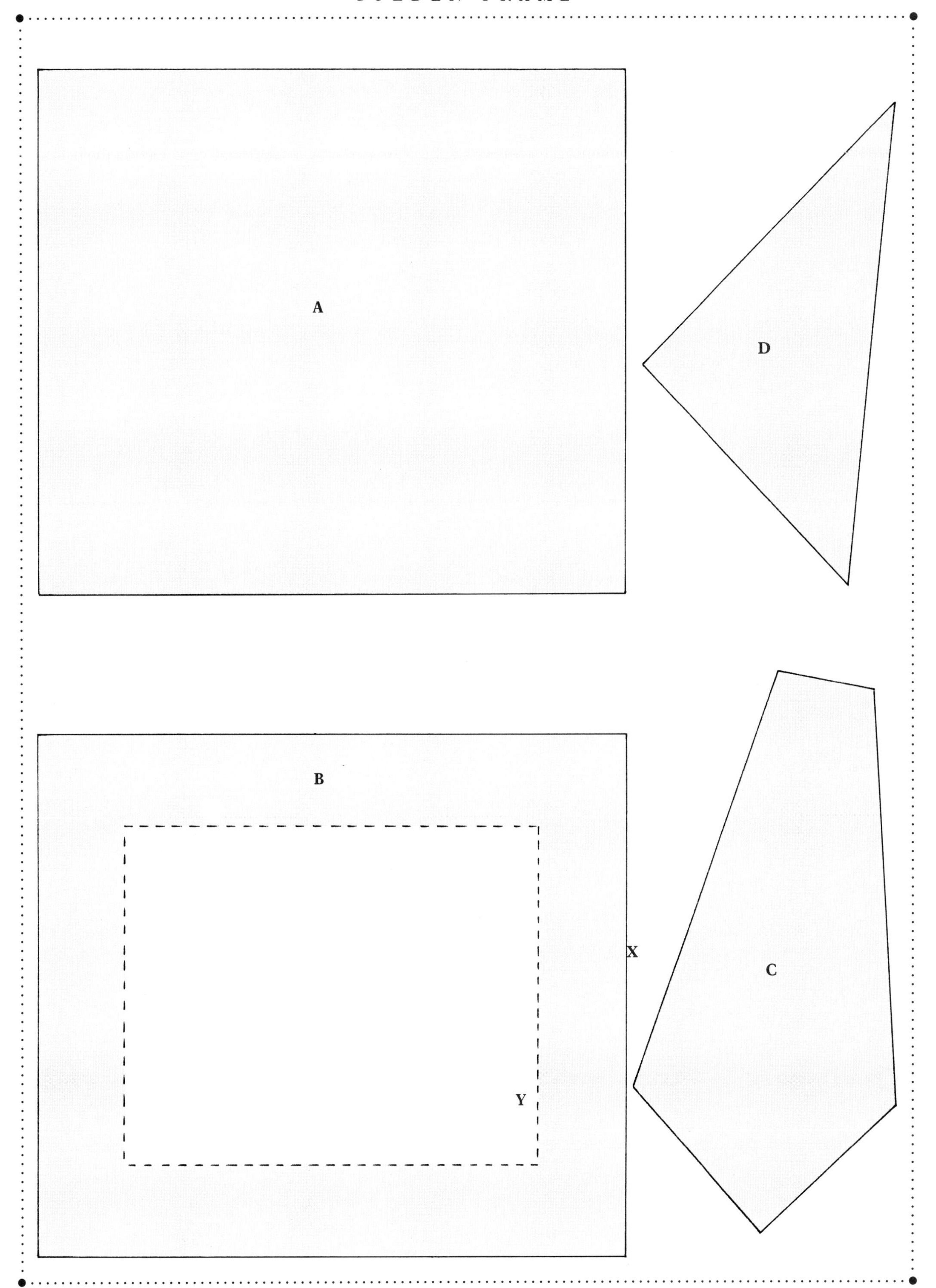
A
D
B
X
C
Y

Floral Box

Rich tones of peach, pink, gold, and cream are used to embroider the rose and bud that adorn this elegant box, which is really two boxes – an inner and an outer one. Tiny gold beads top the stamens. This design can be framed or stitched on a cushion.

SIZE
Embroidery: 4¾ × 6⅛ in
(12 × 15.6 cm)
Box: 7 × 5⅝ × 2⅜ in
(17.5 × 14.25 × 6 cm)

MATERIALS
32-count evenweave linen, at least 10 × 12 in (25 × 30 cm), white
Fabric shown: Zweigart "Belfast," shade 101
DMC stranded cotton, 2 skeins: 353
DMC stranded cotton, 1 skein:

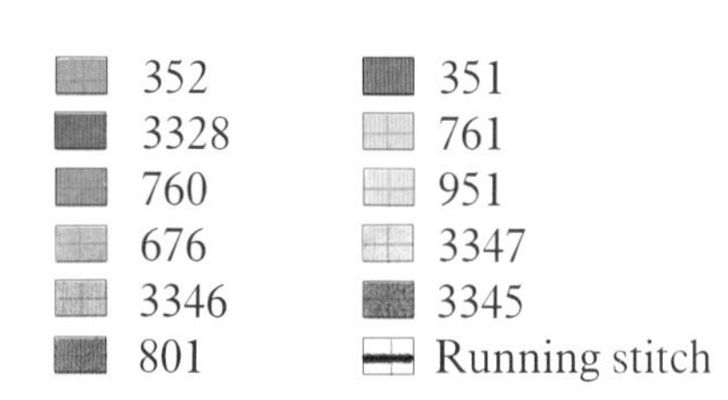

Combined colours:
676 and 951
353 and 676
352 and 676

Gold beads, 7 small
Peach dupioni silk, ¼ yd (20 cm)
Cream-coloured lining fabric, ⅜ yd (35 cm), at least 36 in (90 cm) wide
Cream-coloured felt, ¼ yd (20 cm)
Foam padding, ¼ yd (20 cm), at least 28 in (70 cm) wide and ¼ in (6 mm) thick
Cardboard, 14 × 30 in (35 × 75 cm)
Transparent adhesive tape
Glue stick
Cutting board and craft knife
Steel ruler

CHART FOR FLORAL BOX DESIGN

Working the embroidery

1 Bind the fabric edge with tape or overcast stitches. Mark the centre with basting stitches and mount in an embroidery frame.

2 Following the chart from the centre out, embroider the design in cross stitch. Use two strands of thread throughout. Some areas of the design need two shades in the needle. Small straight stitches are used for leaf points. Stamens are worked in backstitch using 676 (*see page 98*).

3 Press the finished embroidery face down on a padded ironing board.

4 With matching sewing threads, sew a bead to the top of each stamen in the positions shown. Alternatively work French knots (*see page 126*) using six strands of shade 676.

Working the outer box

1 Photocopy the templates on page 81 at 200 per cent, so they are twice the size at which they appear. Then photocopy them again at 200 per cent, so the templates are four times the original size. Using the enlarged templates, cut the outer box pieces from cardboard. Bind the edges of all pieces securely with tape.

2 Cut a strip of felt 25½ × 2⅜ in (65 × 6 cm). Glue front, back, and side pieces of the box to the felt; stagger layers (*see illustration below*).

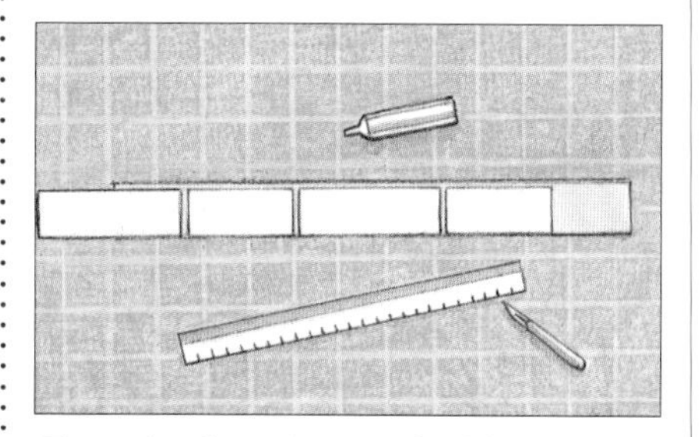

Fastening box pieces to the felt

3 Form the strip into a rectangle and glue the flap of felt to the free end of the back so they join in the centre. (Trim the felt to avoid overlapping the other edge.) Glue the base piece to the felt and trim around the edges.

4 Cut a strip of peach fabric 26¼ in × 4 in (67 × 10 cm). Join and stitch ends, right sides together; use ⅜ in (1 cm) seam allowance. Press seam open; turn strip right side out.

5 Place fabric strip over the sides of the box, positioning seam at a back corner. Turn the raw edges to the inside and lace together with strong thread (*see illustration below*).

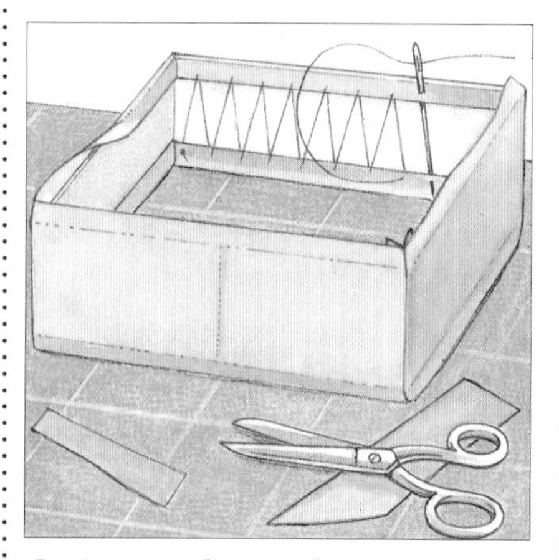

Lacing raw edges together

6 Cut a piece of peach fabric 9½ × 8 in (24 × 20 cm) and place on a flat surface. Smooth out any creases carefully. Add glue to edges of base, then place base in centre of fabric.

Press fabric edge against glued edges of base piece. Trim off any excess fabric neatly at the corners.

7 Place base inside box sides. Stick fabric onto the lower part of the box sides. Using the base template, cut out shape from foam and lining fabric. Layer lining fabric, then foam, then lid. Fold fabric over the edges and pin to the edge of the cardboard (*see illustration below*).

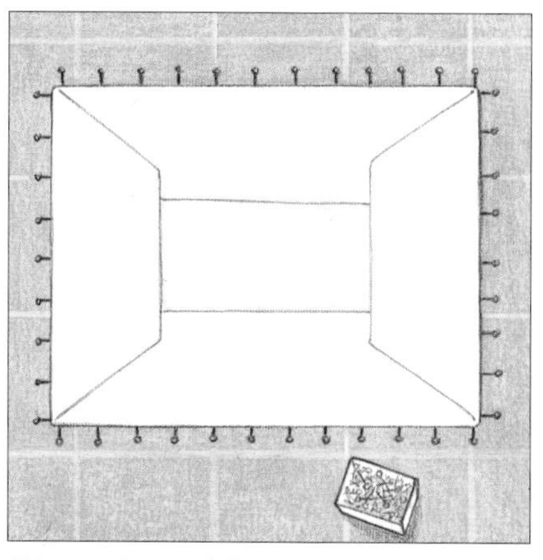

Pinning lining fabric in position

8 Centre embroidery onto top of lid; pin in place by inserting the pins into the edge of the cardboard. Place lid face down and trim embroidery fabric 1¼ in (3 cm) larger than lid. Trim corners diagonally as shown to within ¼ in (6 mm) of the corners of the board (*see illustration below*).

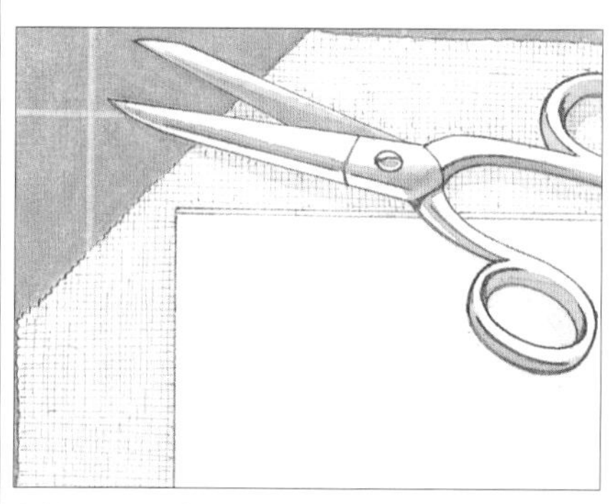

Trimming the corners diagonally

9 Beginning in the centre of one long side, glue the fabric edges to the wrong side of the lid. Pull fabric taut; glue diagonal edges under corners and secure.

Working the inner box

1 Photocopy the templates opposite at 200 per cent, so they are twice the size at which they appear. Then photocopy them again at 200 per cent, so the templates are four times the original size. Then, using the enlarged templates, cut all pieces from cardboard, and bind edges with tape. Cut matching pieces from foam. Cut matching pieces from lining fabric, but add ¾ in (2 cm) of seam allowance.

2 Cover each cardboard shape with foam and lining fabric as follows: Place lining face down on a hard surface. Position foam in centre, then place cardboard piece on top. Fold lower edge up over cardboard and glue firmly in place; glue side edges; glue top edge securely.

3 Place inner base and four side pieces inside box to fit snugly.

4 Make hinge as follows: Cut a piece of lining fabric 13½ × 3 in (34 × 8 cm). Join and stitch ends, right sides together, using ⅜ in (1 cm) seam allowance. Press seam open. Turn hinge right side out and position seam at centre. Press seam flat.

5 Remove inner back piece from box and glue hinge to cardboard side, leaving 1½ in (4 cm) free (*see illustration below*). Glue hinge to back and replace in box. Repeat with left-hand side and front piece.

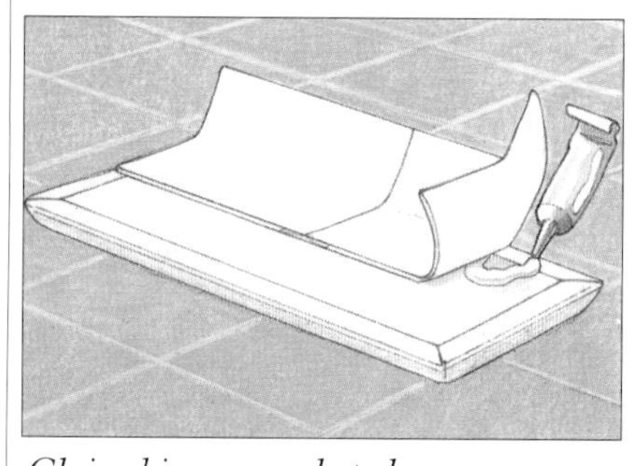

Gluing hinge securely to box

6 Cut a strip of lining fabric 8 × 1¼ in (20 × 3 cm). Turn under ¼ in (6 mm) strip of lining fabric along one long edge; press. Then turn under another 3/16 in (5 mm); press. Along the other long edge, turn under 3/16 in (5 mm); press. Fold strip, then machine stitch along both edges (*see illustration on opposite page*).

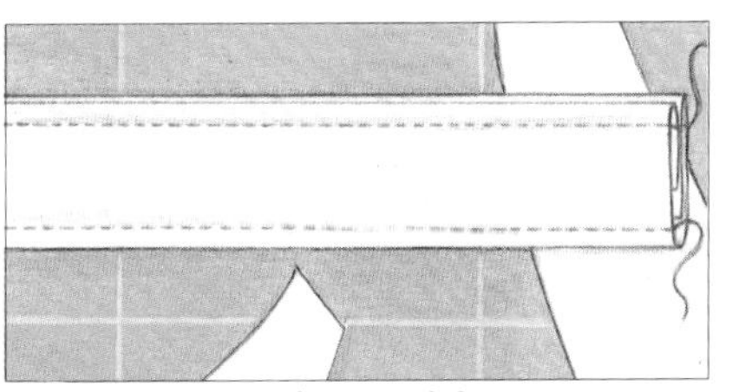
Stitched edges of lining fabric

7 Remove the right-hand side piece from the box and glue the strip to it, making a 45° angle and leaving about 6 in (15 cm) free (*see illustration below*). Glue the right-hand side piece back into the box.

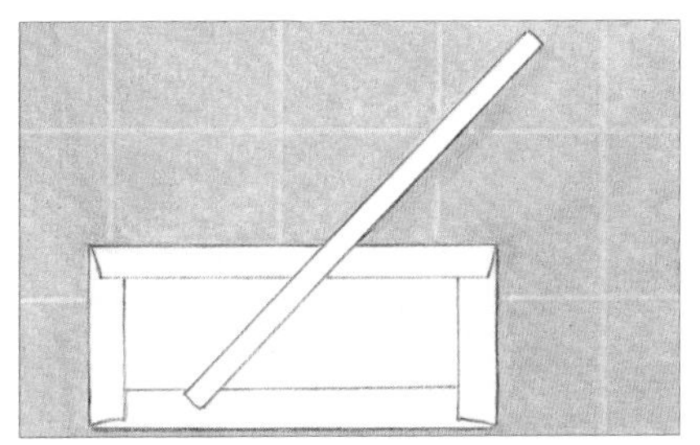
Attaching the right-hand side piece

8 Glue free part of hinge to inner lid, leaving a 1/8 in (3 mm) gap so lid can open easily. Glue strip on wrong side of inner lid.

9 Place embroidered lid right side down. Open box and place inner lid on outer lid, aligning embroidered piece with back edge. Mark front corners with pins (*see illustration below*).

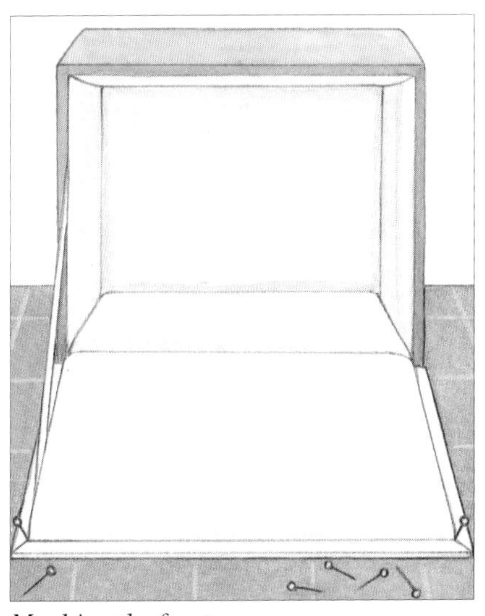
Marking the front corners

10 Glue on lid between pins, with embroidery outside. Dry under weight.

TEMPLATES FOR OUTER BOX

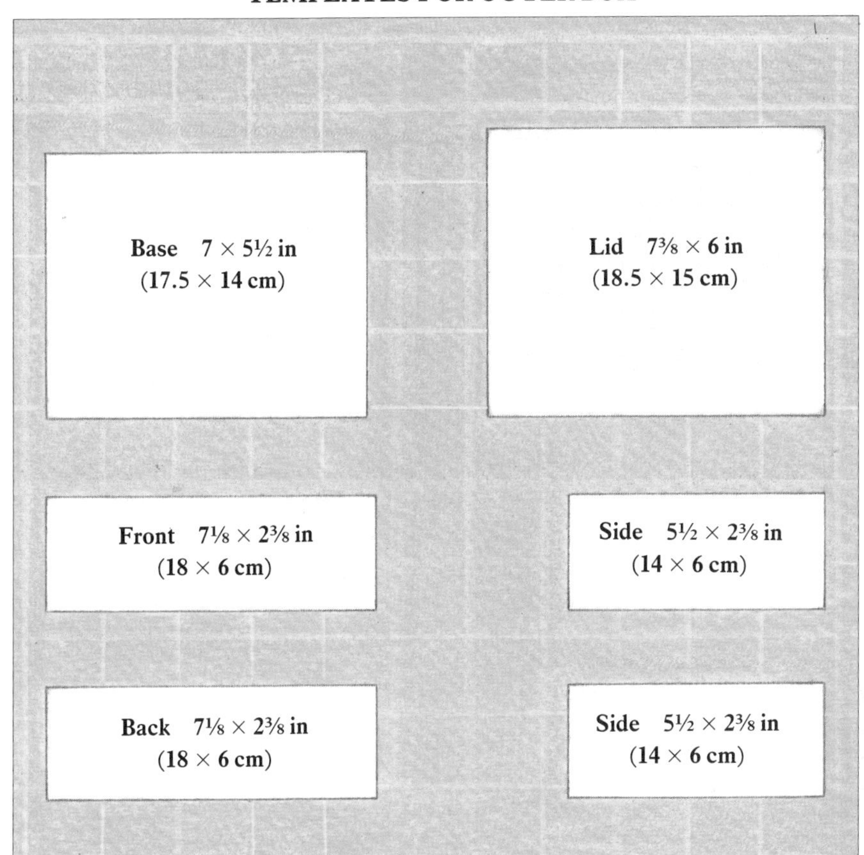

TEMPLATES FOR INNER BOX

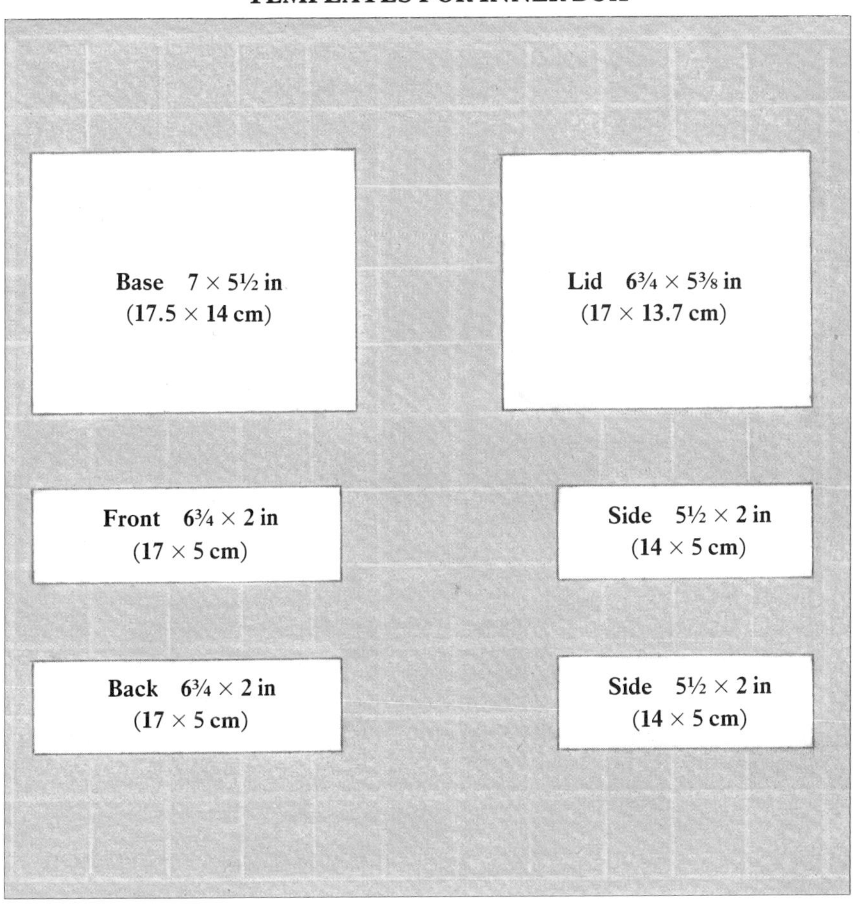

Peacock Napkin and Placemat

The elegance of traditional Assisi work is ideally suited to table linens. The peacock and vine motifs are richly embellished with scrollwork.

SIZE
Placemat: 11¾ × 18 in (30 × 46 cm)
Napkin: 19¼ in (49 cm) square

MATERIALS
For 4 placemats and napkins: 25-count linen, 2⅜ yd (2.1 metres), at least 47 in (119 cm) wide
Fabric shown: Zweigart "Dublin," 222

DMC stranded cotton, amount per colour as shown:

■ 310, 3 skeins

■ 347, 6 skeins

DMC crochet cotton no. 8, ball: ecru
Tapestry needle, size 24

CHART FOR NAPKIN DESIGN

Embroidering and making up the napkins

1 From the fabric, cut a piece 43 × 43 in (109 × 109 cm). Mark the centre in each direction with a line of basting. The corner motifs will be positioned around this centre point.

2 At each corner count in 32 fabric threads and work short lines of basting – about 2 in (5 cm) between the 32nd and 33rd threads. This marks the inner edge of the hemstitching. Count in another six fabric threads; over the seventh and eighth threads, work a single line of cross stitch in red. Continue for 17¾ in (45 cm) in each direction, then turn 90° and work across to complete the border.

3 Mount the fabric in a 6 in (15 cm) round hoop. Beginning at one corner of the border, count 28 stitches to the left; mark this stitch. Count eight threads up from this point and start the scrollwork motif (*see above*). Then work the lower edge of the scrollwork pattern.

4 Work the inner border in cross stitch, 29 stitches on each side. Outline the main motif in Holbein stitch and fill with cross stitch. Complete the border (*see Assisi work technique section, page 29*).

5 When all four napkins have been embroidered, cut along the central lines of basting. Trim the two outer edges of each napkin 38 threads from the border so that all edges are equal. Turn up hems and hemstitch (*see page 153*). Press napkins.

Embroidering and making up the placemat

1 Preshrink fabric (*see page 18*) if necessary. Straighten the end, using scissors, and trim off selvedges.

2 Cut a fabric rectangle 17½ × 23½ in (45 × 60 cm). Cut the longer edge across the width and bind edges.

3 Starting at the top right-hand corner of the chart, measure 3½ in (9 cm) in from top and right-hand edges. Work 134 cross stitches down the right-hand side. Use three strands of red; work over two fabric threads.

4 Count down to the 67th stitch from the top. Run a line of basting or running stitches from the centre of this stitch across the fabric between the two fabric threads. This marks the horizontal centre of the piece (*not* the centre of the fabric).

5 Starting at the mid-point, work the right-hand side of the scrollwork pattern in Holbein stitch (*see page 29*) and cross stitch. Use two strands of black and eight strands of red throughout. Work the inner right-hand border in cross stitch (83 stitches), then the top and bottom borders (29 stitches) and finally the left-hand border. Each square of the chart opposite represents *two* fabric threads.

6 Work main motif; outline in Holbein stitch, then fill in with cross stitch. When outline goes diagonally across the square, fill in with small diagonal stitches worked over only one fabric thread intersection; tuck the stitch under the black outline.

7 Complete scrollwork around the peacock motif.

8 Complete outer border, working clockwise from lower right-hand corner. There are 59 cross stitches before the first scrollwork motif, 61 before the next, and 59 to the left-hand corner. Centre the motif on the left-hand side on the basting line. Work 60 stitches up to this motif, then 57 stitches to the top left-hand corner. Complete top border to match bottom one.

CHART FOR PLACEMAT DESIGN

9 Remove fabric from frame. Count six threads away from the cross stitch border on all edges, then pull out two fabric threads for hemstitching. Count outward 10 threads and pull out the 11th; repeat, pulling out the 11th after that. Count another 8 threads; pull out the 9th. Trim fabric along the last pulled thread.

10 Fold over twice to make a double hem along the outer two pulled threads; mitre the corners. Hemstitch (*see page 153*) with crochet cotton, using four vertical threads with each stitch; press.

Sampler Border Bookmarks

Decorative, useful, and easy to make, these bookmarks make excellent little presents. They are worked on perforated paper or Aida band and are easy to finish. The attractive border motifs were inspired by antique American samplers.

ROSEHIPS BOOKMARK

SIZE
Bookmark: 5¾ × 1¾ in (14.5 × 4.5 cm)

MATERIALS
14-count perforated paper, 6½ × 2½ in (17 × 6 cm)
DMC stranded cotton, 1 skein each colour:

3363
930
347

Tapestry needle, size 22

CHART FOR BOOKMARK DESIGNS

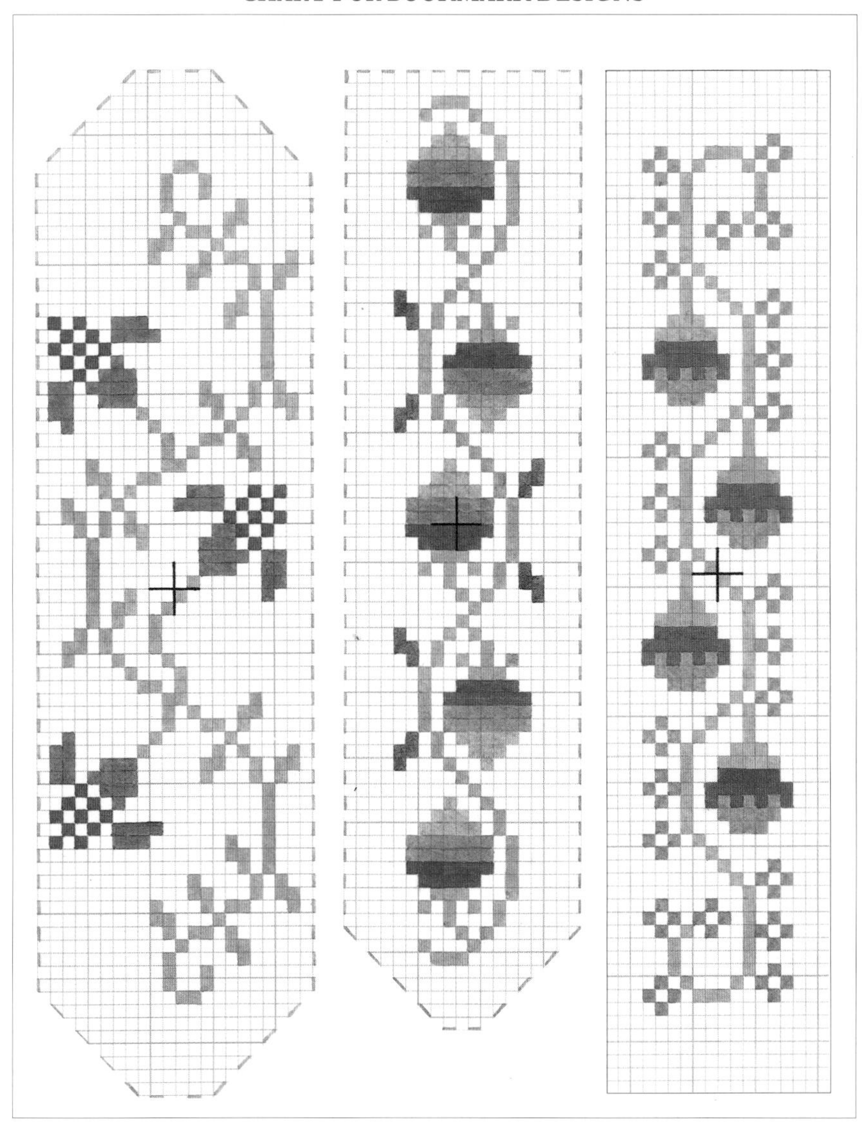

Embroidering and making up the rosehips bookmark

1 Embroider the main design in cross stitch using three strands of thread and following the chart opposite. Each square represents one stitch. Keep the work as neat as possible on the wrong side.

2 Using three strands of shade 3363, work running stitch around the main motif, as indicated on the chart. Work into each hole of the paper; the diagonal stitches will be longer than other stitches. Fasten off neatly.

3 Carefully trim away the excess paper, leaving one line of holes outside the running stitch. You will need to angle the diagonal cuts at one end to form a point.

4 Using shade 347 (or one of the other colours, if preferred), make a small tassel (*see page 156*). To tie the tassel, use three strands only. One by one, thread the two ends (each consisting of three strands) into a needle. Take the needle through the centre hole at the tip of the bookmark and the two adjacent holes. It is a good idea to repeat the stitches several times for security. Tie the two ends firmly together, and trim close to the knot. Trim the tip of the paper just below the fastening point.

TRAILING BUDS BOOKMARK

SIZE
Bookmark: 5½ × 1⅜ in
(14 × 3.5 cm)

MATERIALS
14-count perforated paper, 6½ × 2½ in
(17 × 6 cm)

DMC stranded cotton,
1 skein each colour:

3363
347
422
520
3045

Tapestry needle, size 22

Embroidering and making up the trailing buds bookmark

1 Work the main design in cross stitch, using three strands of thread and following the chart on page 85. Each square represents one stitch. Keep the wrong side neat. Continue to work as for the rosehips bookmark on page 85.

2 Make a small tassel (*see page 156*) using shade 3363. Thread the tassel ends into the bottom two holes on the tip (see rosehips bookmark). Fasten securely into adjacent running stitches on the wrong side.

FRINGED BOOKMARK

SIZE
Bookmark: 8¼ × 2 in
(21 × 5 cm)

MATERIALS
14-count cream Aida band, 12 × 2 in
(30 × 5 cm)

DMC stranded cotton,
1 skein each colour:

3363
347
931

8 in (20 cm) of cream or white ribbon, 8 × 1¾ in (20 × 4.5 cm) wide

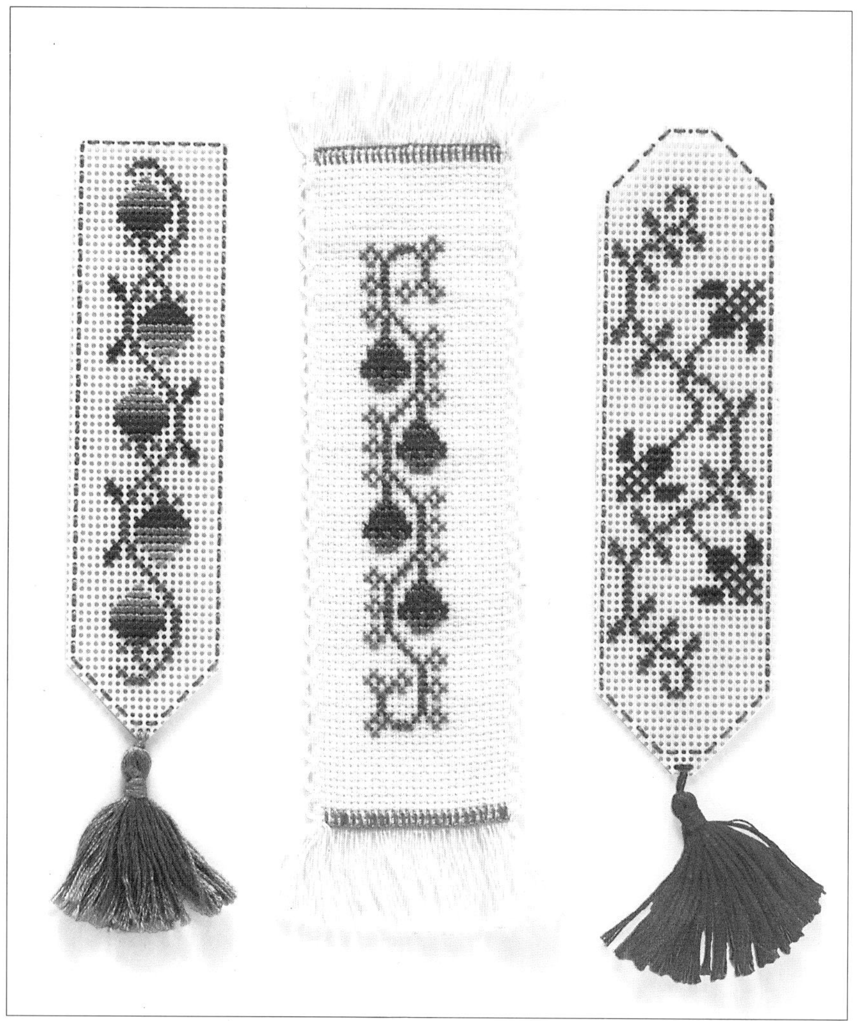

Completed stitched bookmarks

Embroidering and making up the fringed bookmark

1 Mark the vertical centre of the Aida band (14 threads from each edge) with a line of basting or running stitch. Work the design in cross stitch with two strands of thread, centring it along the basted line; follow the chart on page 85.

2 Count 12 threads from one end of the design. Using two strands of shade 3363 work buttonhole stitch (*see page 155*) across one end inside the scalloped edges. Work stitches across one vertical thread and over two horizontal threads. Repeat at the band's other end.

3 Trim the ends to within 1 in (2.5 cm) of the stitching. Pull out the horizontal threads (up to the stitching) to form a fringe. Press the work from the wrong side.

4 Turn under ¼ in (6 mm) on one end of the ribbon. Hem this over the buttonhole stitches on the wrong side of the band, working very small stitches with care. Continue hemming the ribbon in place along all four edges. At the corners, catch the threads of the scalloped edge to hold the ribbon securely in place. Press.

Pattern Darning and Blackwork

These counted thread techniques offer a natural progression from cross stitch. Wonderfully intricate designs, with a crisp, geometric quality, can be created simply by working lines of running stitch through the fabric in a regular pattern – a technique known as pattern darning. Even richer effects are possible in blackwork, where the use of one colour emphasises the depiction of tones and textures.

Pattern Darning Techniques

Darning is probably as old as stitching itself. The charm, versatility, and simplicity of pattern darning have contributed to its continuing popularity as a technique for decorating items as varied as children's clothes, skirts, shawls, and household linens.

BASICS OF PATTERN DARNING

Although pattern darning is worked using only a simple running stitch, it can create very diverse effects. It can, for example, vary considerably in the amount of fabric covered by the stitches. In some styles, the background occupies almost as much space as the stitches, so that the results closely resemble weaving. In others, the stitches predominate, producing work similar to satin stitch. The stitching itself can also be used as the background, with the motifs left unworked.

All types of pattern darning are reversible, although the pattern on the wrong side is usually less interesting than that on the right side. The stitches can be worked vertically, horizontally, or diagonally, or in both directions in the same space. Juxtaposing areas in which the darning lines run in both directions produces an interesting effect.

In double darning, the fabric is completely covered by lines of double running stitch. This is normally worked in two different colours.

Choosing materials for pattern darning

Most evenweave fabrics can be used for pattern darning, although coarser weaves are not suitable if the stitches on the wrong side should not be visible. Because the darning is normally worked along every horizontal thread of the fabric, fine fabrics require considerably more rows of stitching to create a pattern than coarser weaves do.

The embroidery thread should be approximately the same weight as the fabric thread. If the stitches are intended to retain their identity, forming a linear texture over the fabric, a single strand of coton à broder or perlé cotton (*see page 15*) will be the most suitable.

If the stitches are intended to blend together in a satiny effect, stranded floss will work better, since many strands are required to cover the fabric you are using.

If the fabric is coarse, several strands of crewel yarn would be a good choice for your work.

PATTERN DARNING

The pattern in pattern darning is created by the juxtaposition of the stitches and the unstitched areas on the fabric. Pattern darning is worked in straight lines over a predetermined sequence of counted threads to create a pattern. It can be stitched vertically, horizontally, or diagonally and uses running stitch, the most basic stitch of all.

Working simple pattern darning

It is possible to work pattern darning by holding the fabric in the hand if a smooth, relaxed tension is always maintained. However, some stitchers prefer to work double darning in a frame. In either case, take care not to pull the stitches; the fabric should lie flat and be unpuckered.

- Anchor the thread securely with one or two backstitches (*see illustration opposite page:* **1**).
- To work running stitch on evenweave fabric, bring the needle up in the space at the beginning of the line you wish to fill and pull the thread through. Count the number of

STARTING AND FINISHING

Depending on your design, you can start to stitch at the centre (*see illustration right:* **1**) or along one edge of the fabric. If possible, work with a length of thread long enough to complete at least one row of stitching.

Anchor your working thread with backstitches (**2**) that can be removed later. If you are starting in the centre, leave a tail of thread to stitch into the first line (**3**).

If the edges of the worked pattern will be sewn into a seam, fasten the end of the thread with one or two backstitches in the seam allowance. Otherwise, take all ends to the wrong side of the work and darn them into the stitching as neatly as possible.

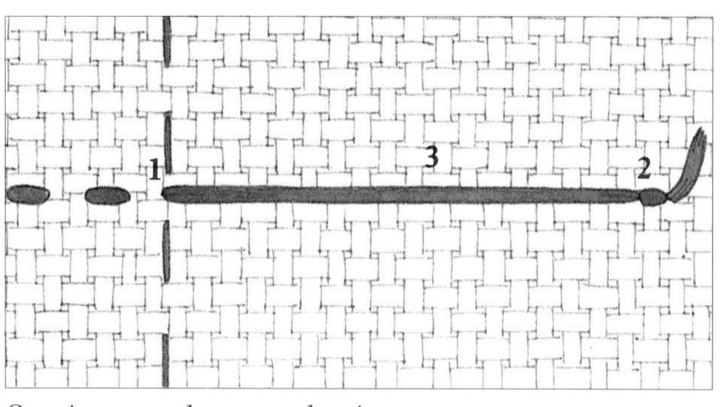

Starting to work pattern darning

threads required by your pattern and then take the needle down into the next space (**2**).

- Count the number of threads required for the next stitch and bring the needle up, then count and take it down as before (**3**).

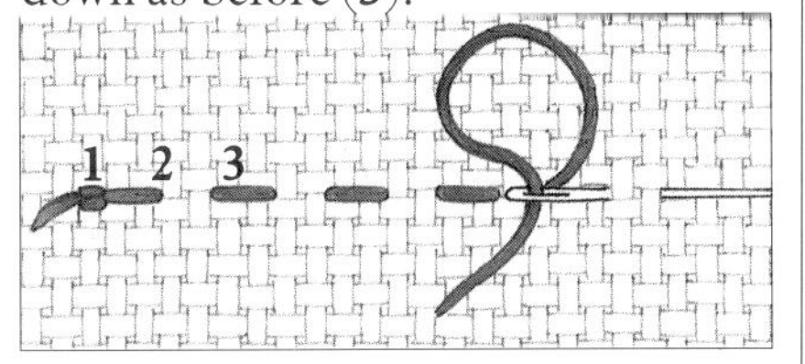

Working running stitch with a backstitch anchor

- Continue moving in and out through the fabric until you reach the end of the line of stitching.
- Then begin stitching the next line of the pattern and work in the same way, counting threads carefully as you work along the line.

You can work pattern darning either from right to left or left to right, over different numbers of threads and in any direction. Some examples are shown here (*see illustration below*).

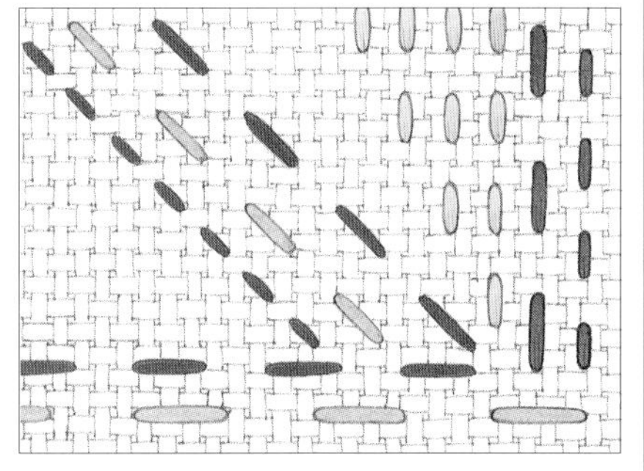

Running stitch worked in various directions

DOUBLE DARNING

Double darning is a form of pattern darning that involves working a pattern of stitches in one colour first and then filling in the spaces with a second colour.

Working double darning

- Using the first colour, begin by stitching a line as for simple pattern darning to establish the pattern.
- Using the second colour, fill in the gaps in the pattern as shown (*see illustration below*). Remember that the needle will be brought up into a hole already containing a stitch. It is easier to achieve a neat effect if you hold the needle vertically.

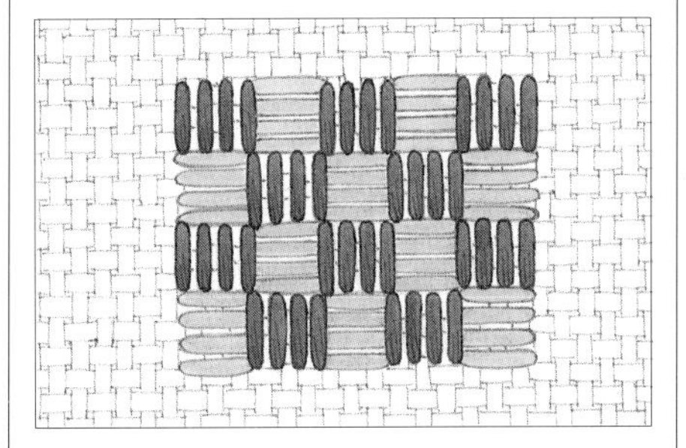

A two-colour darning pattern

- Work each line of the pattern in the same way. You may find it handy to keep two needles threaded, one for each colour thread.

Pattern darning variations

Using two shades of the same colour, especially on diagonal patterns, produces the look of woven damask.

In another attractive variation of double darning, a single fabric thread is left between each stitch.

PATTERN DARNING DESIGNS

Even complex darning patterns are easy to stitch once you have carefully established the pattern.

Positioning the pattern

- To begin, mark the vertical centre of the fabric with a line of basting or running stitches (*see page 18*).
- Begin the pattern darning at this point and, using darning stitch, work one line of the pattern out to the left. (This can be the top line of the pattern, but it need not be.) Leave a long tail of thread at the centre starting point of the pattern.
- When you reach the left-hand edge, return to the centre starting point and darn to the right-hand edge. If possible, use the tail of thread left at the starting point.

Subsequent lines can be worked from right to left across the whole width to build up the patterns (*see illustration below*).

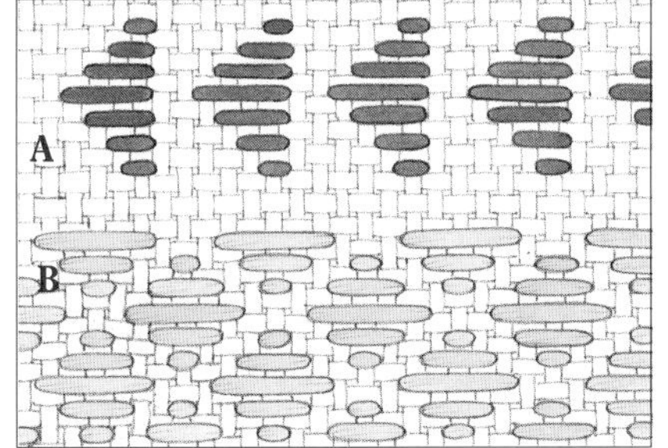

Establishing two different patterns

Counting the fabric threads at the edges of a pattern can also help to establish a pattern on the fabric.

PLANNING A DESIGN

It is quite easy to create your own designs for pattern darning. Chart the design on graph paper first and treat the grid lines as fabric threads. Then experiment with the design on spare fabric.

The attractive sampler shown (*see photograph*) was worked on 27-count evenweave fabric using three or four strands of stranded floss. A wide range of pattern darning designs can be developed. Experiment with different effects by changing either the pattern or the fabric or the thread. Read all the instructions on pattern darning carefully before starting to plan your individual design.

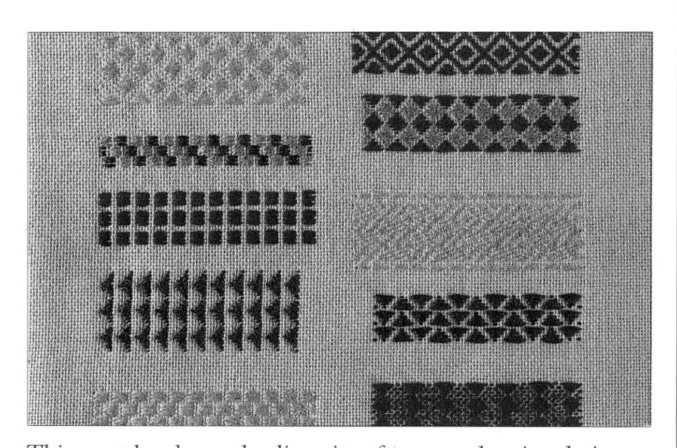

This sampler shows the diversity of pattern darning designs

Pattern-Darned Guest Towels

This quick, easy project is ideal as a present, bazaar item, or accessory for your home. All you need are Aida-band towels, a few skeins of stranded cotton, and a free evening or two.

SIZE
Towels shown: 18 × 16¼ in
(45 × 26 cm)

MATERIALS
2 towels with 14-count Aida band at least 2¼ in (6 cm) wide

DMC stranded cotton
in contrasting colours, 2 skeins
Colours shown are:

995
943

Tapestry needle, size 20

BLUE PATTERN

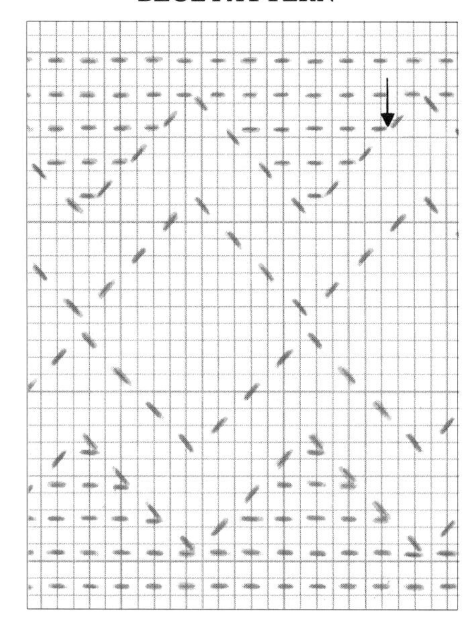

BLUE AND GREEN PATTERN

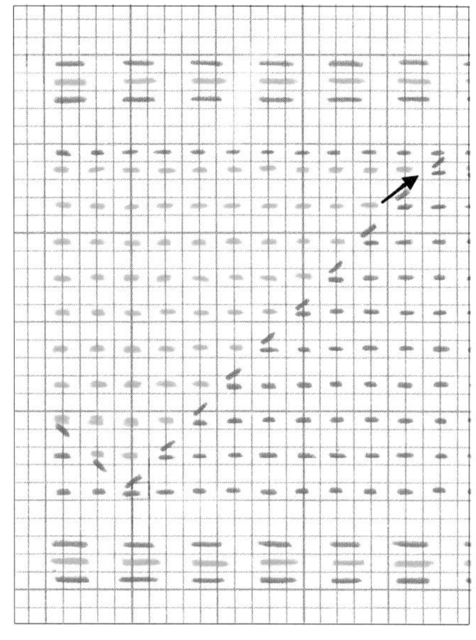

Working the blue pattern

1 Mark vertical centre of Aida band with a line of basting.

2 Work the top two lines of darning across the width of the towel, using all six strands of thread and following the chart (*above left*). Each line shown on the chart represents one group of fabric threads.

3 Work top of pattern from centre to left-hand edge. Begin at the arrow and work the lines for the first point to the left of the centre mark. At the bottom of the point, work the diagonal line up to the top left.

4 Repeat for next point to the left, leaving right-hand diagonal line unworked. Continue in this way to the left-hand edge of the towel.

5 Work back to the right, filling in the unworked diagonal lines. On the wrong side, secure the thread under a couple of previously worked stitches.

6 Finish top of pattern from centre to right-hand edge by reversing method in steps 3–5. Then work two centre zigzag lines, taking care to follow the chart exactly.

7 Turn work upside down and repeat steps 3–6 to work the lower points. Add the outer two lines of darning. Press the completed work lightly and carefully on a well-padded ironing board.

Working the blue and green pattern

1 Mark vertical centre of Aida band with a line of basting.

2 Work the top three lines of the pattern, using all six strands of thread and following the chart (*above right*). Each line on the chart represents one group of threads. Then skip three horizontal fabric threads and work the top line of the main band in blue.

3 Starting at the arrow, work the first green triangle to the left of the centre mark; fasten off. Work the next (partial) green triangle. Work the other green triangles out to the right-hand edge. Fill in remaining spaces with blue thread.

4 Using blue thread, work the diagonal zigzag line between the triangles. Then work the bottom three lines of the pattern. Press completed work lightly over a well-padded ironing board.

Variations

This pattern can be worked over any evenweave linen or cotton fabric to make a traditional guest towel.

Carousel Curtains

This attractive carousel design is ideal for a pair of curtains or a wall hanging for a child's bedroom. The colours shown here can easily be changed to suit any individual colour scheme.

SIZE
Finished curtain: 46 × 31½ in
(117 × 80 cm)

MATERIALS
28-count evenweave fabric, two pieces.
Fabric shown: Zweigart "Annabelle"
(Each piece should be approximately the window width.)

DMC stranded cotton,
5 skeins:

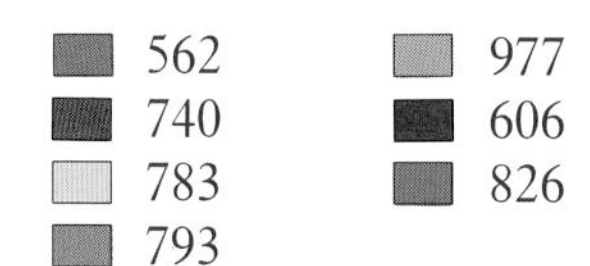

Sewing thread to match
Marking pen with water-soluble ink
Adhesive tape

Template for the carousel horses

Positioning the pattern

1 Measure your window. Add 15 in (38 cm) to length to allow for hemming top and bottom. (This design requires a deep bottom hem: the stitch line of the hem is level with the base of the carousel.) Zigzag stitch top and bottom edges to prevent the fabric from fraying. **Note:** If you have a particularly wide window, it might be better to consider making four curtains rather than two. It is possible to join pieces of fabric together, but the seams look bulky and will detract from the completed embroidered design.

2 Fold up 6 in (15 cm) and press, making sure you follow the weft of the fabric. Measure 5¾ in (14.5 cm) up from the crease and draw a line with a marking pen across the whole width of the fabric (*see illustration below*). This is where the bottom of the carousel will be positioned.

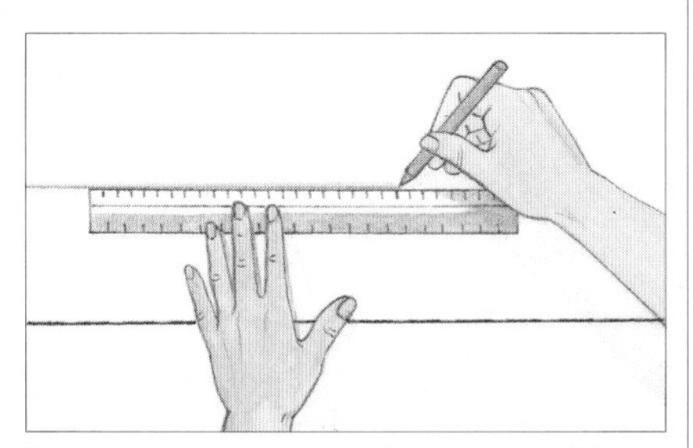

Marking the position of the carousel base

3 Measure ¾ in (2 cm) up from the line. Mark along width of fabric, keeping to a width of one horizontal thread (*see illustration below:* **1**). Measure 4 in (10 cm) in from the side edges, still keeping to one horizontal thread. Draw a vertical line joining the two horizontal lines (**2**). This establishes the depth and length of the carousel platform on the design.

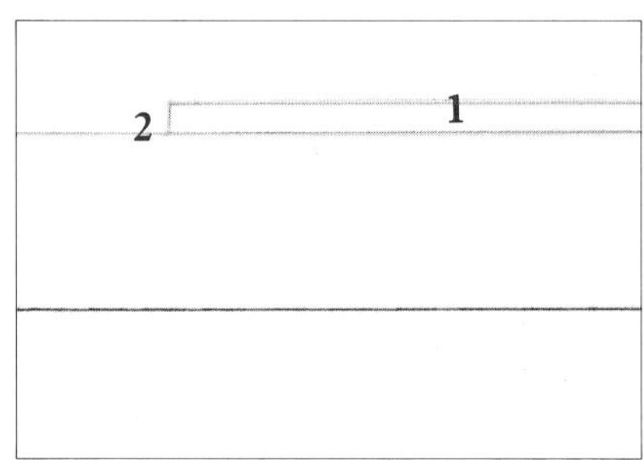

Marking left-hand edge of the platform

4 Measure 7⅜ in (18.5 cm) up from the carousel platform and ⅜ in (1 cm) in from each side. Mark along

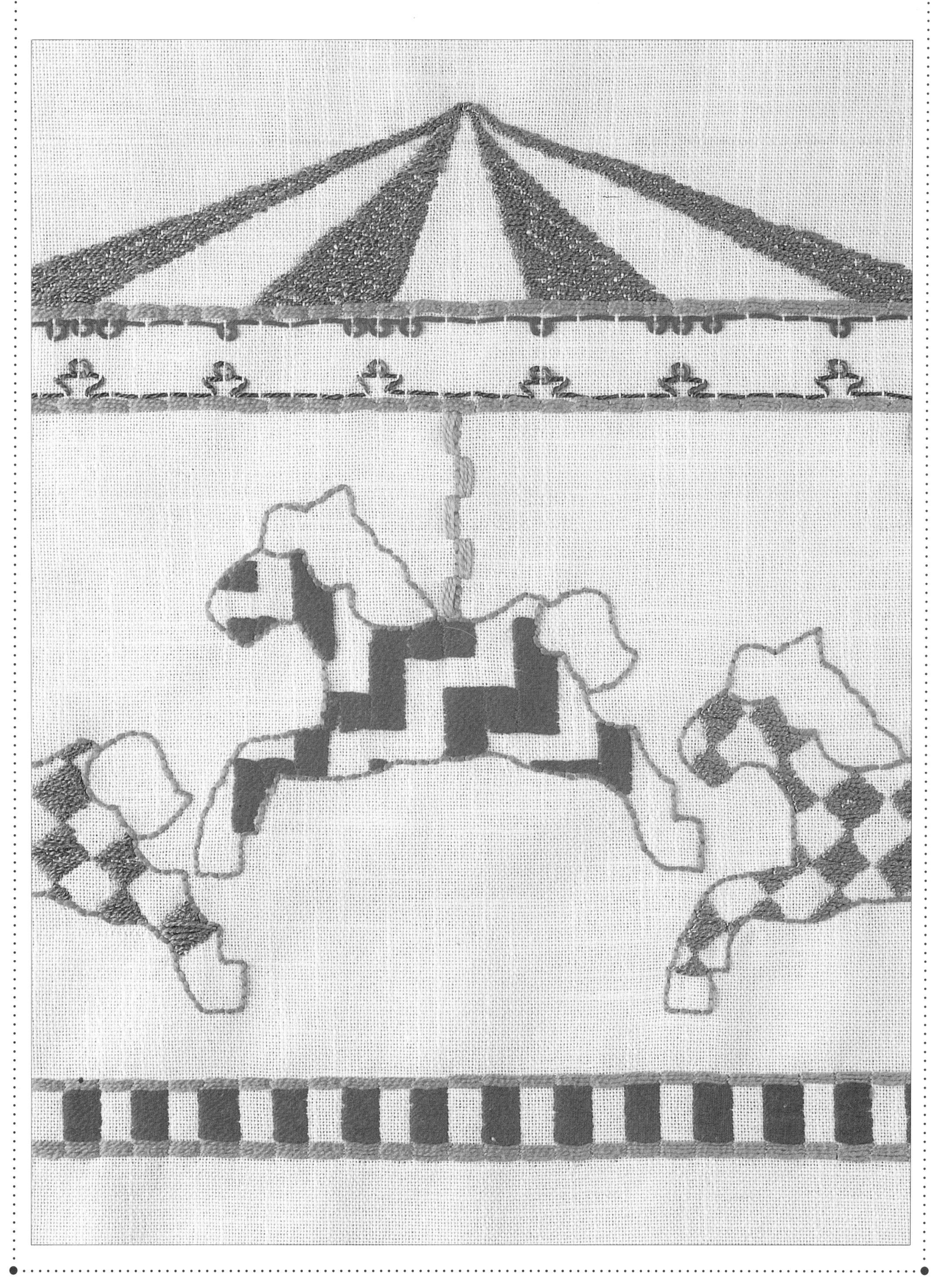

one horizontal thread. This is the base of the roof. Measure 1⅛ in (3 cm) up from this line and mark along one horizontal thread.

Measure 1⅞ in (4.75 cm) up from the centre of the roof line and mark. Measure 7 in (18 cm) in from either side of the fabric and mark. Join these points to the point 1⅞ in (4.75 cm) above the roof line, forming a triangle (*see illustration below*).

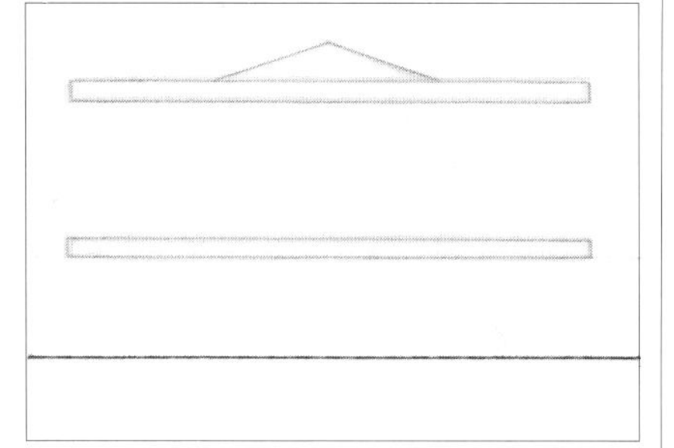

Marking roof line and triangle cap

5 Divide the base of the triangle into seven equal sections (*see illustration above*). Draw a vertical line from the end of each section to the apex of the triangle as shown.

6 Mark in the carousel poles 5 in (12.75 cm) apart. The short poles are 2 in (5 cm) long; the long poles are 4¾ in (12 cm) long. Start by drawing a short pole down from the centre of the roof base, and then alternate long and short poles (*see illustration below*). The number of poles will depend on the width of your fabric.

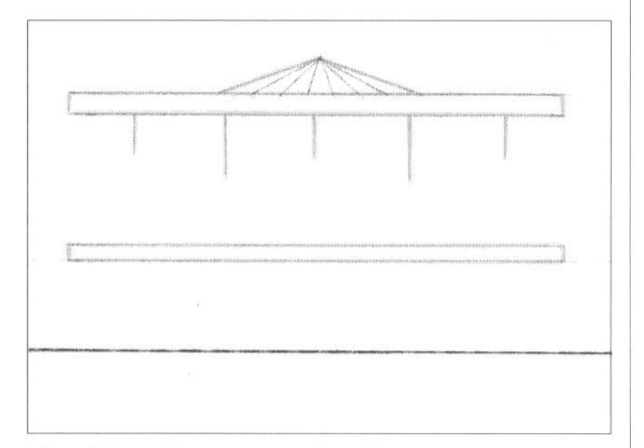

Marking the carousel poles

7 Photocopy the horse template (*see illustration on page 94*) at 130 per cent, so that it is about one-third larger than the size in the book. Then place the horse template onto the fabric, positioning it carefully at the end of each pole. Draw around it.

Working the embroidery

1 Work backstitch (*see page 98*) along each of the carousel poles and around the edges of the horses to form an outline (*see illustration below*).

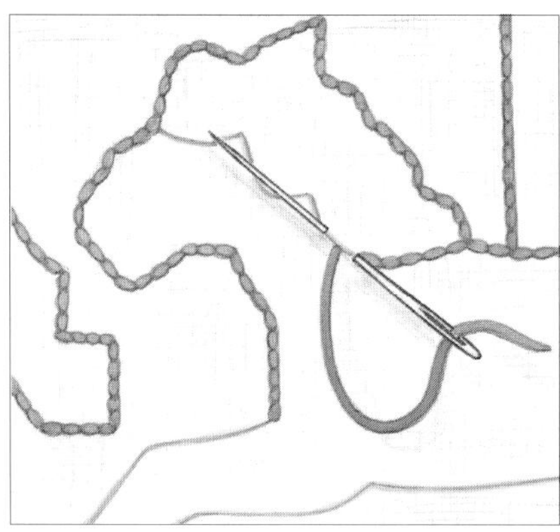

Backstitching the outline of the horses

You may decide to work the outline in different colours on each horse, depending on the number of horses in your design.

2 Work three rows of darning stitch (*see page 90*) in gold thread to mark the top and bottom lines of the carousel platform. All stitches should be equal in length so that you form vertical columns. Use short lengths of thread and a loose tension to avoid pulling the fabric.

3 Using darning stitch, carefully work alternate columns in red thread to create a chequerboard pattern in the area between the gold rows (*see illustration below*).

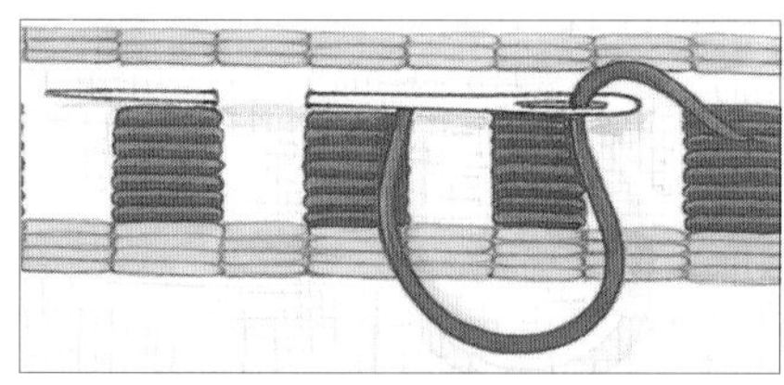

Filling in the chequerboard pattern along the carousel base

4 In the same way, work three rows of gold darning stitch along the top and bottom of the roof base. Work a row of red running stitches below the top gold band with looped stitches at regular intervals, picking up one thread to hold each loop in place.

Work a row of blue running stitches at regular intervals along the roof above the bottom gold band (*see illustration below*).

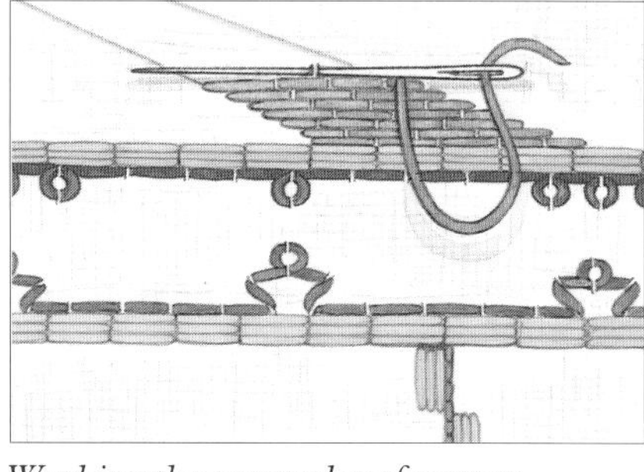

Working the carousel roof pattern

5 Using darning stitch, fill in alternate triangles on the roof in green thread, working from bottom to top. When you are ¼ in (6 mm) from the top, darn straight across the roof to join the sections together.

6 Embroider patterns on the horses. Fill in the diamond patterns on alternate horses in the same way as on the roof. Fill in the chevron pattern in the same way as in the red chequerboard pattern on the base of the carousel (*see illustration below*).

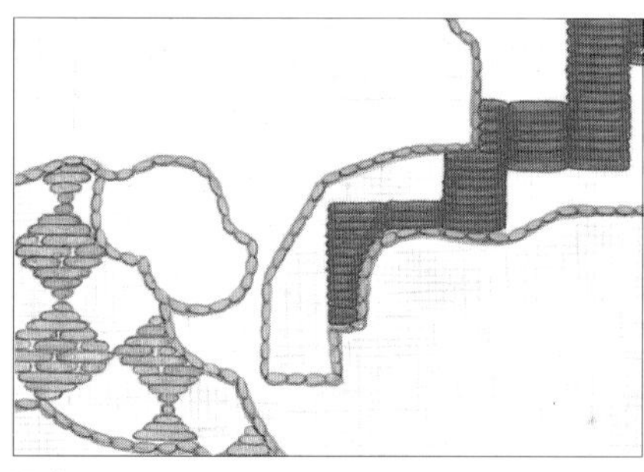

Filling in chevron and diamond patterns

7 Carefully press the completed embroidery using a steam iron. Fold in the side edges 1¼ in (3 cm), press, and slipstitch. Turn up 6 in (15 cm) at the bottom, turn zigzag edge under ¼ in (6 mm), and slipstitch. Attach tape to top of the curtains.

Variation

The measurements given for this set of curtains can be adapted to suit your own particular window. The base and roof could also be worked in simple outline stitch rather than the darning stitch.

Blackwork Techniques

The centuries-old technique of blackwork can be used on a wide variety of items from household linens to pictorial panels. Its geometric designs can be worked as everything from motifs on table napkins to borders on curtains.

BASICS OF BLACKWORK

Blackwork is easier than it looks. Patterns are created using only a few stitches: for example, backstitch, running stitch, Holbein (also known as double running) stitch (see page 29), *cross stitch* (see page 26), *Smyrna stitch* (see page 27), *and Algerian eyelets. Only two or three of these are normally used in any one design. Once you have worked a few motifs of a pattern, it is easy to repeat the motifs as required to fill in the shape or outline of a design.*

Choosing materials for blackwork

Blackwork is normally worked with a single thread that is in scale with the fabric. Linen or cotton evenweaves are the traditional fabrics, but other evenweaves, ranging from silk to canvas, can be used. On fine fabrics, a single strand of stranded floss or sewing thread (silk for a lustrous effect) is most suitable; typically coton à broder or perlé cotton is used on medium-weight fabrics. On coarse fabric, try a softer embroidery cotton. Wool thread or yarn, however, is usually too fuzzy for this technique; blackwork should have a crisp look.

Although traditionally worked in black thread on white fabric, blackwork patterns can be stitched in any two-colour combination (*see the blue and white cushions on pages 102–103*). Various shades of the same colour thread can sometimes be used effectively. For the best effect, however, there should be a good colour contrast between the fabric and the thread used in the project.

BLACKWORK STITCHES

Because blackwork patterns are geometric, they rely on linear designs. These in turn depend on straight stitches, which can be horizontal, vertical, or diagonal. In blackwork the patterns depend on the length and the configuration of the stitches. Patterns can be altered – in some cases radically, in others subtly – by changing the number of threads over which a stitch is worked, or by altering the number of stitches made.

Working backstitch

Almost every blackwork pattern makes use of backstitch.

- The basic principle of the stitch is shown here worked in a line. As in other counted thread techniques, each stitch is worked over the same number of threads, in this case three. Begin working the stitch by bringing the needle out in front of the line to be covered (*see illustration below:* **1**). Then take the needle back once again to the beginning of the line (**2**).
- Bring the needle out an equal distance beyond the stitch just made (**3**) and back again to **1**, thus taking a "step" back.

Note that for the first stitch, the needle is brought up ahead of the starting point.

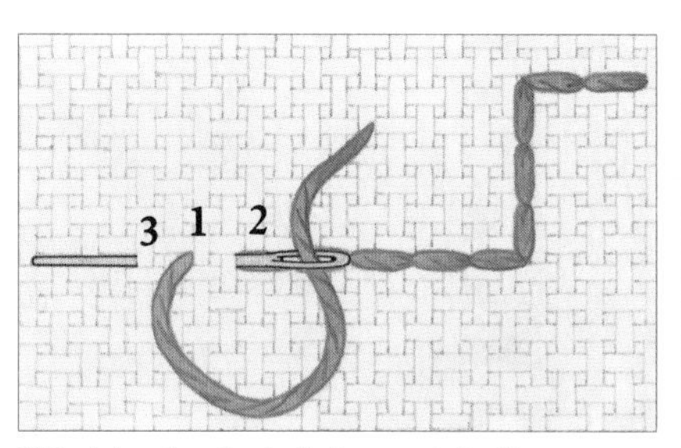

Working backstitch in straight lines

BLACKWORK PATTERNS

There are no hard and fast rules for working a blackwork pattern. Look at the pattern to see what stitches are included and work a few practice motifs, then choose the simplest order of stitching to suit you.

Starting and finishing

Begin and end your work as for cross stitch (*see page 26*). As a general rule, avoid leaving long strands of thread on the wrong side of the work.

Always practise a pattern on a scrap piece of the chosen fabric to make sure that the thread does not show through on the right side of the work. If it does, try using a denser fabric or adjust your order of stitching to make fewer connecting stitches on the back of the work.

Lining the finished work with a darker fabric may help disguise traces of black thread.

Deciding the stitching order

In some cases, each individual motif should be completed before you begin the next. In others, it may be simpler to stitch certain elements in the pattern to provide a framework and then to go back and fill in the other parts of the motifs. The octagonal trellis pattern shown on page 101, for example, needs to have the vertical lines stitched first. Then work the octagon motifs with their central star patterns.

- Backstitch is typically used to form a variety of shapes in blackwork. To work backstitch around corners, simply follow the line of the pattern, working over and under the correct number of threads. Among other shapes, backstitch can form zigzag lines, striped triangles, and squares as shown (*see illustration below*).

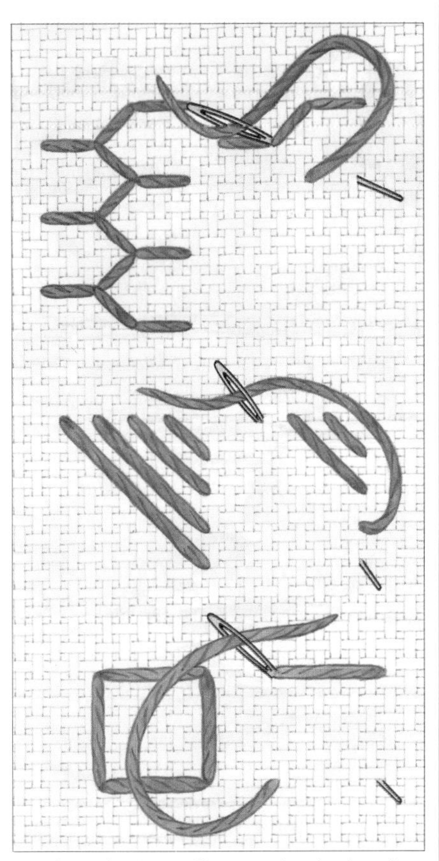

Backstitch zigzag lines, striped triangle, and square

You can substitute Holbein stitch (also known as double running stitch, shown on page 29) for backstitch, if you wish to vary the pattern. Some varied patterns are shown in the box.

Holbein stitch is worked in two runs. The first consists of simple running stitch, worked along a line of stitching. The second run is worked back over the first, filling in the gaps in the running stitching.

Working Algerian eyelet
This stitch resembles Smyrna stitch (*see page 27*), but the threads do not cross at the centre.

- Bring the needle up on the edge of the shape (*see illustration below:* **1**).
- Take the needle down in the middle (**2**), so that you cover the required number of fabric threads in your design.

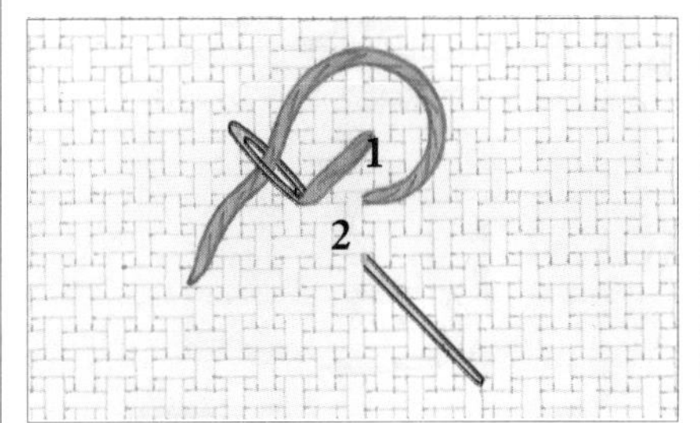

Starting Algerian eyelet

- Continue working around the square following the sequence shown (*see illustration below*). Be careful to take the needle down into the centre hole as you complete the eyelet.

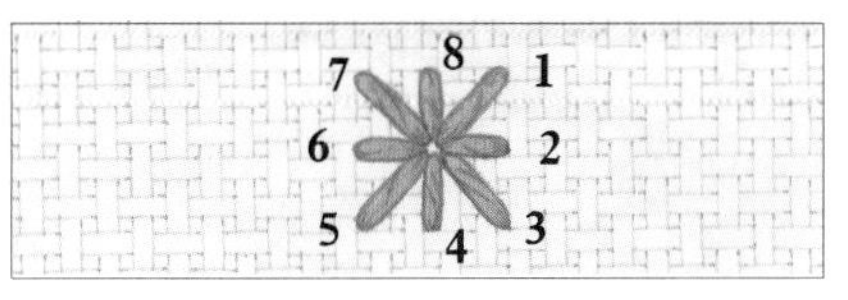

Completing the Algerian eyelet

Positioning patterns
To position a blackwork pattern within a regular shape such as a rectangle or circle, first mark the centre of the fabric with lines of basting or running stitches (*see page 90*). Then work the pattern outward from the central point.

Note that a small-scale pattern need not be centred. It is usually easier to begin near the middle of the shape in order to establish the pattern and then to stitch partial patterns along the edges.

- When using free-form shapes, first transfer the outlines to the fabric (*see page 21*). If the pattern consists of large individual motifs, place one at the focal point of the shape. This can be determined visually, then pinned.

SHADING A PATTERN

The ability to create shading and vary the density of a pattern makes blackwork a very interesting technique. Vary the thickness of thread for a shaded effect (*see photograph below left*).

Many blackwork patterns can easily be varied by adding or subtracting various elements. A simple pattern of squares and cross stitches illustrates the principle (*see photograph below right*). The top row is simply a series of double boxes. The inner boxes in the other rows have been filled in with increasingly complex cross stitches; the outer boxes have been linked first with single, then double, cross stitches.

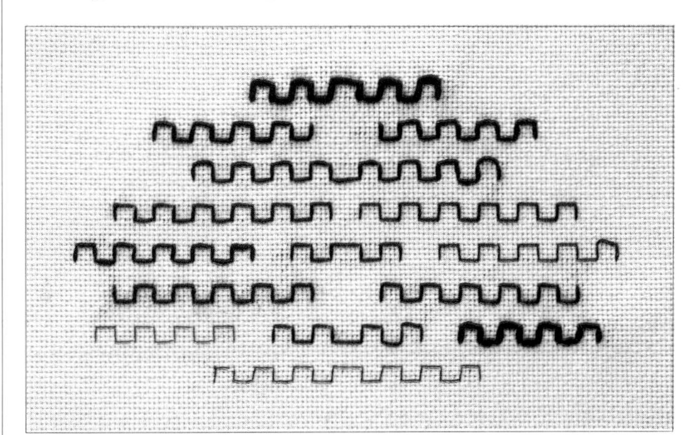

Varying thread thickness to give a shaded effect

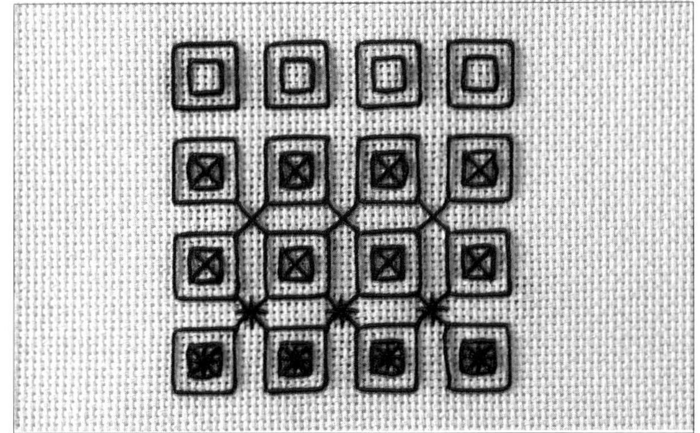

A blackwork pattern combining various elements

• Stitch the first motif, then work outward from it in each direction. You may need to work partial motifs at the edges of free-form or curved designs (*see photograph below*).

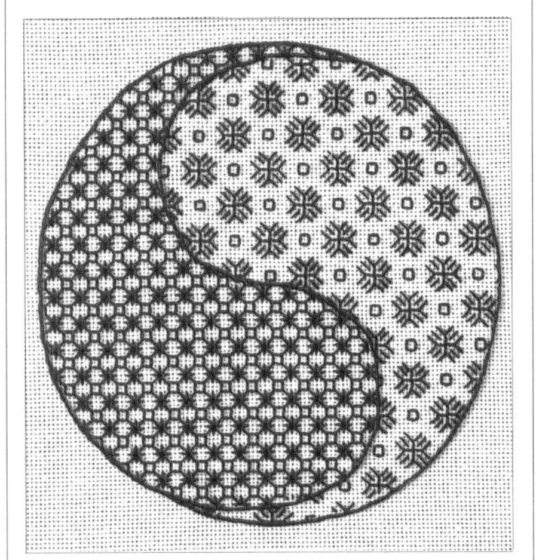

Example of partial motifs

Designing blackwork

Because there are so many blackwork patterns, creating your own designs can be an exciting challenge. If you like the idea of working out your own designs, there are many sources to which you can refer.

To create your own blackwork patterns, staple a piece of coarse evenweave to a piece of grey cardboard and have it photocopied. Use this as a grid for working out your own patterns.

The patterns shown here were worked on 18-count evenweave fabric so that the distinctive structure and effect of each one can be seen (*see photograph below*).

Samples of blackwork patterns

OUTLINING BLACKWORK

When blackwork patterns have been completed, you may define the outlines with any suitable linear stitch you wish. Traditionally, Holbein stitch (see page 29) *or backstitch is used, but stem stitch can also look very attractive. Other surface stitches, such as chain stitch or couching, can also be used and are especially effective on curved or flowing lines. These stitches will, however, create a thicker line. In some modern blackwork, such as the picture on page 107, no edging stitch is used.*

Working stem stitch

• Stem stitch can be worked from left to right or from bottom to top. Bring the needle out at the beginning of the line to be covered (*see illustration below:* **1**).

• Insert the needle further along the line (**2**) and bring it out again so that it comes up at a slight angle (**3**).

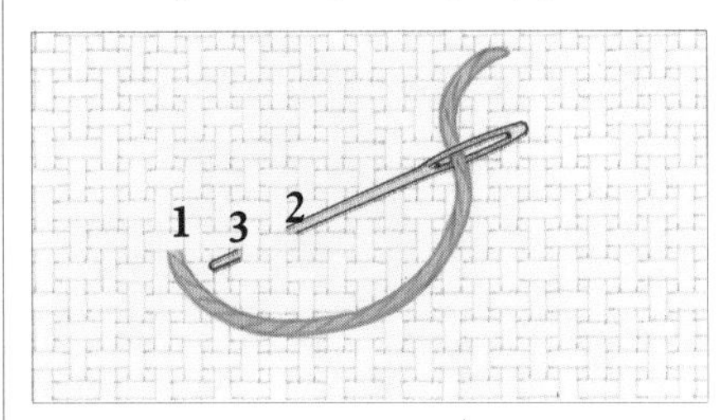

Working an individual stem stitch

• Continue working in this way, keeping each new stitch the same length as the previous one (*see illustration below:* **4**). Take the needle back to the "head" of the line of stitching each time (**5**).

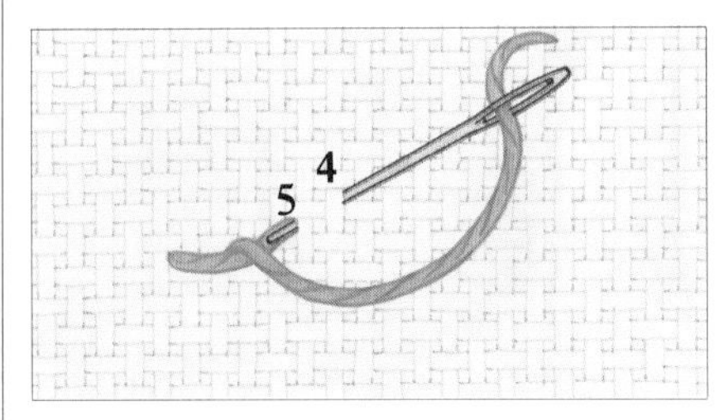

Working a row of stem stitch

For each stitch, keep the thread on the same side of the needle, traditionally below or to the right. Holding the thread on the opposite side is an alternative that alters the look of the stitch slightly.

Working chain stitch

• Bring the needle out at the beginning of the line to be stitched (*see illustration below:* **1**) and hold it down with your thumb. Insert the needle again at **1**.

• Bring the needle out on the stitching line (**2**) and make sure that the thread forms a loop under the needle. Carefully pull up the loop to begin to form the "chain."

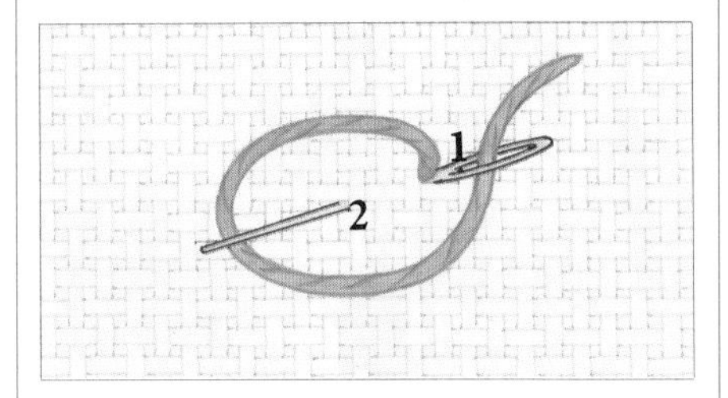

Working the first chain stitch

• Hold the thread down as before and insert the needle again at **2**.

• Hold the loop down as before and bring up the needle (*see illustration below:* **3**). Pull up the loop as before.

• To fasten the final loop in a chain, make a small stitch over it.

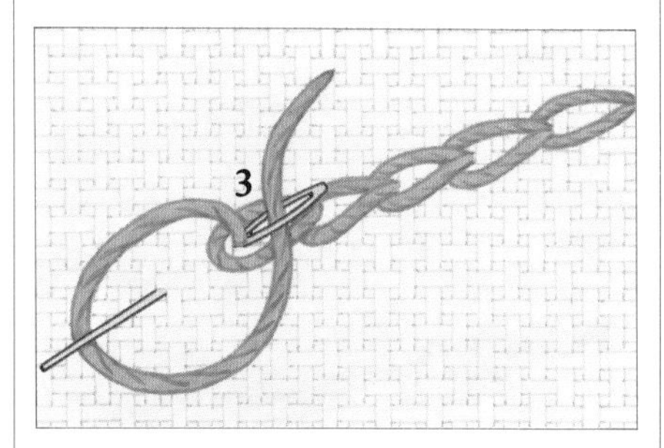

Working a line of chain stitches

Working couching

There are a number of ways to couch threads. One or more threads can be laid down, or "tied", with a variety of stitches. The process of laying the thread can be done simply with a wide range of stitches – for example, a tiny single or double stitch, or using cross stitches, herringbone, blanket stitch, or even an open chain stitch to hold the laid thread in place.

The diagrams on the opposite page clearly show how to work a line of simple couching.

• Bring the thread to be couched up at the beginning of the line to be covered (*see illustration opposite page:* **1**).

- Hold this thread in place with your thumb and bring up another needle and thread (**2**). Take it down on the opposite side of the laid thread (**3**) to make a tiny "tying" stitch.

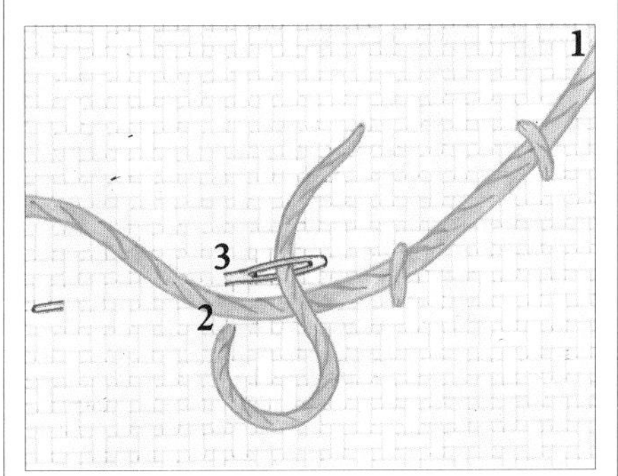

Couching a thread

- Continue in this way, tying the laid thread down at regular intervals.
- To finish off a line of couching, take the laid thread and the tying thread through to the back at the end of the stitching line. Then fasten both threads securely.

Bear in mind that both chain stitch and couching will create a thicker line than either stem stitch or double running stitch.

Blackwork variations
Many general embroidery books contain information on blackwork and samples of patterns. In addition, many portraits show detailed blackwork patterns, particularly from the 16th century. Art books or postcards may also provide patterns that appeal to you.

More samples of blackwork patterns

OCTAGONAL TRELLIS

This is a good example of an attractive pattern that is built up over a framework. There are several ways in which it can be worked, but the following sequence is one of the most straightforward. You might want to try working the pattern in a different order to see which you prefer before stitching a final piece using this pattern.

Working the pattern

- Begin by working vertical lines of backstitch over two fabric threads, spacing them six fabric threads apart as shown (*see illustration below*).

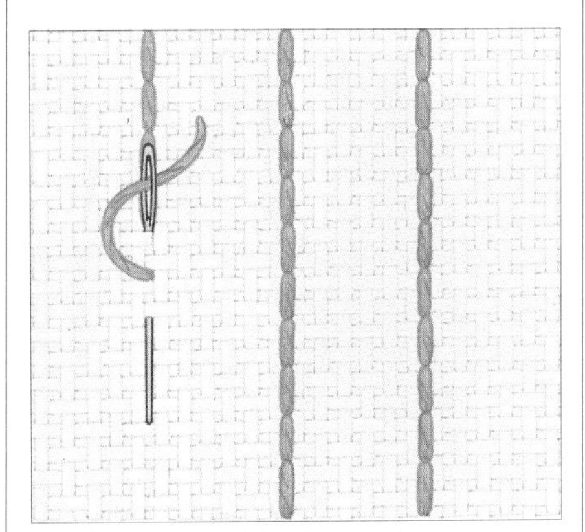

Working vertical backstitch lines

- On every alternate vertical line, work an octagon in backstitch. Note that the diagonal sides of the octagon will cover two thread intersections and the straight sides will cover four threads (*see illustration below*).

Working the octagon

- Work a cross stitch in the centre over four intersections, working in the following order: needle up at the upper right, down at the lower left, up at the upper left, then down at the lower right. Bring the needle up at the point indicated (*see illustration below*).

Working the centre design

- Work two running stitches over four threads, crossing the cross stitch and then the next vertical line of backstitch. Then bring the needle up in position to begin the next octagon (*see illustration below*).

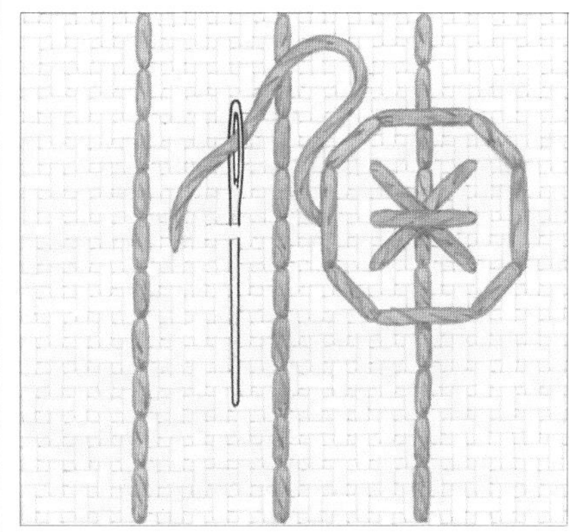

Completing the octagon motif

- Work each octagon until you reach the end of the row.
- On the following row (worked in the opposite direction), place the octagons on the remaining vertical lines. Leave one fabric thread between the bottom of the previously worked octagons and the top of the new ones (*see photograph below*).

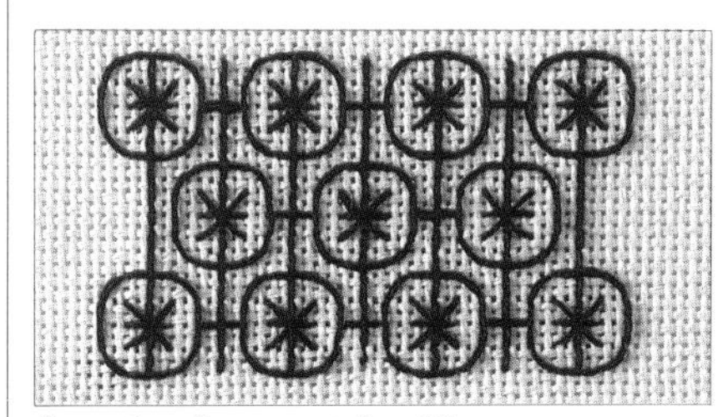

Sample of octagonal trellis

Blue and White Cushions

These three simple patterns in cool blue and white make a striking design, reminiscent of patchwork. Stitched in perlé cotton on coarse evenweave, the embroidery is easy to work and can be stitched quickly in a spare evening or two.

SIZE

Finished cushions: 15 in (38 cm) square

MATERIALS

For each cushion: 20 in (50 cm) of 18-count evenweave, at least 40 in (100 cm) wide
Fabric shown: Zweigart "Davosa", shades 1 and 522
DMC no. 5 perlé cotton, 2 skeins each colour:
798
blanc neige

1⅞ yds (1.7 metres) of narrow cord to match stitching (or extra skeins of the perlé cotton to make a twisted cord)
4 buttons
Sewing thread to match fabric and cord
Cushion pad 16 in (40 cm) square
Tapestry needle, size 20

CHART FOR BLUE AND WHITE PILLOWS

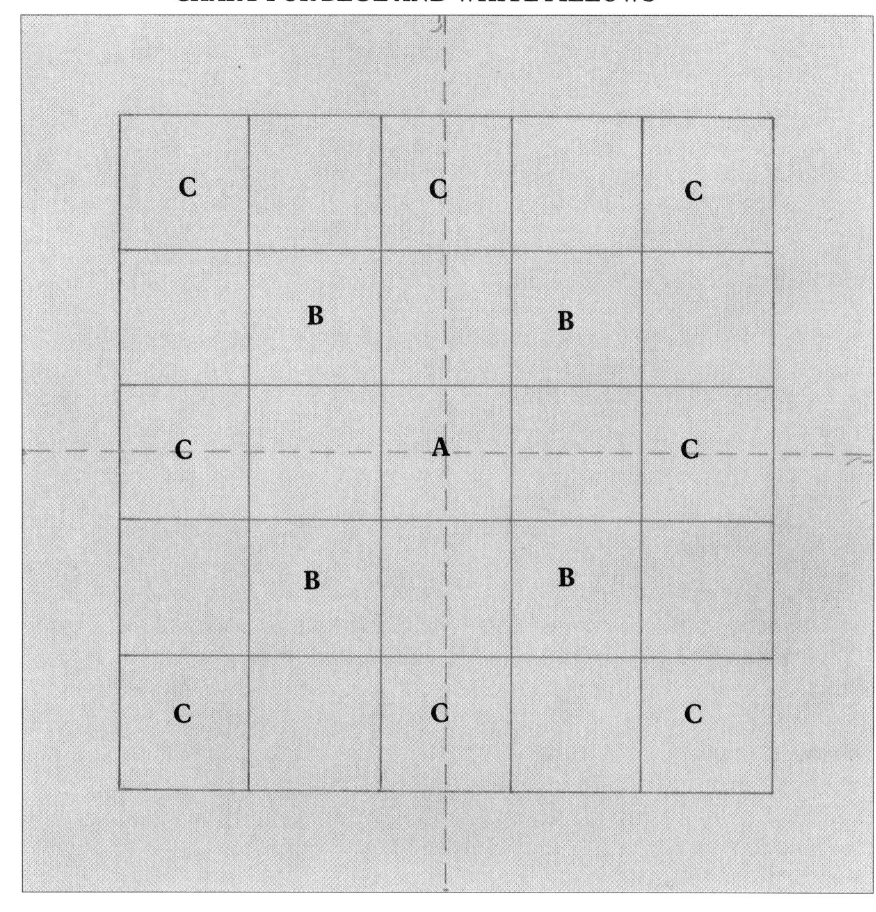

Working the embroidery

1 Cut one piece of fabric 20 in (50 cm) square for the front. To prevent fraying, secure all edges with zigzag or overcast stitch. Alternatively, cover the edges with masking tape.

2 Work a line of basting or running stitches through the centre, both horizontally and vertically.

3 Embroider the design (using the instructions below) and follow the chart. All the small motif blocks are aligned along common fabric threads; that is, there are no threads separating a block from its nearest neighbour. Each small motif block contains 25 individual motifs.

4 Once you have positioned an individual motif in a block, it is easy to position the others. Each single motif covers eight fabric threads and is separated from adjacent motifs by two fabric threads. Embroider the first motif exactly where the basting lines cross, then work the remaining motifs in the pattern.

5 Begin work in the centre of the block following pattern A:

- Work the inner square in backstitch over four fabric threads, then backstitch the outer square over eight threads (*see illustration below*).

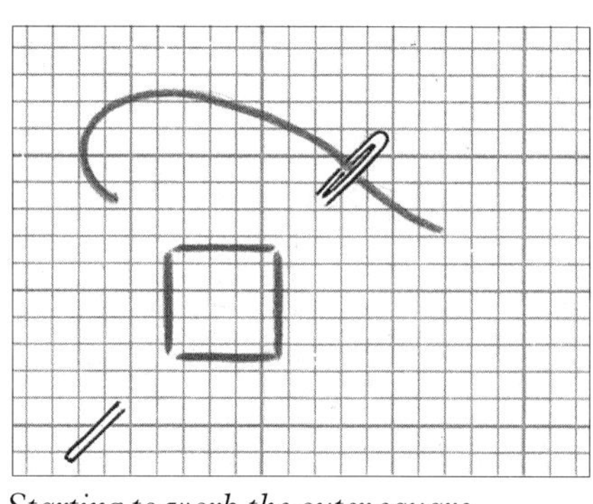

Starting to work the outer square

• Next, work four diagonal straight stitches, coming up at each corner and going down in the centre hole (*see illustration below*).

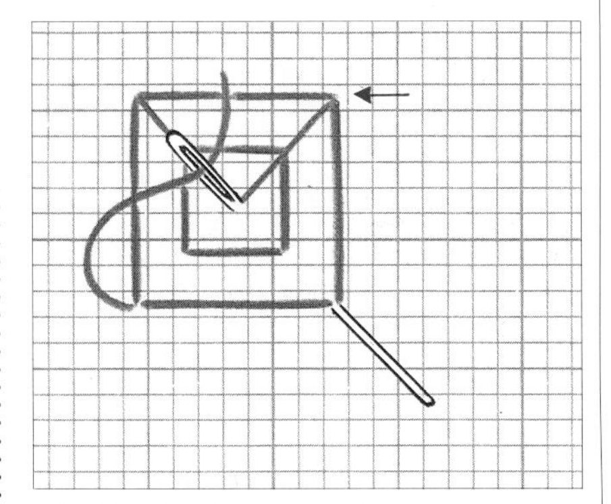

Working the diagonal stitches

6 Work the four blocks of pattern B:
• Start at the lower right-hand corner (*see starting arrow on illustration below*) and make a diagonal stitch across, two threads.
• Repeat the diagonal stitches over four, six, and eight threads in turn.

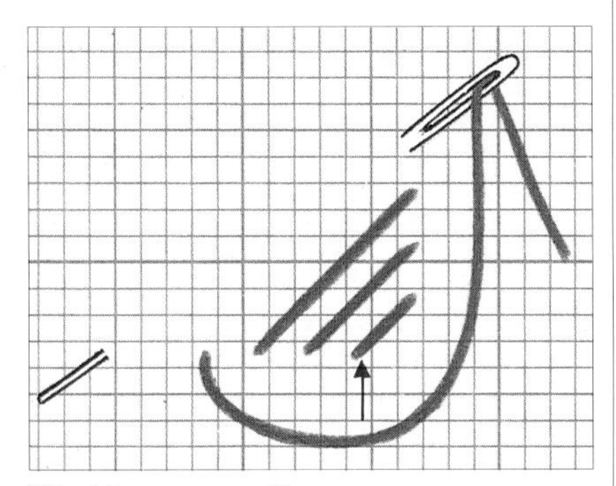

Working pattern B

• To begin the next motif, bring the needle up four threads to the left of the point where the thread last emerged (*see illustration above*).

All the triangles treated in this way should be aligned in the same direction, with the longest stitches to the upper left.

Note that on the upper-right and lower-left blocks, these long stitches will touch the corners (*see main photograph on page 103*).

7 Work the eight blocks of pattern C:
• Start at the upper right of the block, by the arrow. Work four horizontal and four vertical stitches over two, four, six, and eight threads (*see illustration next column*).

You can combine the patterns A, B, and C shown on page 102 in different ways to create your own design.

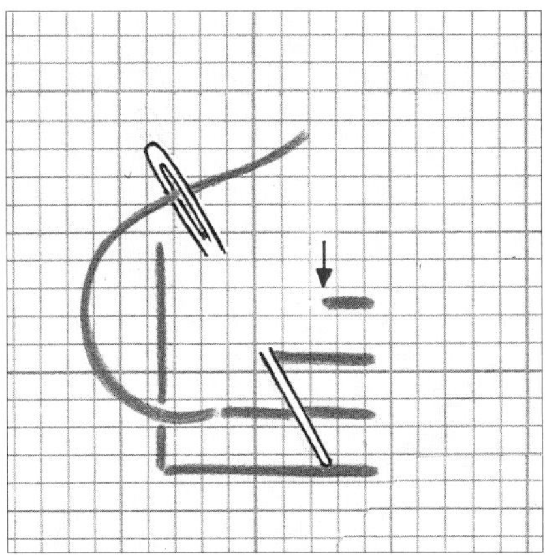

Working pattern C

• Work a single stitch down the middle over all eight threads (*see illustration below*). The needle is in position to begin the next motif.

Note that all of these motifs point towards the upper right-hand corner.

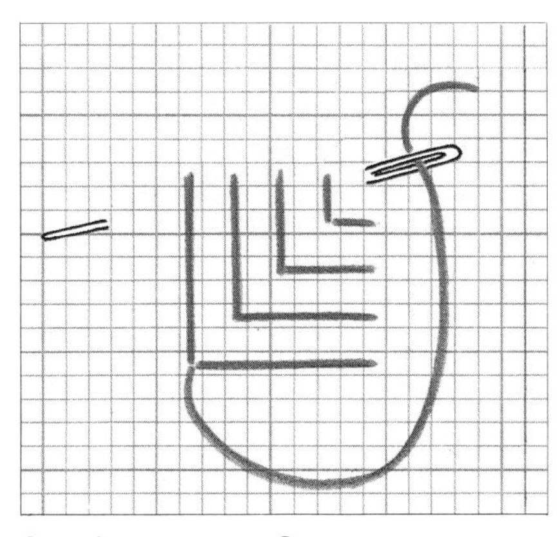

Completing pattern C

8 When all the blocks are complete, work a border of cross stitch around the edge, two threads outside the outer blocks. Work each cross over two fabric threads.

Making up the cushion

1 Press the work lightly from the wrong side. Be careful not to flatten the stitches.

2 Count 18 fabric threads from the border and work a line of basting around all four sides; this marks the seam line. Trim away excess fabric, leaving a seam allowance of ¾ in (2 cm) all around. The piece should now measure 17½ in (44 cm) square. You will probably find a slight variation between the vertical and horizontal measurements, as very few evenweaves are precisely the same in both directions.

3 From the remaining fabric cut two rectangles for the back: one measuring 17½ × 13 in (44 × 33 cm) and one measuring 17½ × 8 in (44 × 20 cm). (Adjust the longer one to match the front, if necessary.)

4 Turn under ⅜ in (1 cm) on both pieces to form a hem along one long edge; stitch. On the larger piece, turn under 1¼ in (3 cm) on the stitched edge; press carefully.

5 Lay the two pieces on a flat surface, wrong sides up, so that the hemmed edges overlap by 2 in (5 cm). The combined measurement should be the same as the width of the front piece; adjust if necessary. Baste pieces together where they overlap.

6 Place the front piece over the back piece, right sides together. Baste the back and front together just outside the basted seamline. Stitch seam, leaving a 1¼ in (3 cm) opening in the lower edge to insert the cord ends. Trim the corners diagonally. If desired, finish seam allowance edge with machine zigzg or overcast stitch. Turn the cushion cover right side out.

7 Sew buttons, equally spaced, to the underlying back section, just beside the folded edge of the other back section. Work a thread loop (*see page 155*) on the overlapping edge opposite each button. If desired, work buttonholes by machine before joining the two back sections.

8 Insert the cushion pad. Sew the cord to the seam (*see page 155*), overlapping the ends smoothly and inserting them in the small seam opening. Slipstitch the edges carefully and securely together around the cord (*see page 155*).

Mediterranean Picture

This lovely panel has the delicacy of a pen drawing plus the textural appeal of fabric and thread. Most of the stitches are counted, but they are occasionally interrupted to give the work a spontaneous quality.

SIZE

Finished design: 10¼ × 5½ in (26 × 14 cm)

MATERIALS

Piece of 32-count evenweave linen, 16 in (40 cm) square

Fabric shown: Zweigart "Belfast" shade 101

DMC stranded cotton, 1 skein, black

DMC no. 8 perlé cotton, 1 ball, black

Cardboard, 20 × 30 in (50 × 76 cm)

Tapestry needles, sizes 22 and 24

Crewel needle, size 5

Working the embroidery

1 Mount the fabric in the embroidery frame, keeping the threads at right angles to each other.

2 Embroider the design, following the chart (*see below*). Start at either the left-hand side (about 3 in (8 cm) from the fabric edge) or the right-hand side (about 4 in (10 cm) from the edge. Stitch with a single strand of thread throughout. You should use stranded cotton for the stitches in black on the chart and either perlé cotton or DMC no. 18 coton à broder for the stitches in red. Each square on the chart represents two fabric threads; all the counted stitches are worked over this two-thread grid.

CHART FOR THE MEDITERRANEAN PICTURE

3 When all counted stitches have been worked, embroider cross stitches randomly over the fabric for the foliage (shown as solid shaded areas on the chart). Use perlé cotton or coton à broder with the crewel needle.

Refer to the chart on page 105 and follow the dotted outline, or baste the outline on the fabric as a guideline.

Mounting the panel

1 Remove the work from the frame. Press it face down on a well-padded ironing board.

2 Mount the work over the poster board (*see page 152*). It is now ready to frame.

Making window mounts

You can either frame your completed picture professionally or create a frame for it yourself. Making mounts is one of the best methods.

There are two main types of mounts, known as square and bevelled mounts. Square mounts are cut with square (straight-sided) interior angles and are easier to make.

1 To make a square-edged mount, measure and mark the four edges of the opening. Using a metal straightedge, lightly draw the rectangle that you want to cut out. Use a set square to position the corners at right angles (*see illustration below*).

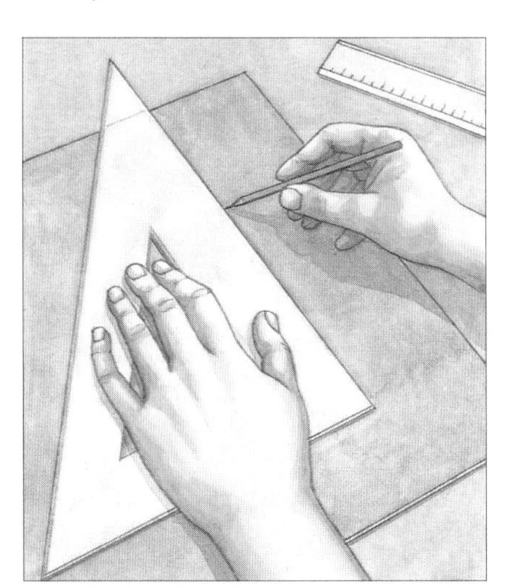

Marking the rectangle

Detail of the Mediterranean Picture

2 Indent each corner with a drawing pin. Cut along pencil lines carefully (*see illustration below*).

Use a sharp craft knife and a metal straightedge or ruler. Stop cutting at the indentation of the drawing pin.

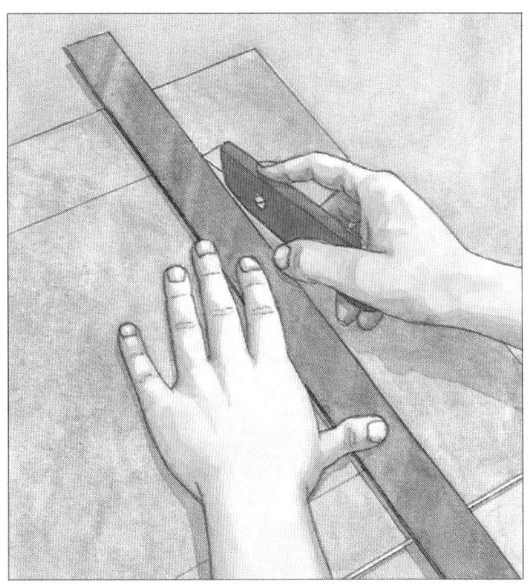

Cutting the rectangle

3 You can also cut mounts with bevelled (angled) interior angles. To work bevel-edged openings, you need a mount cutter. Practise using the cutter on scrap board first, as these cuts require some mastery.

Mount boards are available in a wide range of colours. Choose one that complements the colours in your drawing and the colour of the drawing paper. For the Mediterranean Picture, the creamy background will need a strong contrasting colour in the mount to set it off to best advantage.

Openwork

Openwork is a particularly attractive and varied group of counted thread embroidery techniques. All sorts of marvellous lacy effects can be produced by removing fabric threads or pulling them together and then working over them with various stitches. Openwork techniques have been used for centuries to embellish household linens and clothing. Today they are also used to create purely decorative work such as pictures and wall hangings. Three of the most popular and attractive forms – pulled work, drawn thread work, and Hardanger work – are presented in this chapter.

Pulled Work Techniques

The delicate textures of pulled work make it the most appealing of all the counted thread openwork embroidery techniques. Instructions are given here for a small selection of pulled work stitches which cover a wide range of textural effects.

BASICS OF PULLED WORK

The openwork patterns of pulled work are created by working special embroidery stitches which "pull" the fabric threads together to form decorative holes or perforations. In pulled work designs, ordinary simple surface embroidery stitches are used alongside the openwork textures for outlines and extra contrasting details.

Unlike drawn thread work, pulled work does not entail removing any fabric threads. Thus the finished work, although it may have a lacy appearance, is quite strong. It lends itself to all sorts of household linens and delicate garments.

Choosing fabrics for pulled work

The fabric chosen for pulled work should have an even weave with threads that are easily counted and separated. The particular type of fabric used has varied through the centuries. For example, the very fine muslins that were used in the 18th century are today considered impractical as there is often less time available to work on a particular project. However, an occasional piece of small-scale pulled work can be a satisfying, as well as challenging, project. A somewhat coarse, loosely woven evenweave linen, or cotton, with between 26 and 18 threads to 1 in (2.5 cm), is the best choice for table linens and most soft furnishings. A cheaper alternative, useful for practising the stitches, is linen scrim or hessian.

Some sheer curtain fabrics, such as marquisette, can also be used for this work, and depending on the current fashion, some dress fabrics may be suitable for pulled work.

Choosing thread for pulled work

The thread used for pulled work should normally be the same thickness as the fabric threads; in some cases, however, a thicker one will produce a more interesting texture. It should also be sufficiently strong to withstand considerable tension. Perlé cotton and coton à broder are good choices; buttonhole twist, crochet threads, and lace threads are also suitable. In general, stranded floss is not recommended, because it tends to break or fray.

Choosing colours for pulled work

Today, as in the past, pulled work is usually worked in white or ecru – sometimes placed over a coloured lining, which enhances the contrasting openwork textures. However, the technique is equally successful in colour; the only restriction is that it is normally best to use thread that matches, or nearly matches, the fabric colour. This is because the stitches themselves are not especially attractive; they merely serve to create the textures, which would be somewhat obscured if the stitches were too prominent.

Preparation and equipment

Always use an embroidery frame for pulled work. This makes the individual threads more visible and holds them at an even tension, minimizing any warping of the fabric. Some stitches, however, will tend to pull the fabric diagonally. You can either adjust your working tension to compensate or try to block the finished work back into shape (*see page 151*).

As for other kinds of counted thread work, a tapestry needle is used.

Working filling and border stitches

There are many pulled work filling stitches. These stitches are used both for filling the inside of a motif or for filling the background around a motif. Only a small selection of fillings are described, but a wide range of textures and openwork effects are covered.

Pulled work filling stitches do not fall easily into specific categories as their structures, working techniques, and resulting appearances are so varied. In the following pages they are loosely grouped according to the types of textures they create.

Almost all pulled work stitches are used for filling areas of a design. A few can be used for narrow lines or borders (*see page 117*).

Reading stitch diagrams

Pulled work stitches are quickly mastered with a little patience and practice. Always make a practice sample of the stitches before beginning a pulled work project.

Remember that the working diagrams of the pulled work stitches do not show what the finished fabric looks like because the embroidery stitches are shown as if worked with a slack tension.

Arrow number 1 on the stitch diagrams with numbers indicates the starting point where the needle is first brought up. On the remaining arrows the tail end shows where the needle was taken down, and the arrow head where it is next brought up.

BASIC SATIN STITCH

Ordinary satin stitch is one of the main stitches used in pulled work designs. It is sometimes used for shaped motifs which are worked in conjunction with pulled work motifs or for outlines around pulled work motifs. But satin stitch can also be worked as a counted thread technique, and "counted satin stitch" can, in turn, be worked tightly for various pulled thread effects.

To practise the basic method of pulled work and discover its effects, try embroidering some satin stitch rows and blocks. In most pulled work the stitches are pulled tightly in order to draw the fabric threads together as closely as possible. In some cases, however, only a moderate tension is required, and tensioned stitches are sometimes combined with other stitches worked with a slack tension to provide a contrast in texture. Experiment with different tensions as you gain more experience.

In all the patterns given on pages 118–127, a firm tension is used unless stated otherwise.

Working satin stitch rows

- To work a single row of satin stitch, first bring the needle up at the starting point (*see arrow in illustration below*). Work a stitch over the required number of threads.
- Work the following stitches over the same number of fabric threads (*see illustration below*).

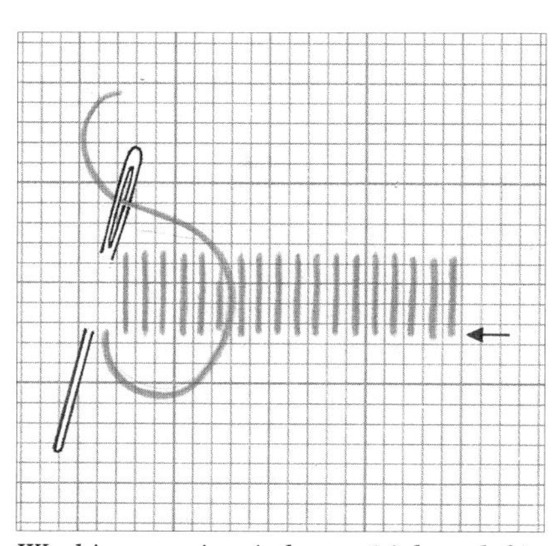

Working a satin stitch row (right to left)

In the bottom row of the photographed sample, satin stitch is worked over four fabric threads: with a slack tension, with moderate tension, and with a firm tension.

In the top three rows, satin stitch has been worked with firm tension over three, four, and five threads (*see photograph below*).

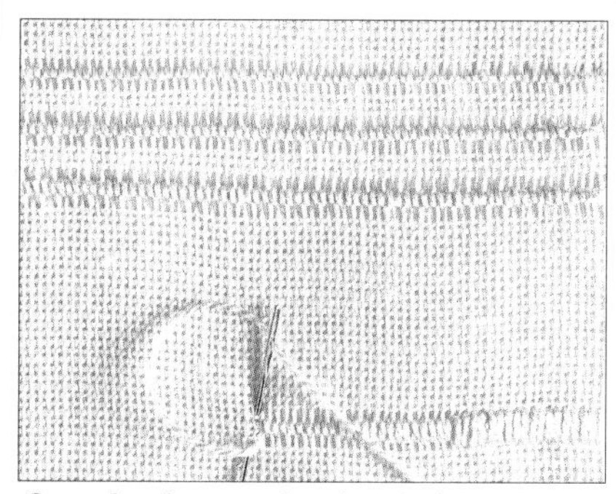

Sample of counted satin stitch rows

Working satin stitch blocks

Satin stitch blocks are stitched diagonally over a chosen number of fabric threads, typically three to five threads (*see illustration below*).

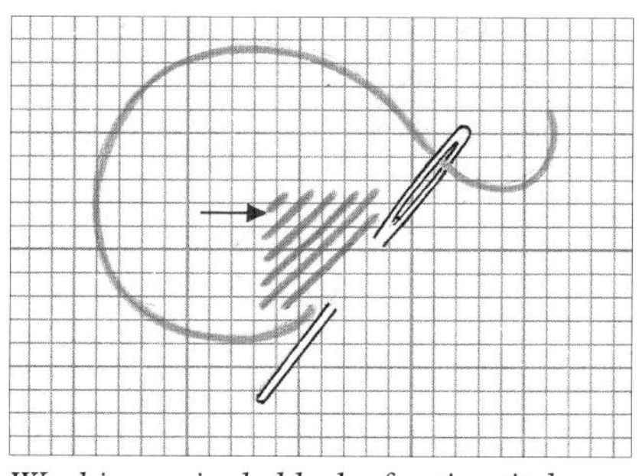

Working a single block of satin stitch

The blocks may all be stitched in the same direction (*see photograph below: top row*) or in alternating directions (*bottom row*).

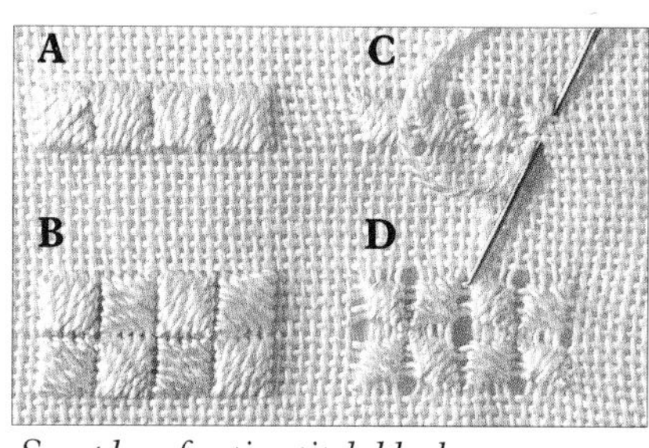

Samples of satin stitch blocks

Experiment with satin stitch blocks with slack tensions (*see photograph above:* **A**, **B**) and moderate tensions (**C**, **D**) to create different effects of texture. Remember that the centre stitch of a satin stitch block should not be pulled too tight or it will distort the shape of the whole.

SATIN STITCH FILLINGS

Chessboard, basket, and step stitch filling patterns are all based on satin stitch. These fillings produce a slightly more solid effect than other fillings included in this section, because they are generally not pulled as tight.

Working chessboard filling

This filling consists of rows of ten stitches worked over three threads, with three rows making up each block. Each successive block is stitched at a right angle to the previous one.

- Bring the needle up in the position shown by the starting arrow (*see illustration below:* **1**) and work the first horizontal row of ten satin stitches.
- After completing the tenth stitch, bring the needle up at the base of the next horizontal row (**2**) and work ten more stitches.
- Bring the needle up at the base of the next row (**3**) and again work a row of ten stitches.
- Bring the needle up in the position indicated (**4**) to begin the next block of stitches, which is made up of three vertical rows.
- Work the first of the three vertical rows upward, the second downward, and the third upward.

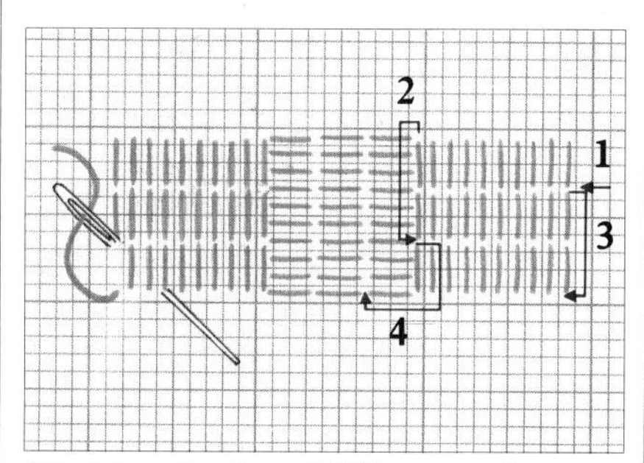

Working chessboard filling over three right-angle blocks

- Work the next block of three horizontal rows of ten stitches in the same way as the first block of three horizontal rows.
- Continue in this way to fill the desired area of fabric, alternating horizontal and vertical rows.

On rows adjoining the row ends of another block, work so that the needle goes *down* into these row ends; this makes it easier to insert the needle between the correct fabric threads, some of which will be tightly bunched together.

Chessboard filling, shown here with a firm tension (*see photograph below*), also looks attractive if worked with a loose tension.

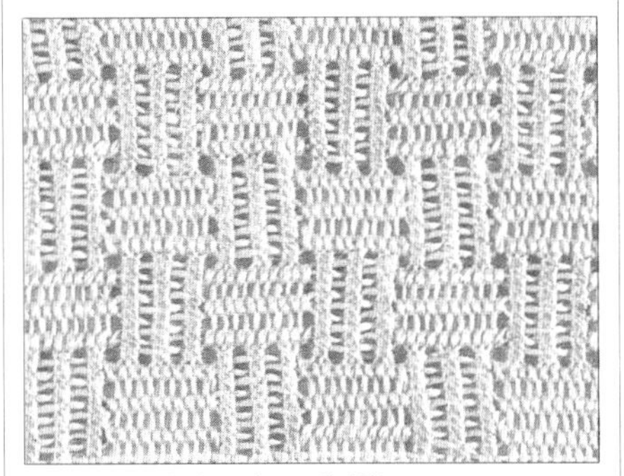

Sample of chessboard filling

Working basket filling

Basket filling is composed of rows of six pulled work stitches worked over three fabric threads.

- Starting at one upper corner of your embroidery, bring the needle up at the position indicated by the starting arrow (*see illustration below:* **1**) and work a horizontal row of six satin stitches from right to left.
- After completing the sixth stitch, bring the needle up at the position to start the next vertical row (**2**) and work the next six stitches.
- Continue in this way, (**3, 4, 5**) working each row of six stitches at a right angle to the previous one.

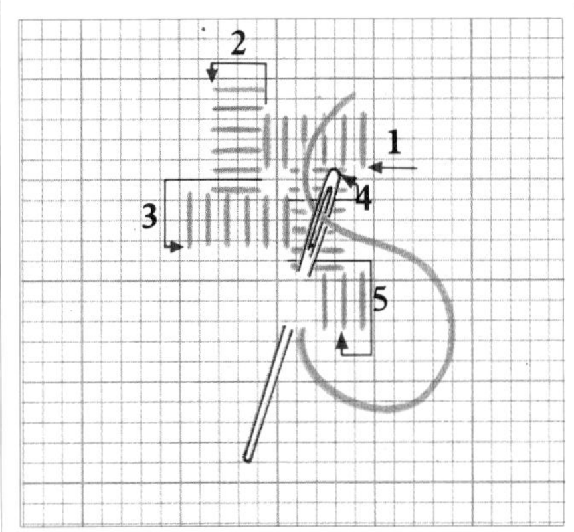

Working blocks of stitches horizontally, then vertically

Although rather time-consuming to work, this filling is finely-textured and ideal for suggesting a screen or grillwork, for example.

Note how different the finished pulled fabric looks from the stitch diagram (*see photograph below*).

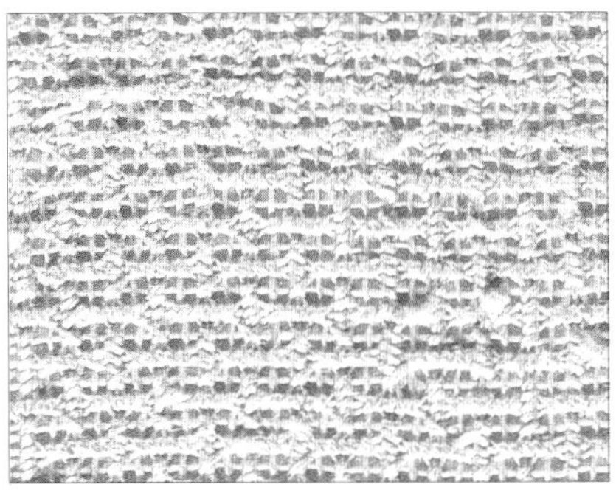

Sample of basket filling

Working step stitch filling

The strongly diagonal effect of this pattern is produced by working blocks of five stitches over four threads and stitching each block at a right angle to the one directly preceding it.

- Bring the needle up at the upper right-hand corner (*see illustration below:* **1**) and work a vertical row of five satin stitches.
- After completing the fifth stitch, bring the needle up at the base of the next horizontal row of stitches (**2**) and work a row of five stitches.
- Working diagonally upward, sew a vertical row of stitches, followed by a horizontal row (**3** *and* **4**).

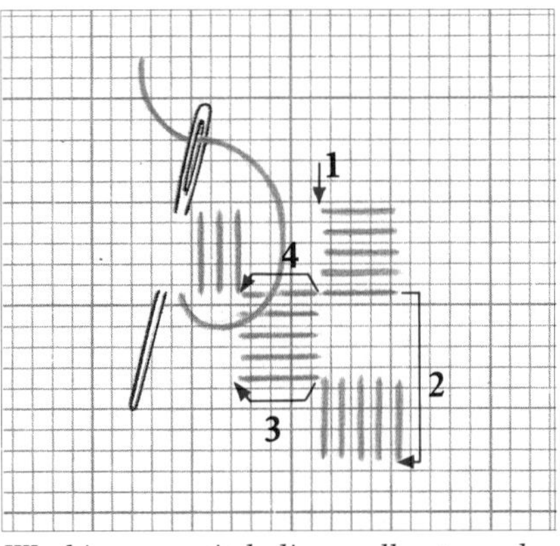

Working step stitch diagonally upward

- Bring the needle up in the correct position (**5**) to begin the next vertical row and work a row of five stitches.
- After completing the fifth stitch in this row, you should bring the needle up at the base of the next horizontal row of stitches (**6**) and then work a row of five stitches.
- Work a vertical row of five stitches, moving diagonally downward, then work a horizontal row of five stitches alternately (**7** *and* **8**).

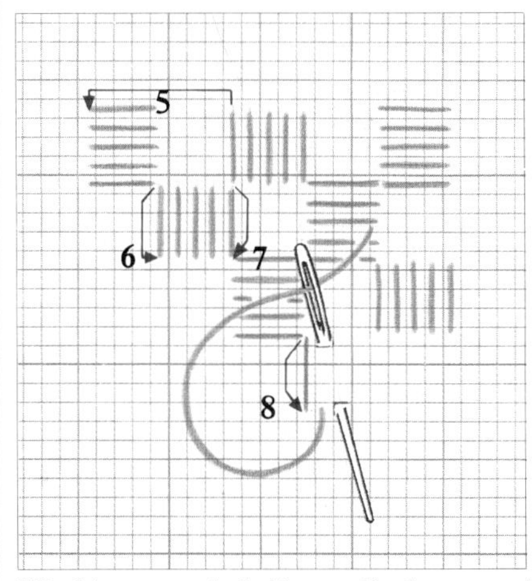

Working step stitch diagonally downward

The filling is created in this way, with the blocks of stitches worked alternately diagonally upward and downward (*see photograph below*).

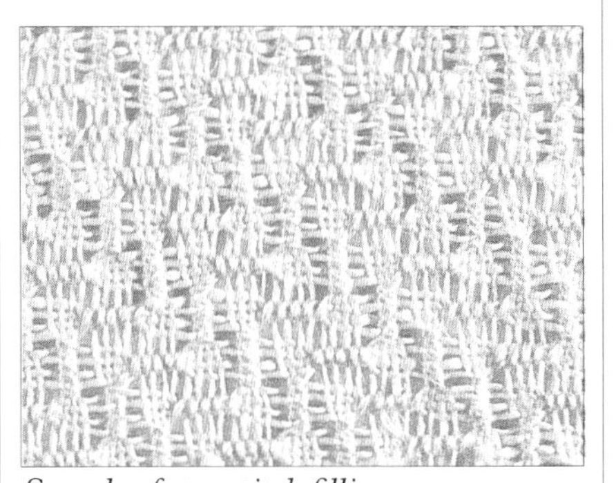

Sample of step stitch filling

EYELETS

Designs formed with eyelets include some of the most attractive patterns in pulled work. The square and single cross eyelets can be used individually, in rows, or grouped. Especially interesting effects can be created by working them asymmetrically (see page 116).

Working square eyelets

This eyelet is simple in structure, but to work it smoothly requires some practice. The square is embroidered over an even number of threads (eight in this example).

- Find the central hole and enlarge it with a bodkin or knitting needle.
- Starting in the centre of one side, bring the needle up (*see arrow in illustration below*) and take it down through the centre.
- Continue around the square, bringing the needle up at the edges and down in the centre. Pull a little more firmly on the side stitches than on the corner ones.

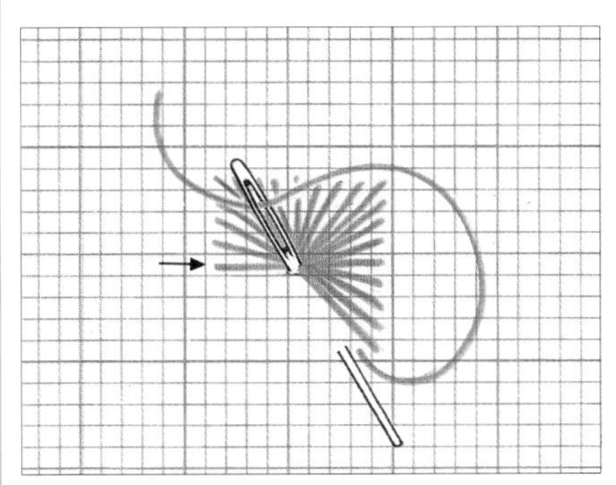

Taking the needle down in the centre and up at the edge

- While stitching, use your fingernail or the needle to coax the stitches to lie as smoothly as possible. Square eyelets form an attractive filling (*see photograph below*).

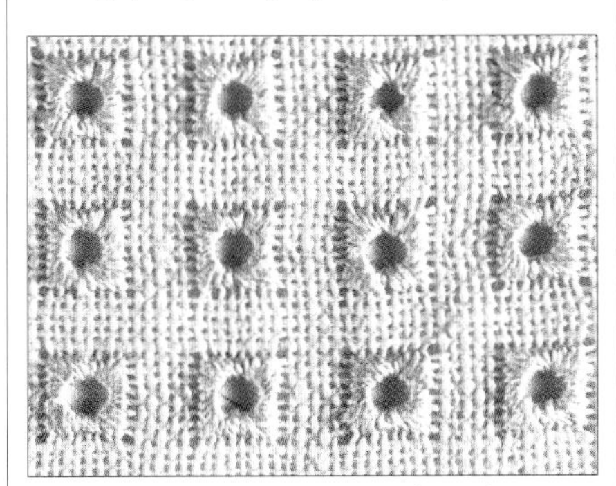

Square eyelets worked five threads apart

Eyelets can also be worked with a very slight tension, which produces a small hole. However, in this case it is best to use a relatively fine thread to minimize crowding at the centre.

Working single cross eyelets

This eyelet is worked over an uneven number of threads (seven in this example) to leave a vertical and a horizontal thread free at the centre.

- Work the stitch as for the square eyelet, but do not cover the fabric thread at the centre of each side (*see illustration below*).

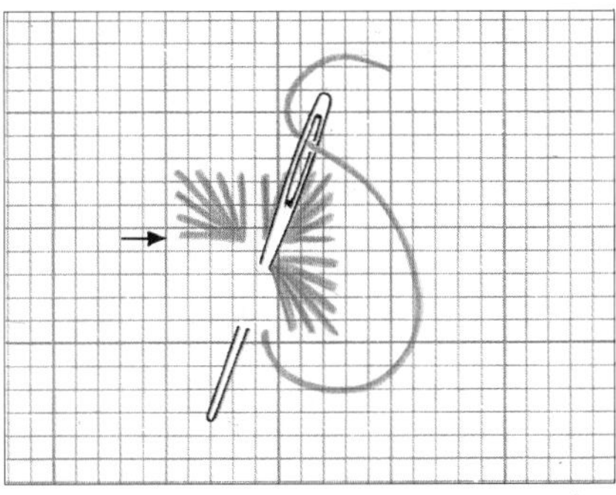

Leaving fabric intersection at centre of eyelet unworked

The vertical and horizontal threads left free at the centre of this eyelet form a distinctive cross in the eye of each stitch (*see photograph below*).

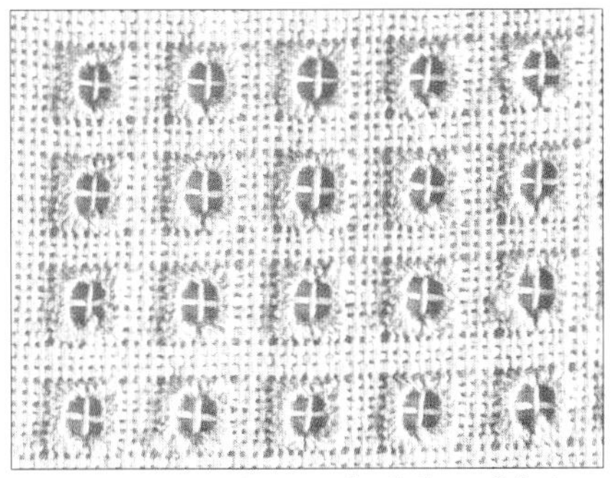

Single cross eyelets worked three fabric threads apart

Eyelet and step stitch filling

This lively pulled work filling pattern consists of diagonal rows of step stitch – six stitches worked over three fabric threads – alternating with square eyelets worked over eight fabric threads. Use a large knitting needle to prepare the eyelet holes, and pull the stitches very tight while working the step stitch filling.

- Beginning at the upper right-hand corner at arrow **1**, work the first eyelet (*see illustration below*).
- Work four bands of step stitch (**2**, **3**, **4**, **5**) then a second eyelet (**6**).
- Begin the third eyelet at the second starting point and continue in this way, working the pattern diagonally.

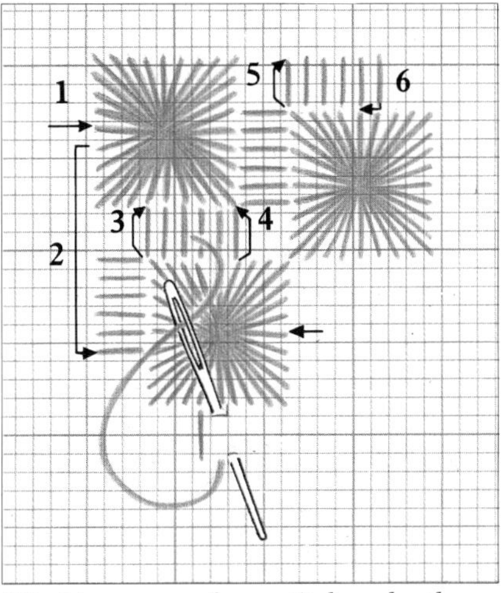

Working a row of step stitch under the third eyelet

When working this filling, begin by establishing the pattern; this will produce sloping sides, which you can then straighten out with partial "steps" and eyelets.

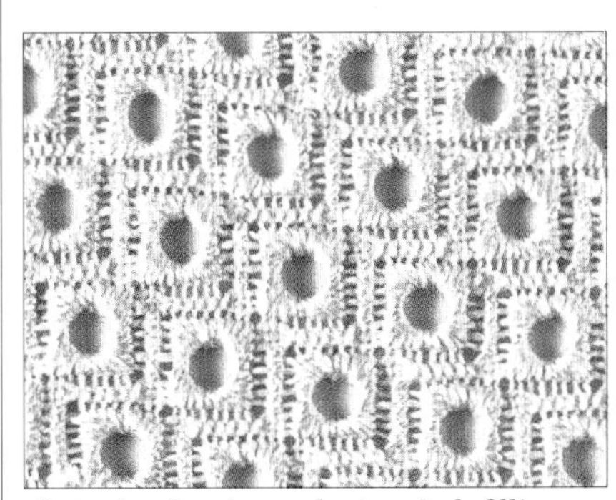

Sample of eyelet and step stitch filling

SIMPLE LATTICE EFFECTS

The three following pulled work filling stitches form simple lattice effects.

Single and double faggot stitch

In essence this stitch is a series of backstitches worked in a zigzag pattern over four threads diagonally across the fabric.

Working single faggot stitch

- To work single faggot stitch, start at the upper left-hand corner and make a horizontal backstitch to the right (*see illustration below:* **1**). Bring the needle up four threads below the starting point (**2**).
- Continue with a backstitch into the starting point, bringing the needle out at the same place (**3**).

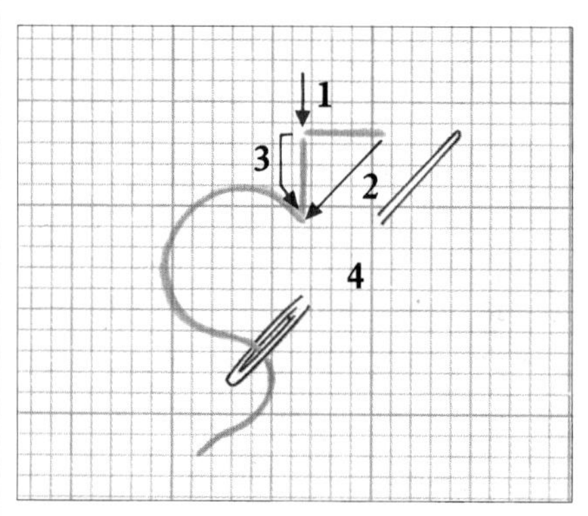

Working single faggot stitch diagonally upward

- Take the needle down four threads below and up four intersections above and right (**4**).
- Take the stitches diagonally up and down across the shape (*see illustration below*).

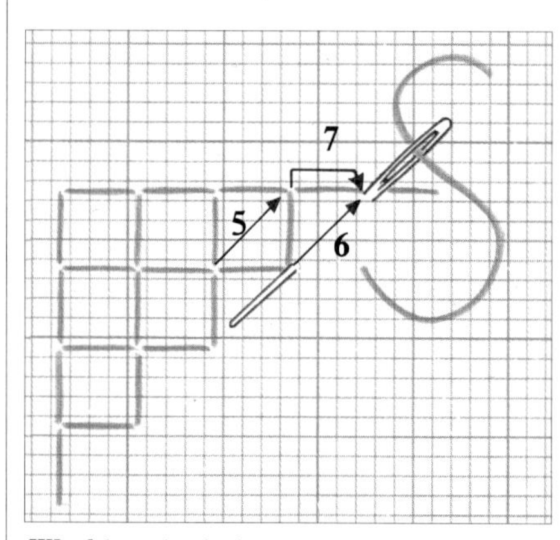

Working single faggot stitch diagonally downward

A completed filling of single faggot stitch has a fine, screenlike texture (*see photograph below*).

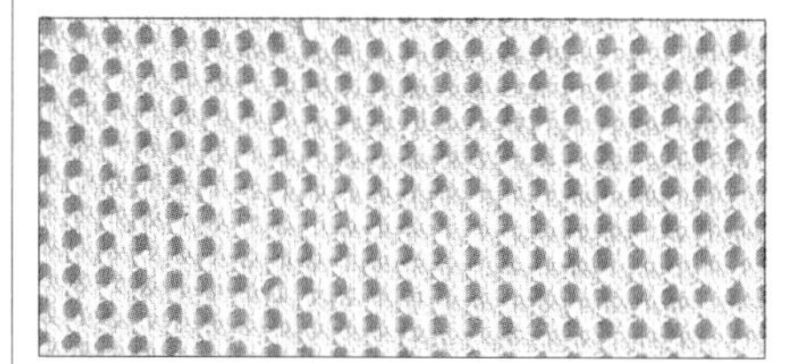

Sample of single faggot stitch

Working double faggot stitch

To create double faggot stitch you simply work each stitch in single faggot stitch twice. This produces a more open effect.

Working diagonal cross filling

Diagonal cross filling is a simple stitch, but very time-consuming.

- Begin at the upper right-hand corner. Work a vertical cross over four threads, with the horizontal arm on top (*see illustration below:* **1** *and* **2**).
- Bring the needle up four threads below the cross (**3**), and work vertical stitches diagonally up to the left (**4**), staggering them as shown.

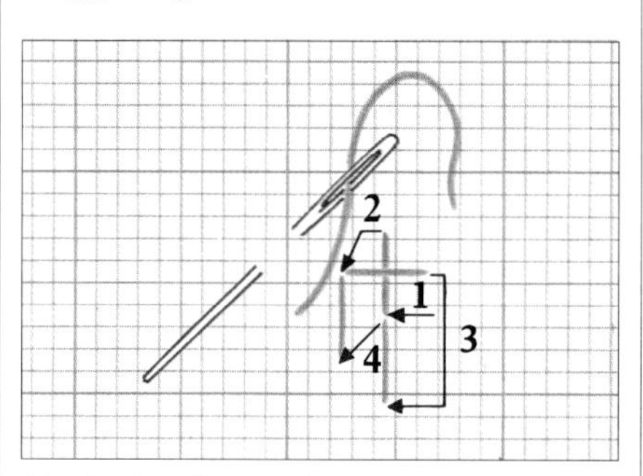

Beginning diagonal cross stitch

- Cross the vertical stitches in the diagonal row with horizontal ones (*see illustration below*).

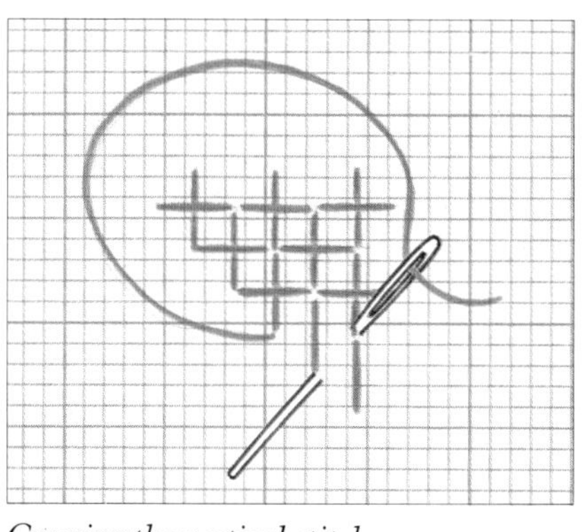

Crossing the vertical stitches

- Continue in this way, working the vertical stitches first and crossing them with horizontal ones. Continue to work the rows diagonally upward and downward until the cross filling is complete.

Working cobbler filling

This stitch is simple and relatively quick to work. All stitches are taken over four fabric threads.

- Begin at the upper right-hand corner. Work the vertical stitches in the first row from right to left (*see illustration below:* **1**, **2**, *and* **3**).
- At the end of the row, bring the needle up at the base of the next row (**4**) and work the next row from the left to the right.
- Continue to work the vertical stitches over as many rows as required by the design.
- Then work all the horizontal stitches as shown, to complete the squares (**2nd starting point**).

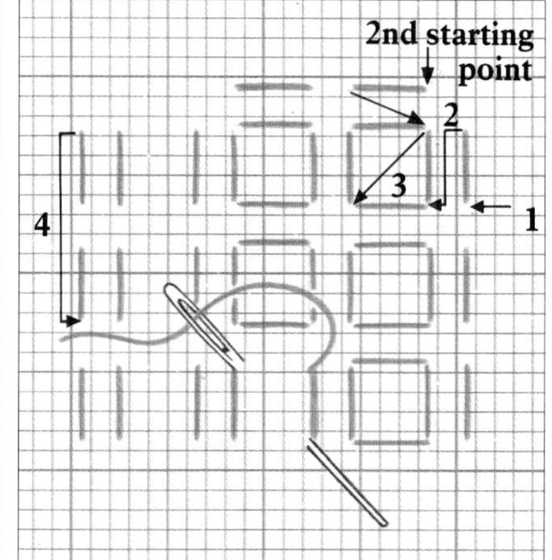

Working the horizontal stitches, after finishing the vertical ones

Completed cobbler filling makes an attractive pattern of thick and thin lines (*see photograph below*).

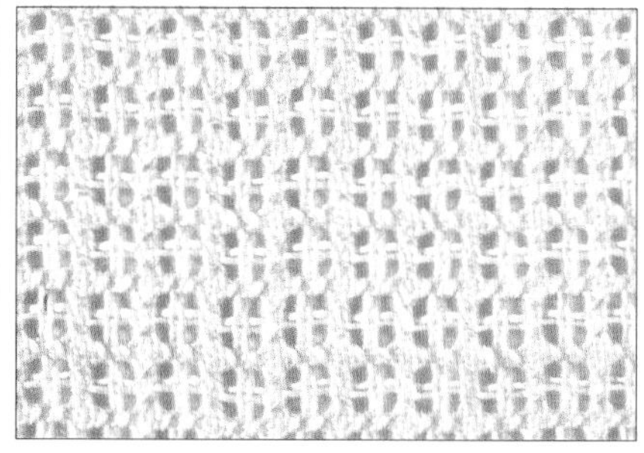

Sample of cobbler filling

RICH TEXTURES

Chequer, ringed backstitch, and small ringed backstitch fillings all produce rich and distinctive pulled work textures.

Working chequer filling

You may find it easier to begin chequer filling with a row of several stitches, rather than starting at a corner. Complete all the lower-right to upper-left rows first.

- Bring the needle up at the lower edge (*see illustration below:* **1**).
- Take the needle down two threads to the left and six above and bring it out two threads to the left and two below (**2**). Continue in this way until you reach the upper edge.
- Take the needle down six threads to the right and two below, then bring it up two to the left and two below.
- Continue to work the filling in this way to the end of the row.

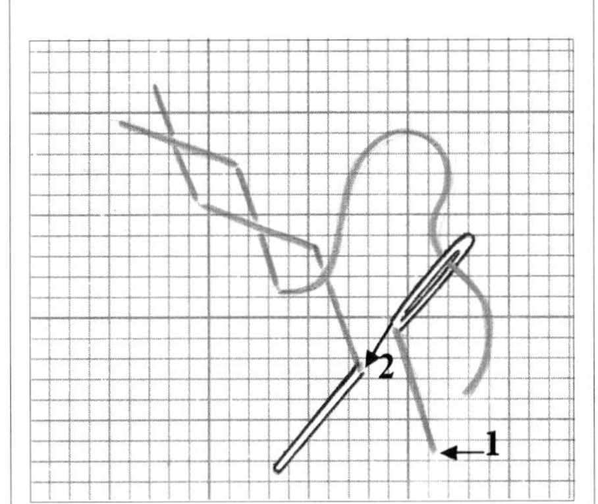

Working chequer stitch in diagonal rows

- Fill the whole space with diagonal rows of oblong crosses in this way.
- Turn the fabric 90° to the right, and work similar rows of oblong crosses on top of the first oblong crosses, working in two journeys as before (*see illustration below*).

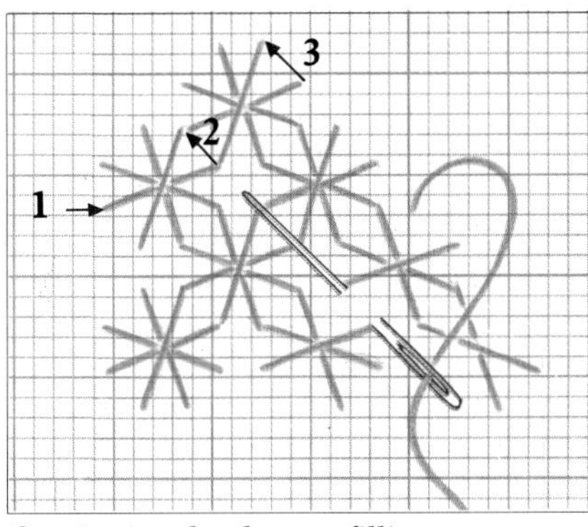

Continuing the chequer filling

Most of the pulling is *across* the line of stitching, under the two-thread intersections. Long stitches on top of the work are under only slight tension (*see photograph below*).

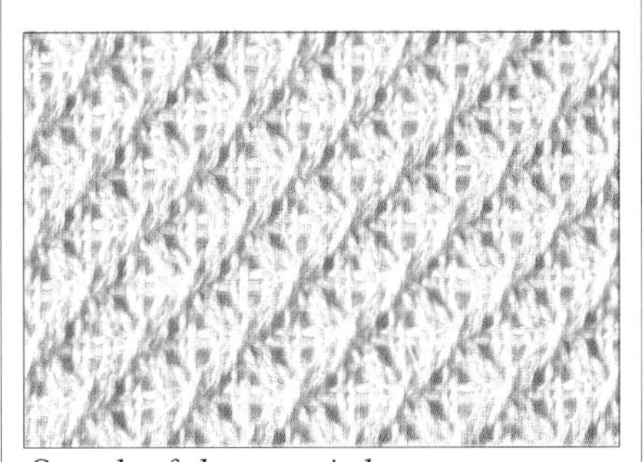

Sample of chequer stitch

Working ringed backstitch

Ringed backstitch is worked in an attractive figure-of-eight pattern.

- Begin at the upper right-hand corner and work each stitch twice over three fabric threads or thread intersections, forming the upper and lower halves of a row of octagons (*see arrow in illustration below*).
- At the end of the row, turn and stitch back to the right, completing the octagons. (The needle is shown completing the centre octagon.)

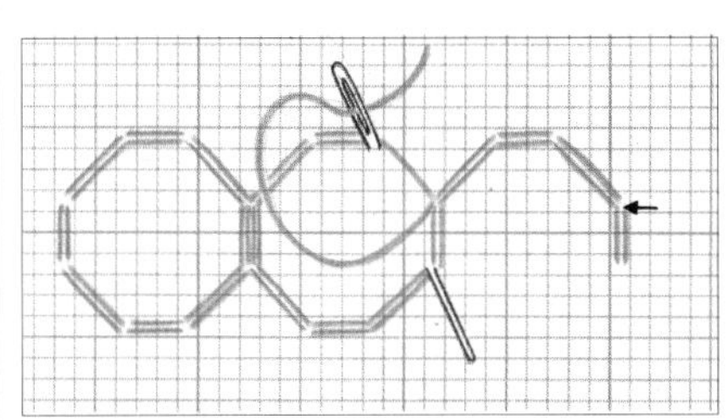

Working the second halves of a row of octagons

Four stitches share the space where the shapes meet (*see illustration above*), creating a solid yet delicate texture (*see photograph below*).

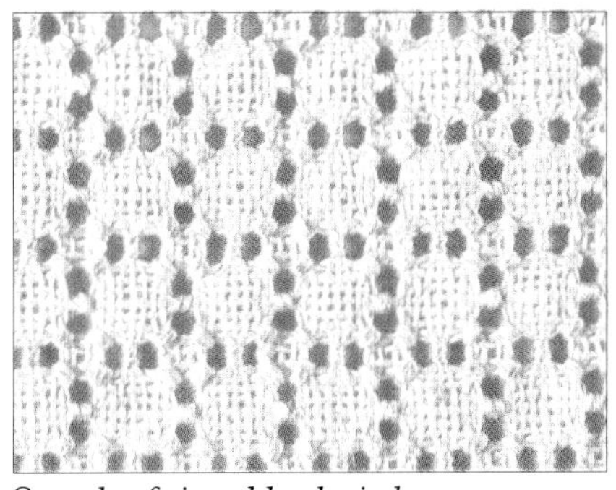

Sample of ringed backstitch

Working small ringed backstitch

Small ringed backstitch is similar to ringed backstitch, but is slightly more complex in structure. It is worked in two journeys.

- Backstitch from right to left, taking each stitch twice over three fabric threads or thread intersections to form the tops of the hexagons and the top and left side of each square (*see illustration below:* **1**, **2**, *and* **3**).
- On the return journey, complete the hexagons and squares. The needle is shown completing a square.

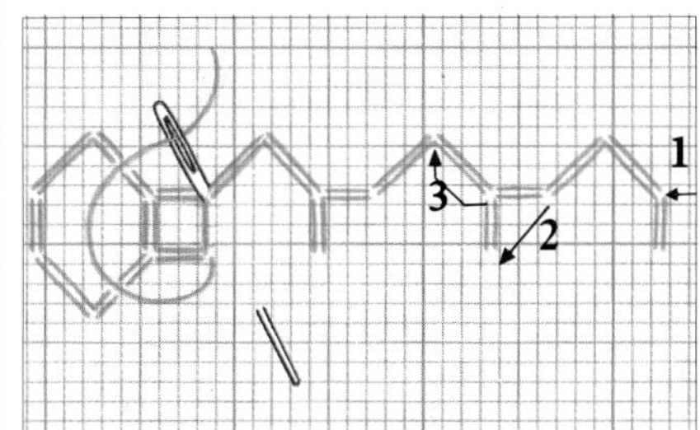

Working the second journey

Small ringed backstitch produces a more delicate effect than ringed backstitch (*see photograph below*).

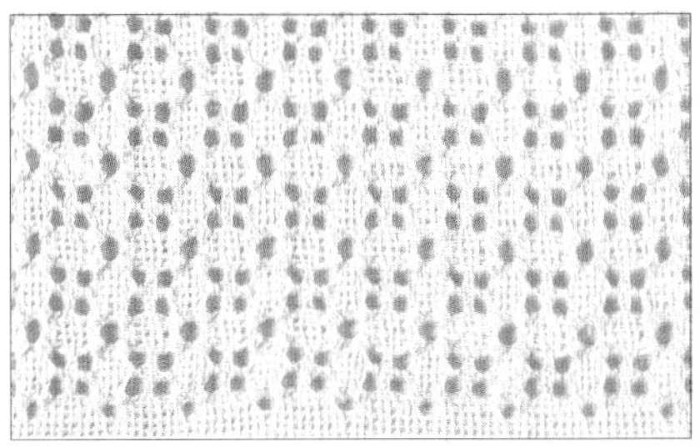

Sample of small ringed backstitch

SOFT TEXTURES

The soft textures of triangle, square, and honeycomb stitches are ideal for use where subtler effects are required in pulled work designs.

Working triangle stitch

Triangle stitch filling is worked in diagonal lines from upper left to lower right.

- Work a backstitch to the right of the starting point, bringing the needle up two threads below it (*see illustration below:* **1** *and* **2**).
- Take the needle down at the starting point (**3**).
- After you have established the corner or the apex of the triangle, make two more backstitches on each side alternately (**4**).
- Continue in this way, carefully positioning the triangles in diagonal rows as shown.

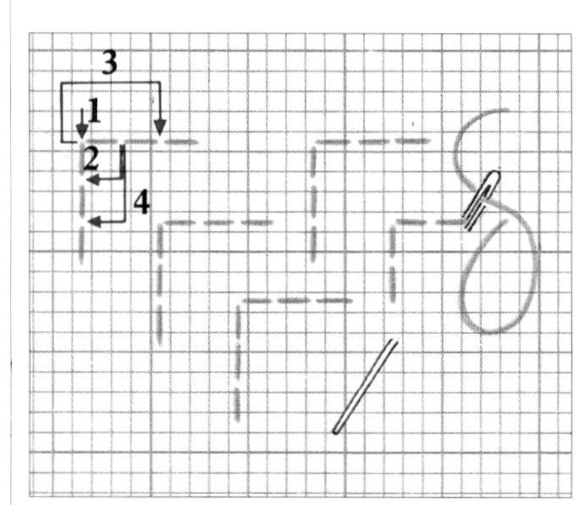

Working in diagonal rows

Triangle stitch produces a subtly textured filling with relatively small holes (*see photograph below*).

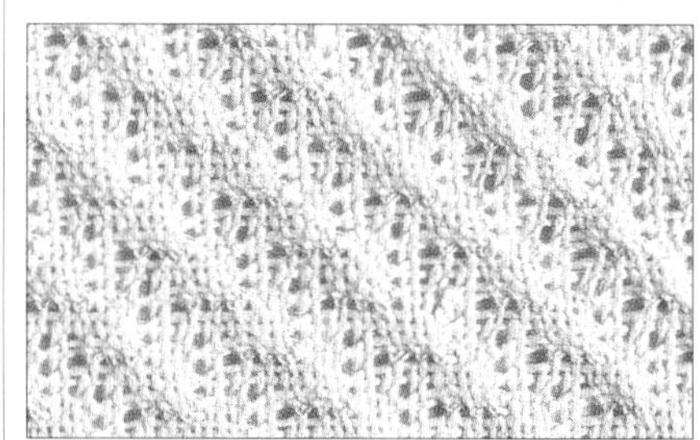

Sample of triangle stitch

Working square stitch

This delicate stitch consists of squares worked over six threads. Work across the fabric in rows as described, either in the same direction (as shown) or in alternating directions.

- Bring the needle up at the upper right-hand corner of the first square (*see illustration below:* **1**).
- Take the needle down two threads below and bring it up at the lower left-hand corner (**2**).
- Then take the needle down again two threads above.
- Continue around the square in a clockwise direction, taking the needle under the fabric and across to the opposite side after each stitch (**3**).
- Bring the needle up at the upper right-hand corner of the next square (**4**) and continue to work squares in the same way across the row (**5**).
- Work the next row of squares below the first row. The needle is shown working the next row.

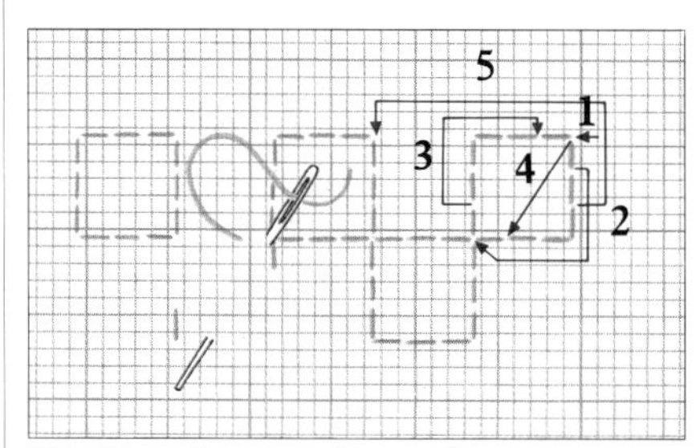

Working the second row of squares

Completed square stitch filling forms a distinctively crisp chequerboard pattern (*see photograph below*).

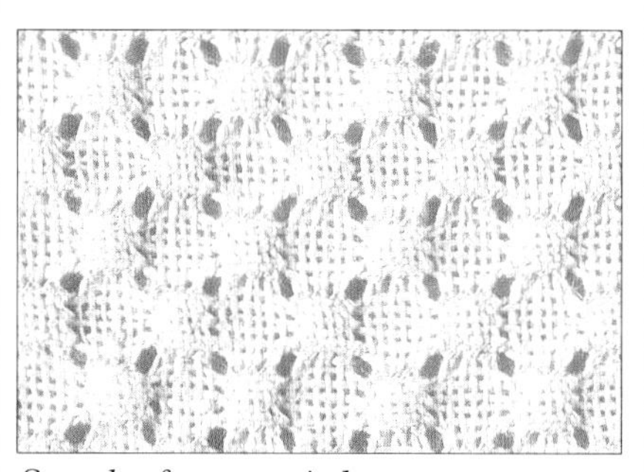

Sample of square stitch

Working honeycomb stitch

Each stitch in honeycomb filling is worked over four fabric threads.

- Start at top right-hand corner (*see illustration next column:* **1**).
- Take the needle down over four horizontal threads. Backstitch over four vertical threads. Bring needle up at same point (**2** *and* **3**).
- Take the needle back up over four fabric threads, and then make another backstitch (**4**).
- Continue working the stitch in this way to the end of the row.
- On the return journey, work in reverse. The needle is shown below working the return journey. Note that two stitches will be made in the same place, where the rows touch. These horizontal stitches are the only ones to be pulled tightly.

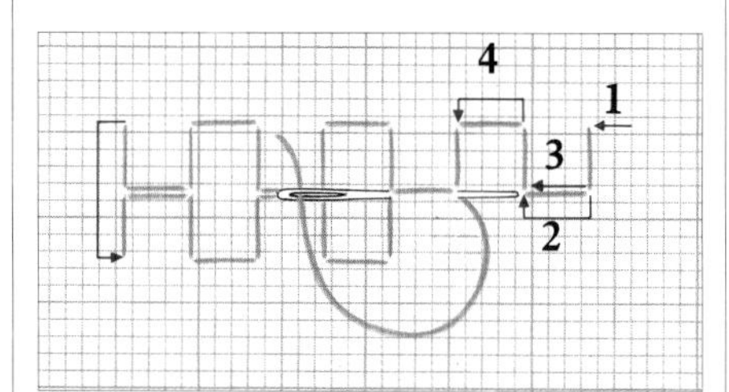

Working the return journey

A relatively thick thread enhances the close texture of honeycomb stitch; here, a no. 3 perlé cotton is used (*see photograph below*).

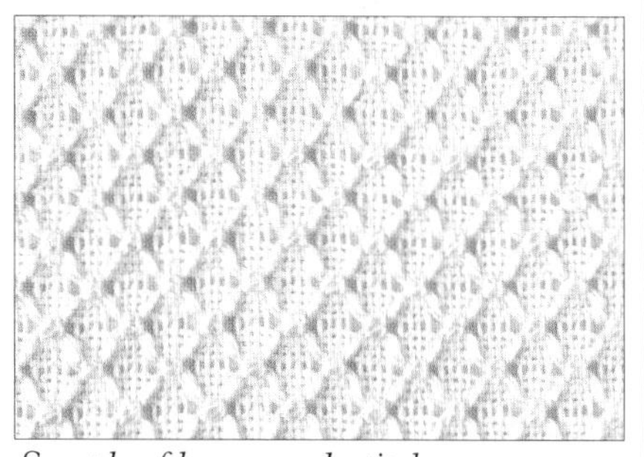

Sample of honeycomb stitch

LINES AND BORDERS

Four-sided stitch and three-sided stitch are pulled work stitches used for lines and borders. Point de Paris is an attractive stitch, used for hemming as an easier alternative to hemstitching. Hemstitching, an important openwork technique, is discussed in more detail on pages 153 as a finishing technique.

Working four-sided stitch

Each four-sided stitch is worked over a square of three fabric threads.

- Bring needle up at lower right-hand corner (*see illustration below:* **1**).
- Take the needle down at upper right and up at lower left (**2**).
- Take the needle down at lower right and up at upper left (**3**) to complete the first three sides of the first square.
- Working from right to left, continue along the three sides of each of the following squares in the same way as the first. A line of stitches is created in this way.

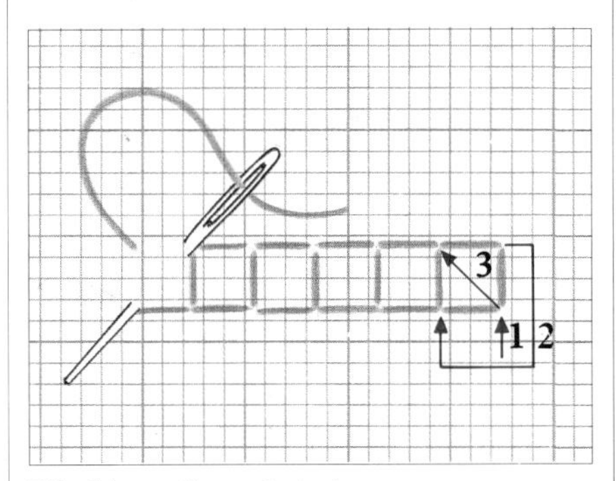

Working a line of stitches

- If you need to turn a corner on the border, it is best to stitch the rows in a counter-clockwise direction, as a neater corner is always produced by turning down than by turning up (*see illustration below*).

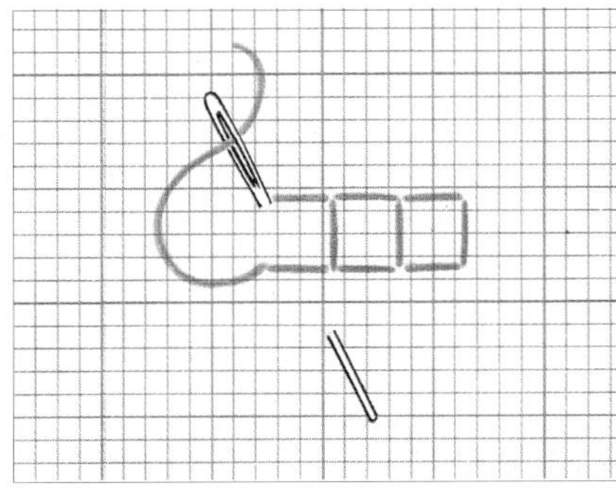

Turning down at the corner

When completed, four-sided stitch makes an attractive, delicate border (*see photograph below*).

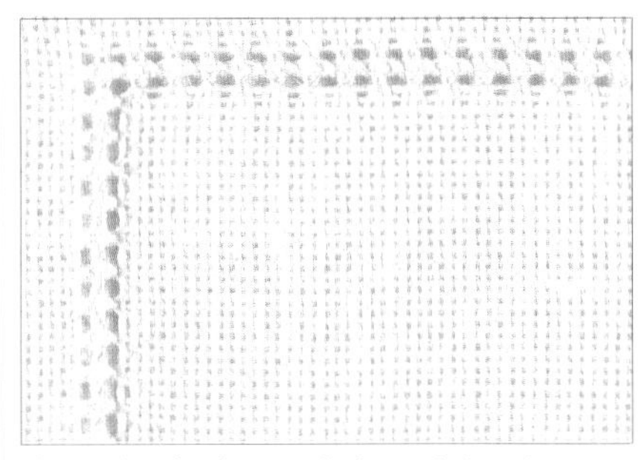

Sample of a four-sided stitch border

Working three-sided stitch

This makes a zigzag line, formed of backstitches, each worked twice over four threads.

- Begin with two backstitches at the upper edge of the border (*see illustration below:* **1**).
- Bring the needle up again at the starting point (**2**). Take it down four threads below, two threads to the right of the starting point.
- Bring the needle back up for the fourth time at the starting point.
- Work a second backstitch in the same place, this time bringing the needle out on the lower edge, four threads to the left (**3**).
- Work a second backstitch on the lower edge, then take the needle down at the starting point (**4**) and work another backstitch in the same place, taking the needle down again at the starting point.
- Continue across the row.

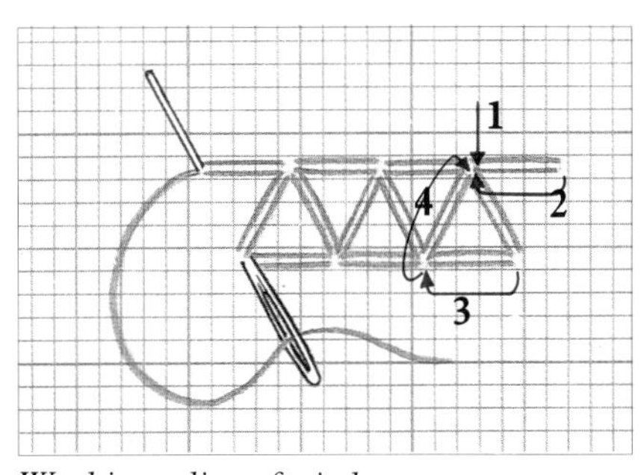

Working a line of stitches

- To turn a corner, first stitch over six fabric threads at the row end.
- Then make two backstitches up to the inner corner. Work over six threads in the new direction and continue as before.

Three-sided stitch creates a more open effect than four-sided stitch (*see photograph below*).

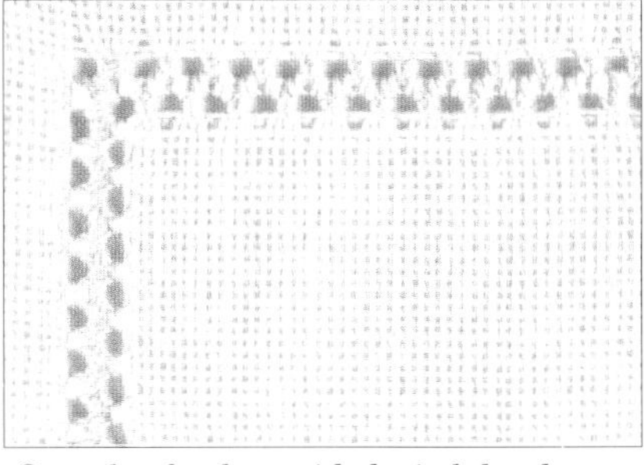

Sample of a three-sided stitch border

Working Point de Paris

Point de Paris is worked along a hem and is easier than hemstitching.

- First turn up a double hem and baste it in place.
- Insert the needle at the starting point, just below the hem fold (*see arrow on illustration below*).

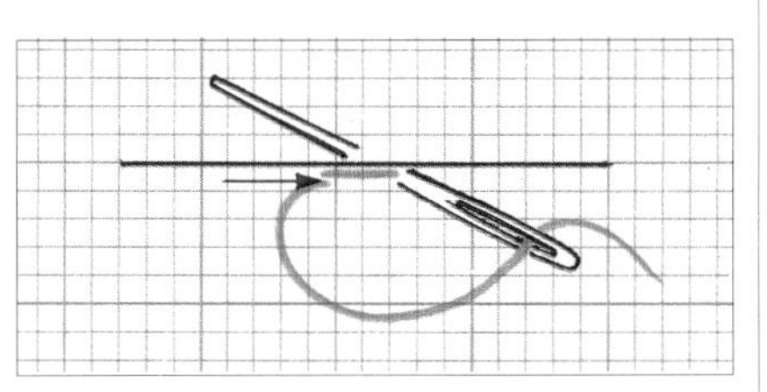

Starting to work Point de Paris

- Bring the needle up three threads to the left and make a backstitch, making sure that you bring the needle up at the same point.
- Make another backstitch, this time taking the needle into the new fold, one fabric thread up and one to the right. The needle is shown in this position (*see illustration above*).
- Take the needle down where it first emerged, forming a small diagonal stitch over the hem fold. Pull all stitches tightly.
- Continue in this way along the hem fold (*see illustration below*).

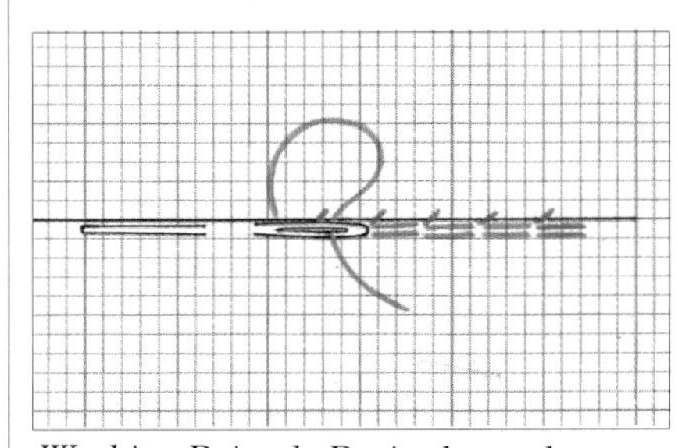

Working Point de Paris along a hem

Pulled Work Lampshade

Pulled work has a lacy, open texture that is especially effective with a light behind it. You can adapt this falling leaf design to fit any shape or size lampshade.

SIZE
Lampshade 6¼ in (16 cm) perpendicular height

MATERIALS
18-count evenweave hessian fabric (To work out how much fabric you need, measure from the bottom edge of your lampshade across the centre of the top opening and down to the bottom edge on the opposite side.)
DMC stranded cotton, colour to match fabric, 3 skeins
Braid to match fabric, 1.3 yd (1.2 m) (To work out how much braid you need, measure the top and bottom circumferences of your lampshade and then add on to this 3 in (7.5 cm) to allow for fraying.)
Fabric glue (must dry clear)

CHART FOR FALLING LEAVES DESIGN

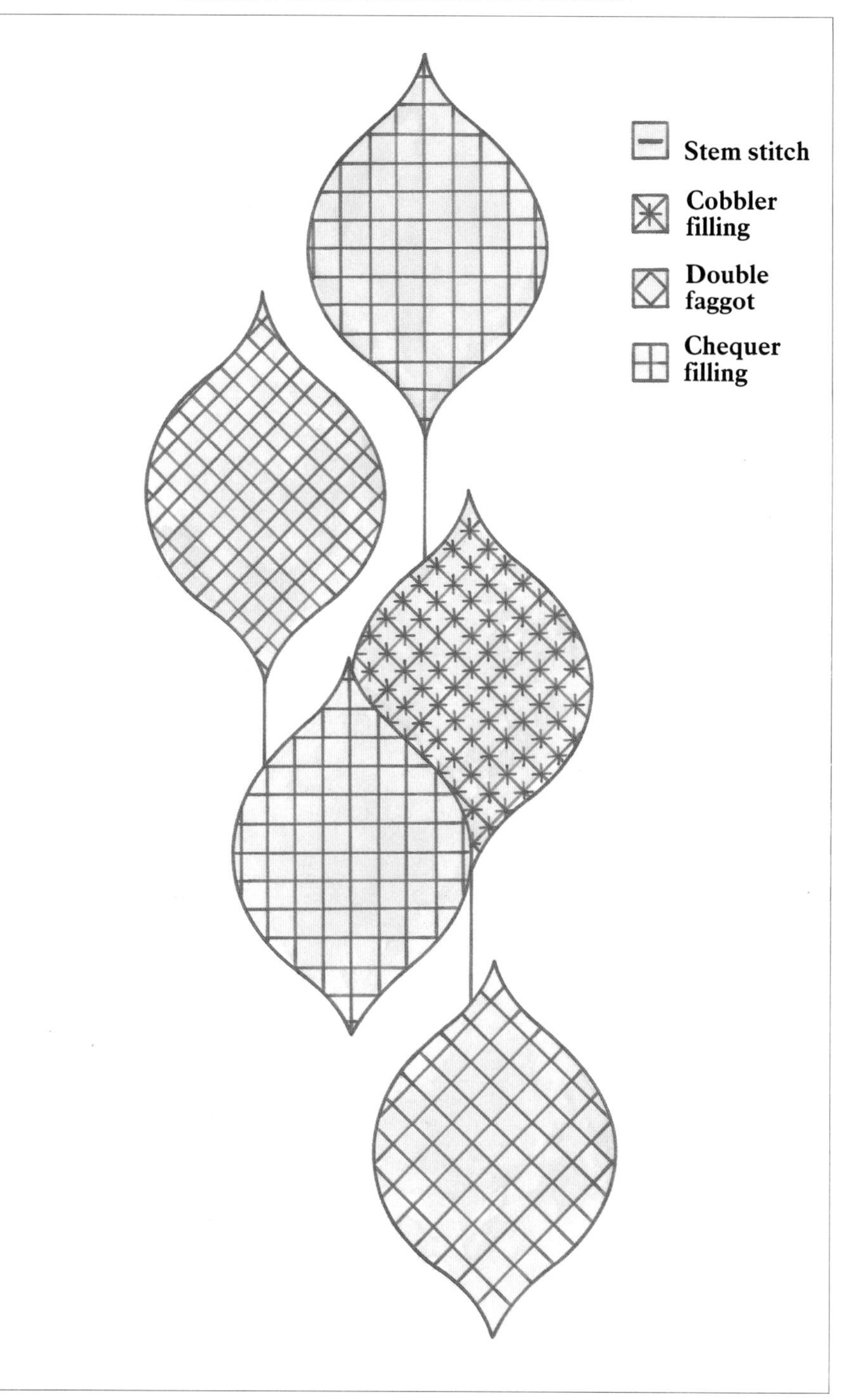

Making the pattern

1 Pin paper to the outside of lampshade. Trace the outline of the shade onto it, allowing an extra ½ in (1.25 cm) all around.

2 Pin the pattern to the fabric and carefully cut around it.

3 To prevent fraying, work blanket stitch around the edges by hand or machine around all edges.

Working the embroidery

1 Following the chart opposite, embroider the falling leaf outlines carefully in backstitch (*see page 98*), using three strands of thread.

As the fabric will stretch when attached to the lampshade, make sure that any embroidery is at least 1 in (2.5 cm) from the seam edges.

2 When the backstitch outline is complete, pass the needle under the backstitch, working from right to left. Be careful to avoid piercing the fabric (*see illustration below*).

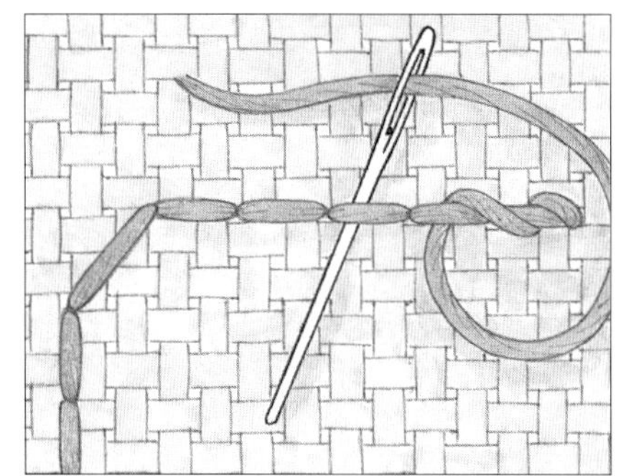

Passing the needle under backstitch

3 Repeat along all backstitches in outline. This whipped backstitch emphasizes the edges of the leaves.

4 Following the chart on page 118, embroider the leaves with filling stitches. Those shown here are double faggot stitch, cobbler filling, and chequerboard stitch, but you can use any other favourite filling stitches (*see pages 111–116*).

Making up the lampshade

1 When the embroidery is complete, place fabric on the shade and pin seam to hold. Pull the fabric taut. Remove fabric carefully, leaving the seam pinned. Then backstitch by hand (use straight stitch if by a machine) along the full length of the seam. Press the seam flat.

2 Slip fabric over the lampshade. Pin around bottom edge to hold in place; pull taut. Trim fabric at the top to edge of the lampshade. Carefully glue under fabric around top edge of shade. Press fabric into glue and allow to dry.

3 Make a line of glue on bottom edge of lampshade, under the fabric. Pull fabric taut and press into glue. Allow to dry and trim off the surplus fabric.

4 Glue the top and bottom outside edges of the lampshade. Attach the braid to each securely.

Variation

If you are using a lampshade without a cover, glue and wind bias binding strips onto the frame. Then sew the cover onto these strips.

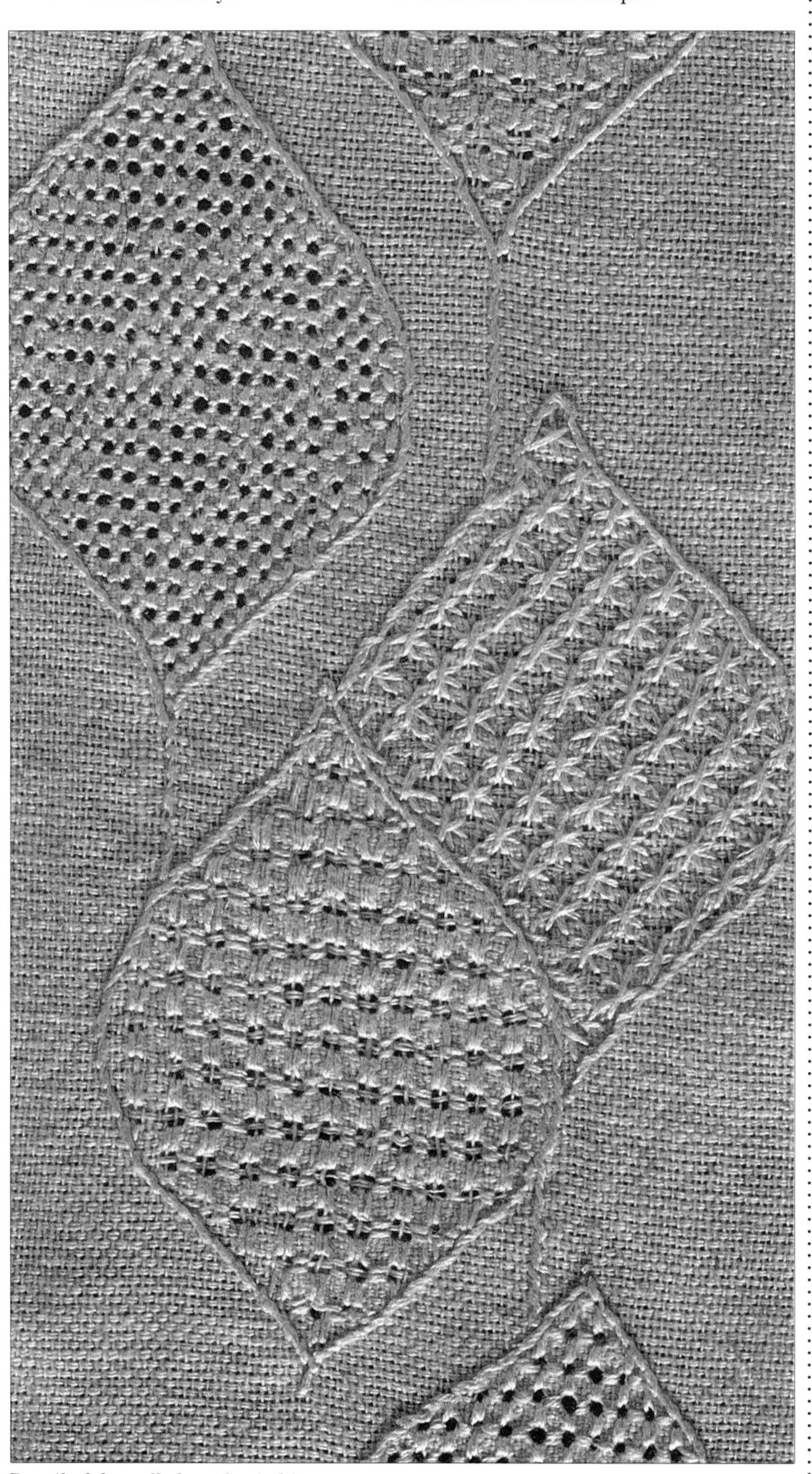

Detail of the pulled work stitching

Pulled Work Petals

Graceful blossoms are created with a combination of simple pulled stitches and surface embroidery on rose linen to decorate this beautiful placemat and napkin set.

SIZE

Finished placemat: 12½ × 18 in (32 × 46 cm); napkins 16 in (40cm) square

MATERIALS

For 4 placemats and napkins:

25-count rose linen, 2⅛ yds (1.9 metres), at least 47 in (120 cm) wide

Fabric shown: Zweigart "Dublin," shade 436

DMC no. 5 perlé cotton, 4 skeins, shade 760

DMC no. 8 perlé cotton, 5 balls, shade 760

Tapestry needles, sizes 22 and 24

PATTERN FOR PLACEMAT MOTIFS

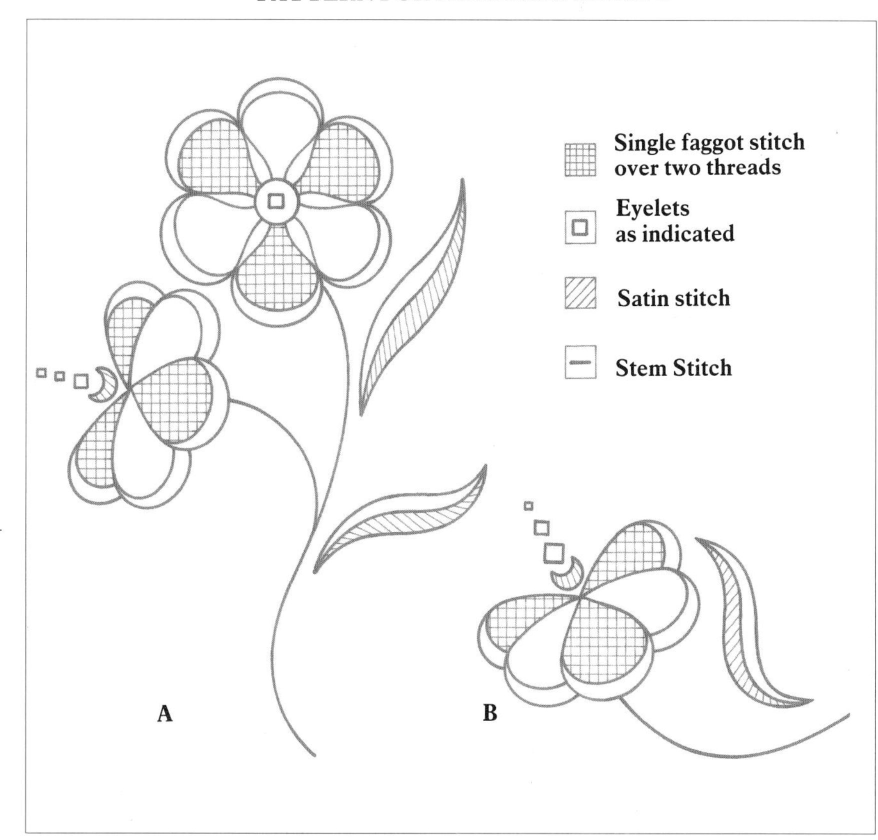

Working the embroidery: *placemats*

1 Test fabric for shrinkage; preshrink if necessary. Straighten ends and trim selvedges. For each placemat, you need to start with a piece of fabric approximately 17¾ × 23½ in (45 × 60 cm). The longer measurement should be across the fabric width.

2 Outline a rectangle 16½ × 22 in (42 × 56 cm) with basting stitches. This will be the cutting line. Overcast the edges (*see page 18*) to prevent fraying, then mount the fabric in an embroidery frame or hoop.

3 Transfer the placemat motifs (*see chart*) onto tracing paper; make four sets. Position motif A in the upper right-hand corner of the marked area; the top petal and the outer edge of the top leaf should be 3¾ in (9.5 cm) in from the basted lines.

4 Transfer the design outlines to the fabric with basting or running stitches (*see page 90*). Gently tear away the tracing paper.

5 Transfer the outlines of motif B to the lower left-hand corner in the same way. The left-hand petal and stem should each be positioned 3½ in (9 cm) from the basted lines.

6 Using a single strand of no. 8 perlé cotton, work alternate petals in single faggot stitch (*see page 114*). Work these alternate petals over only two fabric threads.

7 Using one strand of no. 8 perlé cotton, embroider the eyelets (*see page 113*). Work the stitches carefully over the number of fabric threads indicated on the pattern.

8 Using one strand of no. 5 perlé cotton, stitch all outlines in stem stitch. The short inner line of each petal should be stitched before you start to complete the outer line.

9 Using no. 5 perlé cotton, work satin stitch (*see page 111*) on the leaves and flower centres. This highlights the attractive motifs.

PATTERN FOR NAPKIN MOTIF

POSITIONING MOTIFS FOR THE NAPKINS

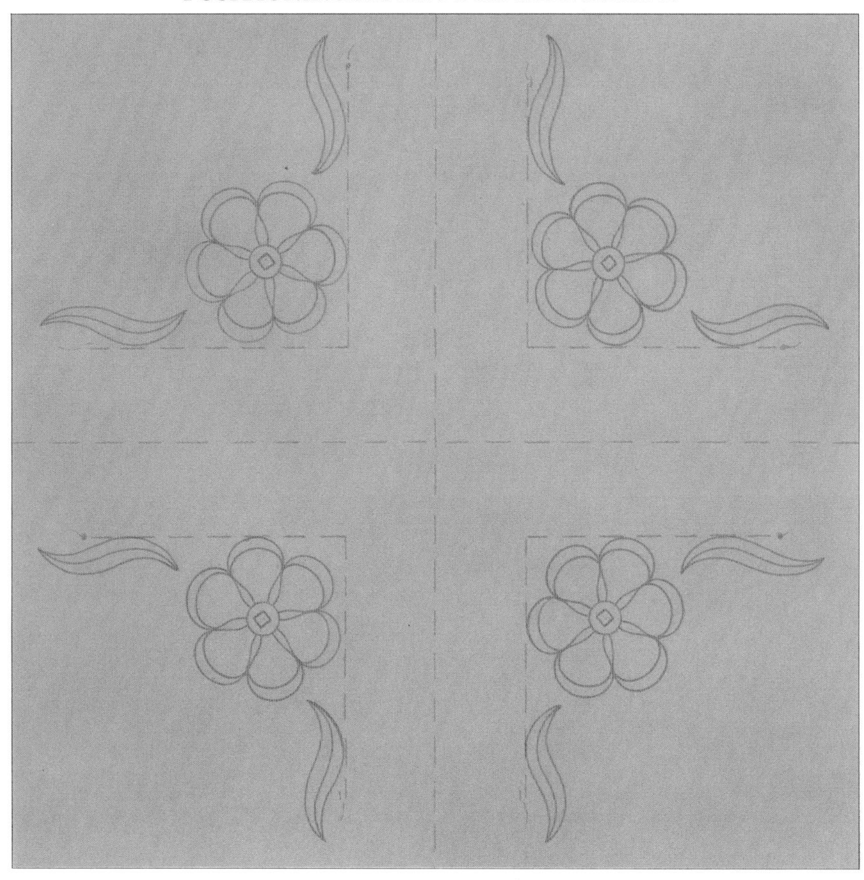

10 Remove the work from the embroidery frame and cut out the placemat along the basted line. Turn up a double 1 in (2.5 cm) hem on all edges, mitring the corners (*see page 153*); baste in place. Using one strand of no. 8 perlé cotton, finish hem with Point de Paris (*see page 117*).

11 Repeat steps 3–10 for the remaining three placemats.

12 Press the completed placemats on a well-padded ironing board.

Working the embroidery: *napkins*

1 Cut a piece of fabric 40 in (100 cm) square. Mark the centre in each direction with a line of basting stitches, dividing the fabric into four equal squares (*see chart*).

2 Mark the position of the two leaves of the napkin motif in one square, placing the pins 4¼ in (10.5 cm) from the basting stitches. Then carefully mount this section in an embroidery frame or hoop.

3 Transfer outlines of the napkin motif to fabric with basting stitches.

4 Embroider design on the napkin, following steps 6–7 of the placemat instructions.

5 Repeat steps 2–4 above for the remaining three squares.

6 Cut fabric along basting lines. Turn and stitch hem of each napkin, using one strand of no. 5 perlé cotton. Stitch all outlines first, then the short inner line of each petal. Finally complete the outer line.

7 Press the completed napkins carefully with a warm steam iron on a well-padded ironing board.

Butterfly Cushion

Fluttering against a delicate screen of step stitch, these butterflies are defined and embellished with surface stitches and eyelets. A border of three-sided and satin stitches completes the design.

SIZE

Pillow: 15 in (38 cm) square
Design: 12½ in (32 cm) square

MATERIALS

For design: 28-count evenweave linen, 20 in (50 cm) square
DMC no. 8 perlé cotton, 1 ball, colour to match fabric. Shade shown: 712
DMC stranded cotton, 4 skeins, colour to match fabric
Tapestry needle, size 24
Crewel needles, sizes 7 and 9

For cover: ⅝ yd (57 cm) medium-weight fabric, 38 in (97 cm wide)
Fabric shown: duchesse satin
Cushion pad 16 in (40 cm) square
4 buttons
Narrow cord, 2¼ yds (2 meters) or an extra ball of perlé cotton to make a cord
Tracing paper, at least 12½ in (32 cm) square
Sewing thread to match

PATTERN FOR BUTTERFLY CUSHION

Working the embroidery

1 Enlarge the butterfly pattern to measure 10¾ in (27 cm) square. Copy the pattern onto the tracing paper. (Keep the original design for use in step 11.) Each square of the grid represents 2 in (5 cm).

2 Mount the fabric in a stretcher or scroll frame (*see page 20*). Baste a 10¾ in (27 cm) square on the fabric, leaving 4¼ in (11 cm) all around. Take care to keep the basting or running stitch of the square between the fabric threads.

3 Pin the tracing to the fabric, aligning edges with basted outlines. Baste carefully around all butterflies. Gently remove the tracing paper.

4 Beginning in the upper right-hand corner and using one strand of the perlé cotton in the tapestry needle, work step stitch (*see page 112*) for the background around the butterflies. At the left-hand and lower edges you may need to end the stitching one or two threads to either side of the basting line, in order to end with a complete group of stitches.
Note that the lower right-hand corner does not touch the rest of the background. To align the pattern on the bottom edge, count the threads across the wing at the right-hand edge, then resume stitching at the correct place on the background.

5 When the background is complete, work a border of three-sided stitch (*see page 117*), leaving at least ¼ in (6 mm) all around it. Use one strand of perlé cotton. At a corner, count the remaining threads to determine whether the corner will turn at the proper point. If this is correct, there will be the same number of threads in the space on the adjacent side. If not, work one of the stitches over three or five threads, as required in order, to position the corner correctly.

6 Embroider a line of counted satin stitch (*see page 111*) with one strand of perlé cotton ¼ in (6 mm) outside the three-sided stitch. Work over three fabric threads and leave the stitches unpulled.

7 Embroider the butterflies, using stranded cotton. Begin by working the outlines in stem stitch, using three strands and the larger crewel needle. Remove the basting as you work around the butterfly outline.

• To work stem stitch, bring the needle up at the starting point and take it down one stitch length – about ⅛ in (3–4 mm) – ahead (*see illustration below*: **1**).

• Bring the needle up halfway between these two points (**2**). Continue in the same manner, always keeping the thread on the same side of the needle. Shorten stitches as required to go around corners.

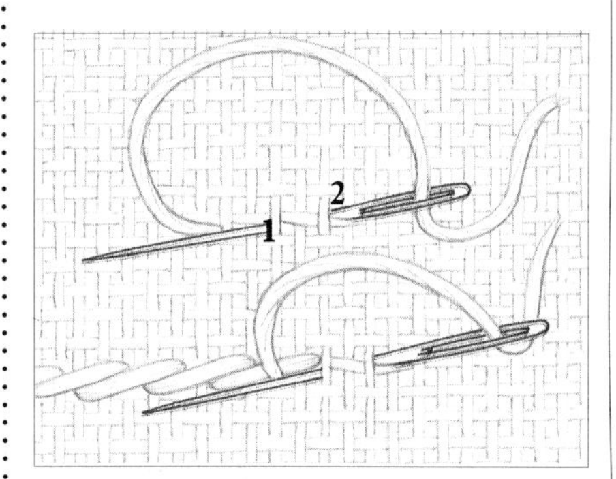

Working stem stitch

8 Stitch the antennae, using either stem stitch or trailing stitch. Trailing stitch is more suitable, but this stitch is also more difficult to keep smooth over the openwork.

• To work the trailing stitch for the antennae, cut a length of stranded cotton about 4 in (10 cm) long; do not separate the strands. Lay this on the work in a V shape.

• Using three other strands of thread, take a single stitch over the point of the V to fasten it to the body.

• Continue to work stitches over the core thread and through the fabric with close parallel stitches (*see illustration below*). Holding the core thread straight with your free hand take the needle down and up under the core thread, not to one side.

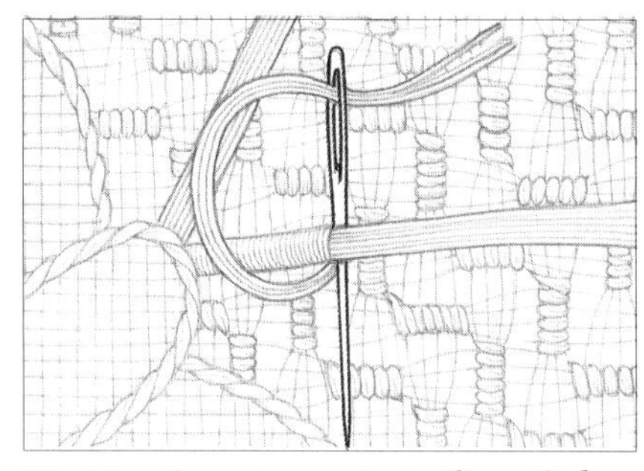
Working the antennae in trailing stitch

Continue to work trailing stitch for ¾ in (2 cm). For the large butterfly use unseparated strands in the needle and work for 1 in (2.5 cm). Do not fasten off, but park the needle out of the way and thread the core threads into a tapestry needle. Make a loose French knot at antenna end.

• To make the French knot, bring the needle up at the end of the antennae. Wrap the thread once around it (*see illustration below:* **A**) and reinsert the needle close to the starting point (**B**).

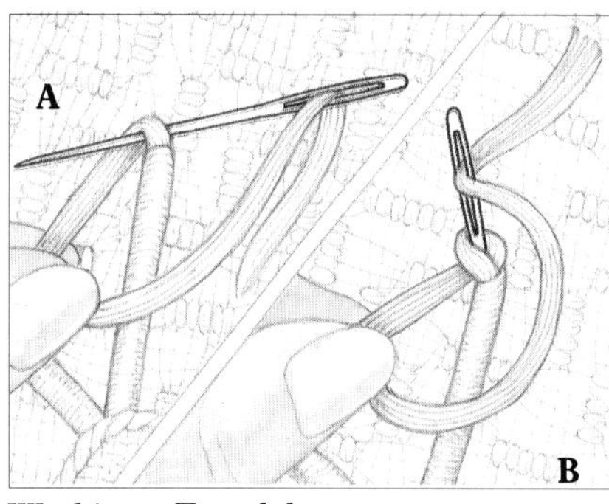

Working a French knot

• Pull the needle through smoothly, holding the thread securely in your hand until the last moment.

• Take both threads to the wrong side. Remove the tapestry needle and tie the threads together securely.

9 Work the bodies of the butterflies in padded satin stitch over the stem stitch outline:

• Starting near the centre of the design area, work diagonally towards one end with close, parallel stitches (*see illustration below*).

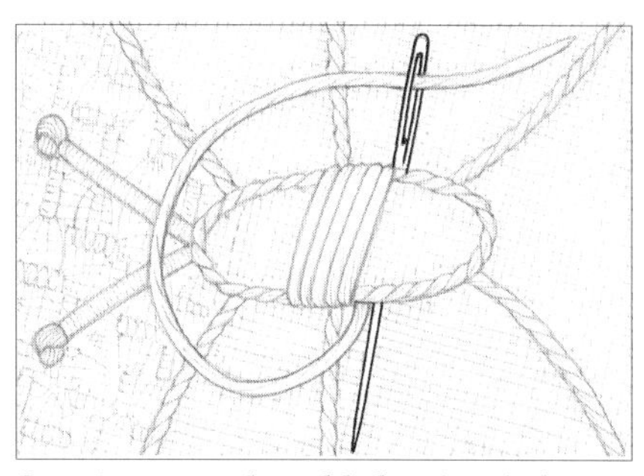
Starting to work padded satin stitch

• Rejoin the thread at the starting point and work to the other end.

• Work the second layer as before, but work in the opposite direction (*see illustration below*). Take care to keep the acute slant of the stitches.

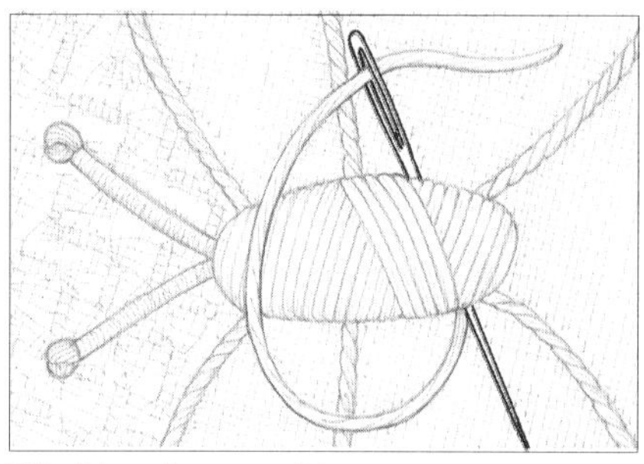
Working the second layer

10 Make eyelets (*see page 113*) in a pattern of your choice on the wings. The eyelets shown are worked over six or four threads; one is worked over eight threads.

11 Stitch the veins, using a single strand of thread (two strands for the large butterfly), in the smaller crewel needle. Work them freehand in a pattern of your choice.

Alternatively, you could draw the veins on the enlarged design. Place this carefully underneath the work and lightly trace the outlines onto the fabric with a water-soluble ink pen.

Making up the cushion

1 Remove the embroidery from the frame. Place it right side up on a well-padded surface, dampen slightly, and pin to shape along the outer edge of the satin stitch border, using rustproof pins, ruler, and set square. Adjust the pins as necessary to ensure that the embroidery has straight lines and square corners and that it is held securely.

2 Dampen the work thoroughly and leave it until almost dry. Remove the pins and place them along the edge of the fabric, pulling the work taut. If the embroidered area is not quite square, pull to straighten.

Dampen the embroidery again around the edges, and let the work dry thoroughly. The edges of the fabric should now be smooth.

3 From the cover fabric cut three pieces: one piece 16½ in (42 cm) square, one piece 16½ × 12¾ in (42 × 33 cm), and one piece 16½ × 8 in (42 × 21 cm).

If the fabric has a lengthwise weave, as satin does, make sure that the weave runs along the longer measurement in the last two pieces.

4 Baste the embroidered piece to the square backing piece with right sides and edges aligned. Finish cushion as instructed on page 154. Trim the seam allowance of the larger front backing piece to ⅜ inch (1 cm). Cut all corners diagonally. Overcast both pieces together on the diagonal edges.

5 Press the seam allowances open; finger-press into the corners. Turn the cover right side out. Attach buttons at 3 in (8 cm) intervals.

Carefully add thread loops (*see page 155*) to the overlapping edge of the fabric using perlé cotton.

6 To finish the cushion, sew cord around the edges by hand (*see page 155*). Begin at the top left-hand corner with the mid-point of the cord, then work in both directions to the lower right-hand corner.

Detail of butterfly cushion

7 Form the ends into a bow, stitching in place with invisible stitches. Knot ends at the desired length; trim if necessary.

Variations

You could use another pulled stitch instead of step stitch. Single or double faggot stitch (*see page 114*) would be quicker to work and very effective. Honeycomb stitch or small ringed backstitch are also attractive alternatives. This design was created with cut paper shapes, traced from life-size pictures of butterflies. You could create a similar design, for example with birds of your choice or flowers.

Remember that there is scope for flexibility in your design. Do not worry if the veins are a little irregular. For example, real butterfly wings are not precisely symmetrical.

Hardanger Work Techniques

Named after the area around the Hardanger Fjord in western Norway, Hardanger embroidery is a form of counted thread openwork embroidery that has become popular around the world. Modern Hardanger is often used on furnishings such as table linens.

BASICS OF HARDANGER

The basic structure of Hardanger embroidery consists of regular groups of satin stitches (see page 111), *called kloster blocks. These stitches surround open areas that are created by cutting and removing fabric threads. The fabric threads remaining inside the open area are then covered with overcast stitches or needleweaving to build up the distinctive geometric patterns that closely follow the weave of the fabric.*

Bars created by needleweaving or overcasting can be enhanced with picots, and the spaces between them can be decorated with various filling stitches. Other embroidery stitches, such as eyelets (see page 113) *or satin stitch in various shapes, are often used to embellish the remaining areas of the fabric. Some pieces of Hardanger embroidery have a decorative edge that is worked in buttonhole stitch.*

Choosing Hardanger materials

The embroidery is generally worked on Hardanger cloth, a strong, firm evenweave fabric woven with pairs of threads. It does not fray when the threads are cut and withdrawn, and is available in traditional white or cream, and in a variety of other colours. Hardanger can also be worked on other evenweave fabrics, provided the threads can be counted easily.

Perlé cotton is the prefered thread; its crisp, glossy texture complements the rectangular character of the work and gives it an attractive sheen. For the kloster blocks, choose a thread slightly thicker than the fabric threads. No. 5 perlé cotton, for example, is well suited to 22-count Hardanger cloth, while a finer thread, such as no. 8 perlé cotton, is more suitable for covering the bars and working filling stitches. Other threads such as coton à broder or various matt-finished threads can also be used.

Traditionally, Hardanger embroidery was worked in white thread on white fabric. However, it can also be worked effectively using coloured thread on either white or off-white fabric, as shown in the sample (*see photograph below*). It can also be worked successfully using coloured fabric and matching thread.

Sample of spider's web filling, using coloured thread and white fabric.

Hardanger should be worked with a tapestry needle, the size of which depends on the chosen fabric.

Some professional embroiderers work Hardanger in the hand, but it is a good idea to begin by working in an embroidery frame or hoop (*see page 19*). This makes it easier to count threads and maintain an even tension in your work.

USE OF SIMPLE HARDANGER MOTIFS

Hardanger designs vary widely, and there are no precise rules that will cover all of them. However, most typical motifs can be worked on the principles described below. Kloster blocks of satin stitch combine with overcast or woven bars, which can then be embellished further if required. The simple cruciform motif illustrated in this section is a good one to use to practise basic Hardanger stitches to create kloster blocks. After you have practised making overcast and woven bars, try out the more complicated filling stitches on the following pages.

Positioning Hardanger motifs

The method of positioning the Hardanger motifs varies according to the design, but it is usually essential to mark the centre point with basting or running stitches (*see page 18*). To position the first kloster block, count outward from the centre point.

If the design is a border, you may only need to find either the vertical or horizontal centre.

Working the kloster blocks

Kloster blocks normally consist of five stitches worked over four fabric threads, although they may consist of three, seven, or nine stitches and may also vary in height.

- Begin by anchoring the thread with backstitches, leaving an end to be darned in later (*see page 98*).
- Work five satin stitches over four fabric threads (a pair of threads count as one), bringing the needle up at the lower edge each time. This completes the first kloster block.

- Bring the needle up at the lower right-hand corner ready to work the next block (*see illustration below*).

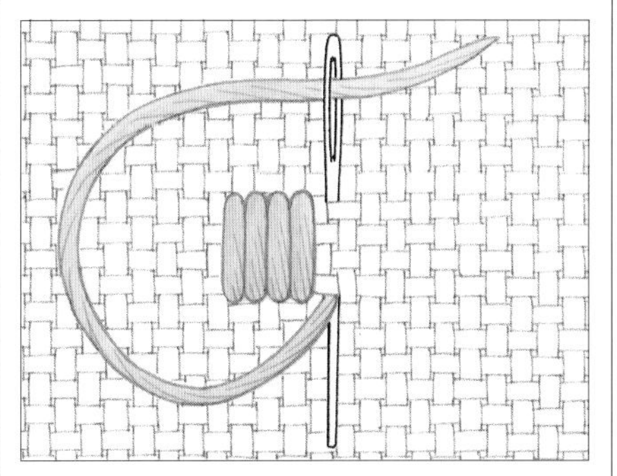

Working the first block

- Work the second block over four threads at a right angle to the first.
- Work the third block at a right angle. Bring needle up four threads down from last stitch of the second block (*see illustration below*).

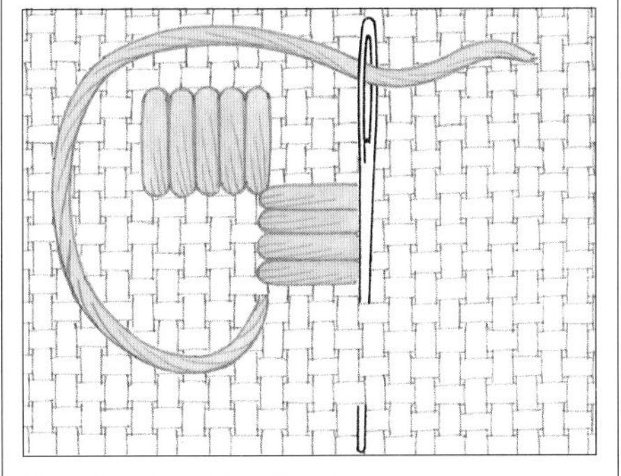

Starting the third block

- Continue in step formation back to the starting point (*see illustration below*). Darn the thread under several kloster blocks; trim the end.
- Pull out the backstitches at the starting point and darn the end in under several blocks.

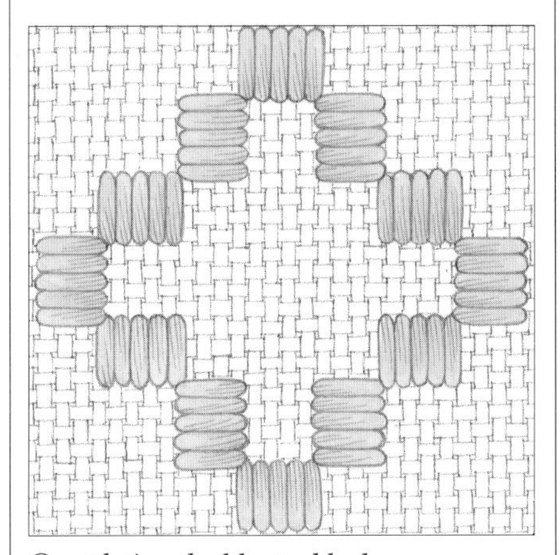

Completing the kloster blocks

Removing fabric threads

- Cut the fabric threads using sharp-pointed scissors. Cut only those threads running between the bases of two opposing kloster blocks.
- Cut the four fabric threads at the base of one block; do **not** cut the stitches or the crosswise threads.
- Cut the same four threads at the base of the opposite block and pull the cut threads out with tweezers.
- Remove all cut threads in one direction, then in the other. Only threads between unstitched edges remain (*see illustration below*).

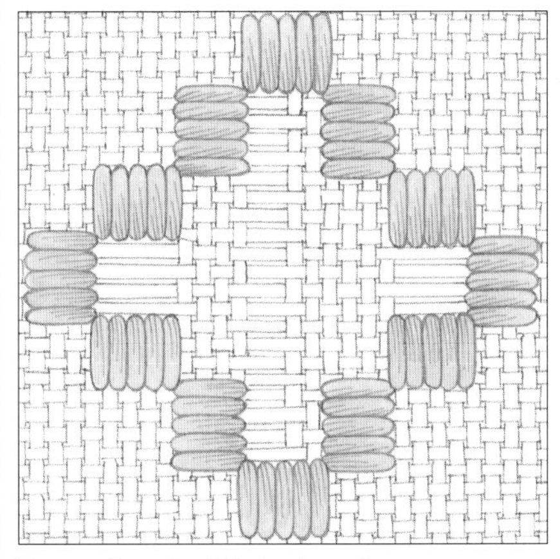

Removing the fabric threads

Working overcast bars

- Bind groups of remaining fabric threads with needleweaving or overcasting, using a finer thread.
- Fasten off the end of the thread and work over it.
- Take the working thread over the fabric threads, covering them completely (*see illustration below*). When moving to the next bar, take the needle under the work.

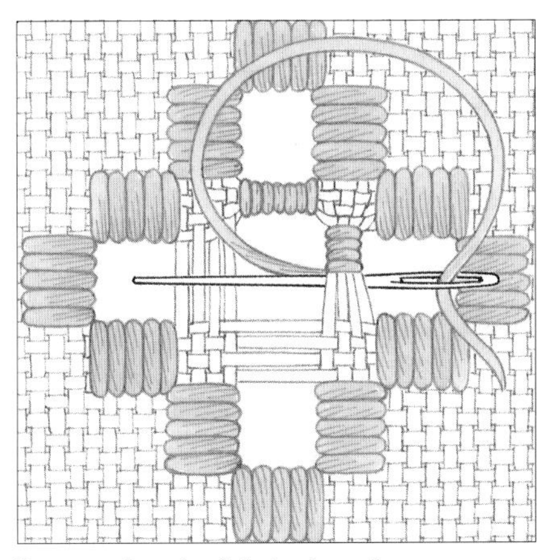

Overcasting the fabric threads

Working woven bars

- Woven bars are an elegant alternative to overcast bars. To work these, bring the needle up in the centre of the group of threads, then take it over those to the right and left alternately (*see illustration below*).

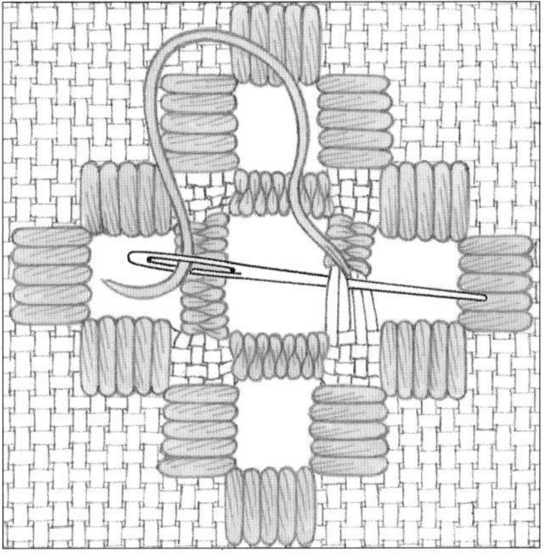

Working woven bars

This basic motif with woven bars has been embellished with examples of other Hardanger motifs. The eyelets at the top and bottom are worked like those on page 113, but positioned diagonally to the grain of the fabric and worked without pulling (*see photograph below*).

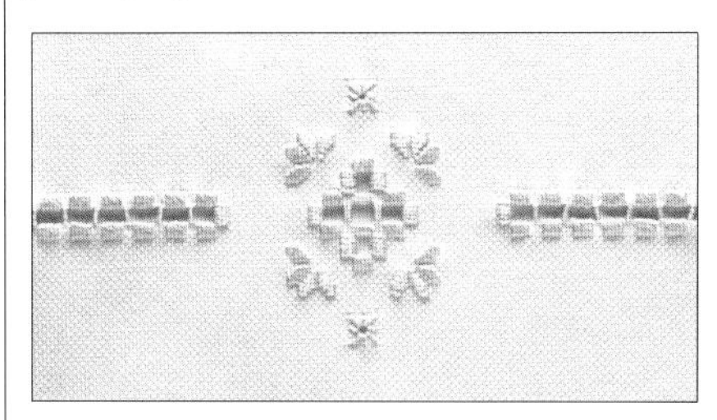

Hardanger motif worked with woven bars and embellished

EMBELLISHMENTS

Rich and delicate effects can be achieved in Hardanger work by decorating the bars and open spaces with picots and various filling stitches. It is the interplay between the crisp outlines of the kloster blocks and the lacy fillings that gives Hardanger work its charm. Attractive embellishments also give the technique more flexibility and allow individual creativity to shine through its somewhat rigid framework. Embellishments need practice, but are not difficult to work.

In the past, Hardanger embroidery was used mainly to decorate festive clothing, such as headdresses and bridal shirts. Many kinds of embellishments were added to basic kloster blocks to achieve a celebratory look.

Preparing to practise techniques of Hardanger embroidery

- Prepare several squares consisting of two groups of five-stitch kloster blocks on each side.
- Remove appropriate fabric threads so that a single cross made up of four threads is left in each square.

Working picots

Picots are a form of loop used as decorations on Hardanger embroidery. They are worked on a woven bar and can be placed on one or both sides of the bar.

- Work needleweaving along the bar to the halfway point.
- On the next weaving stitch, bring the point of the needle up through the centre of the threads, then loop the working thread under it as shown (*see illustration below*).

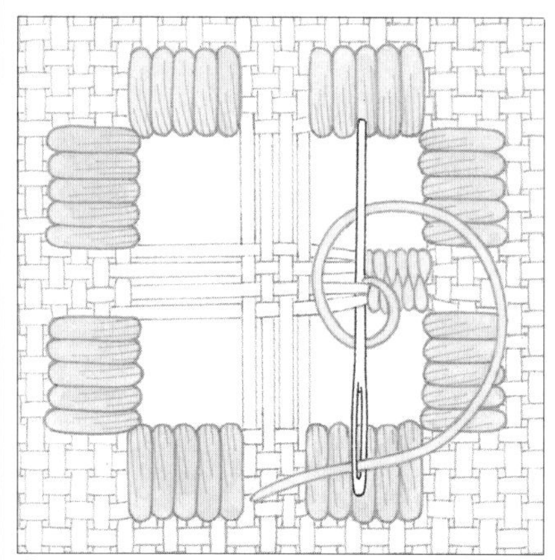

Starting to work the picot

- Pull the thread through carefully to form a picot.
- Take the needle back under same two threads and up through centre as before (*see illustration below*).

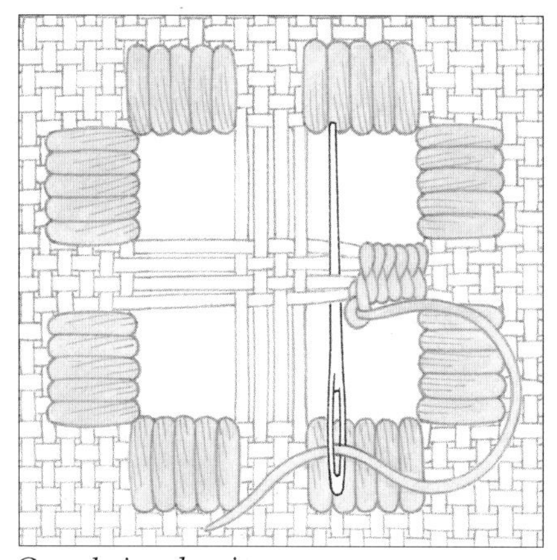

Completing the picot

- Continue needleweaving in this way to the end of the bar. Another picot can be formed on the opposite side of the bar immediately after completing the first one if desired (*see illustration below*).

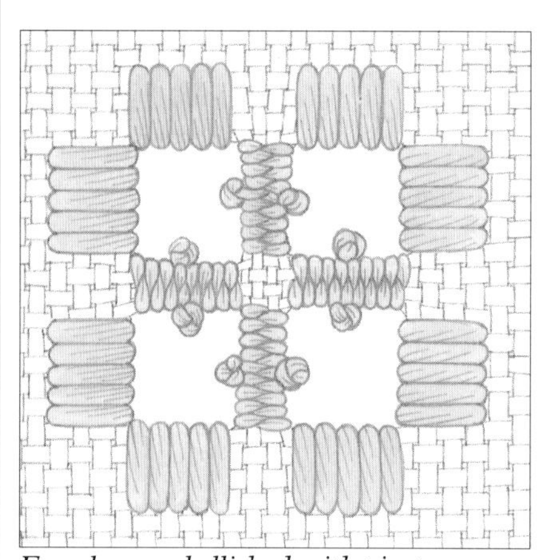

Four bars embellished with picots

Working oblique loops

This filling can be worked in any kind of square, including those formed by kloster blocks, overcast bars, or a combination of blocks and bars. The starting point will vary, depending on the sequence of the work.

- Overcast the top and left-hand bars of the square.
- Bring the needle up at the lower left-hand corner of the square.
- Take the needle down through the lower right-hand corner (here the centre of the square) and bring it up over the thread to form a loop as shown (*see illustration below*).

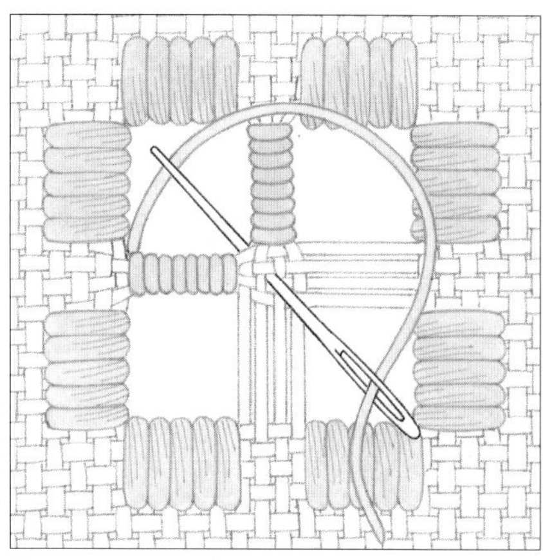

Beginning an oblique loop

- Take the needle down at the top right-hand corner, then up over the thread (*see illustration below*).

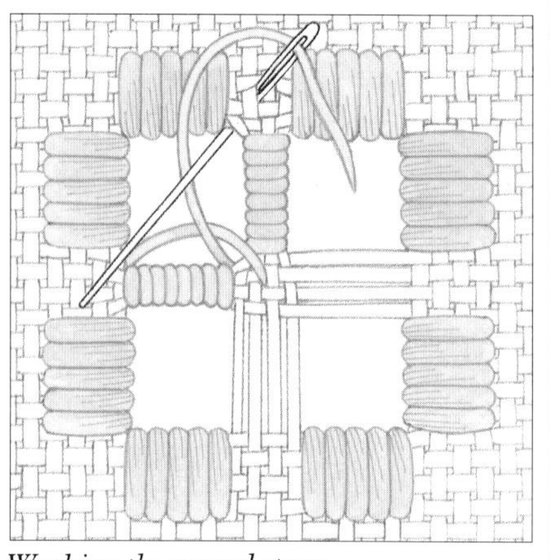

Working the second stage

- Repeat at the upper left-hand corner. To complete filling, take the needle over the third loop as shown, then down under fourth loop into fabric (*see illustration below*).

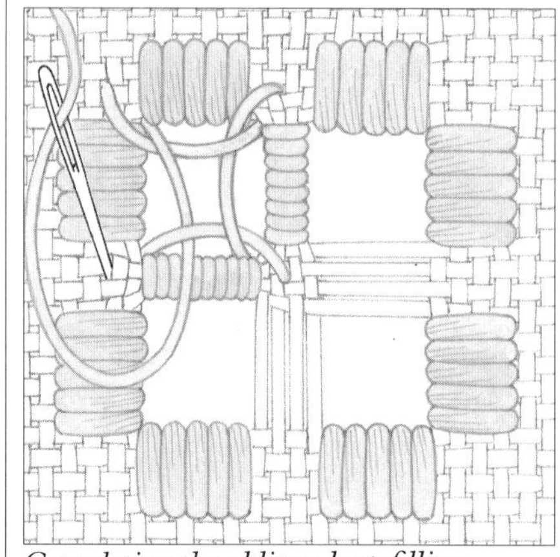

Completing the oblique loop filling

• Work around the motif to fill as many squares as desired.

Working simple lace filling stitch

Straight loops are shown here worked into woven bars and kloster blocks to form a simple lace filling. These loops, like most embellishments in Hardanger work, can also be worked over overcast bars.

• Weave the top and left-hand bars of the square.

• Bring the needle up below the centre stitch of the kloster block, then take it from left to right under the centre stitch of the adjacent block as shown (*see illustration below*).

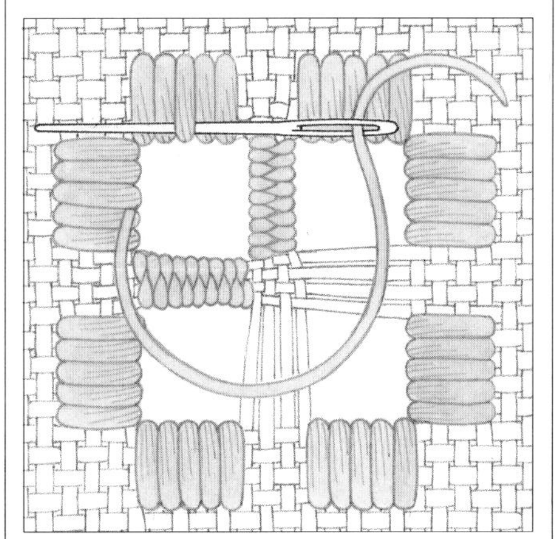

Beginning simple lace filling

• Take the needle over this first thread loop, then down into the centre of the first woven bar and up over the working thread as before (*see illustration below*).

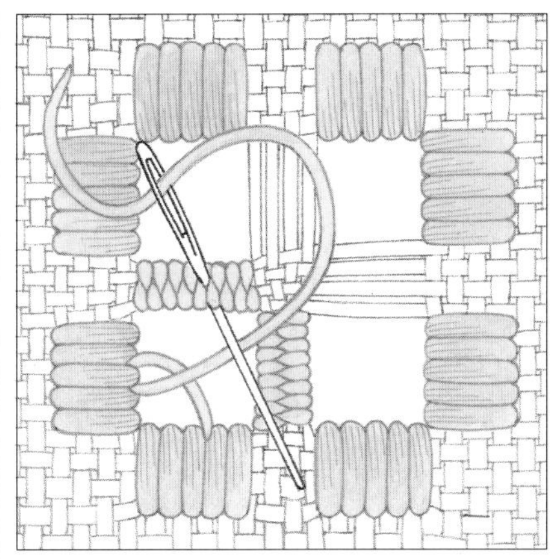

Completing the second loop

• Repeat in the other woven bar, then take the needle over the last thread and under the first thread leading from the kloster block (*see illustration below*). This completes the simple lace filling.

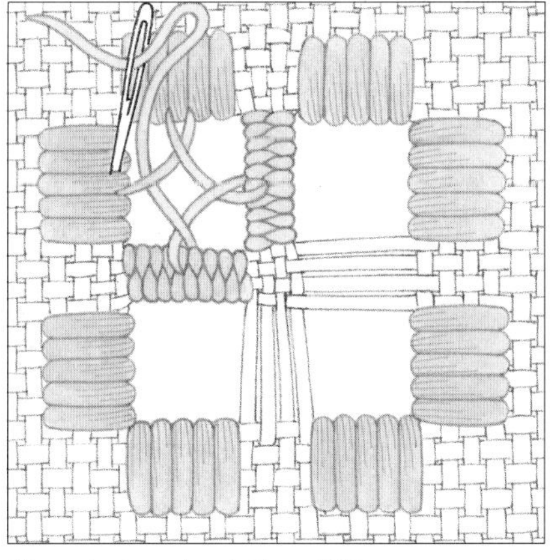

Completing simple lace filling

• Work around the motif to fill as many squares as desired.

• Lace filling can also be worked inside four bars. Begin the first loop in the middle of the fourth bar after completing half the overcasting or needleweaving on that bar. Work all the loops, then cover the rest of the bar (*see illustration below*).

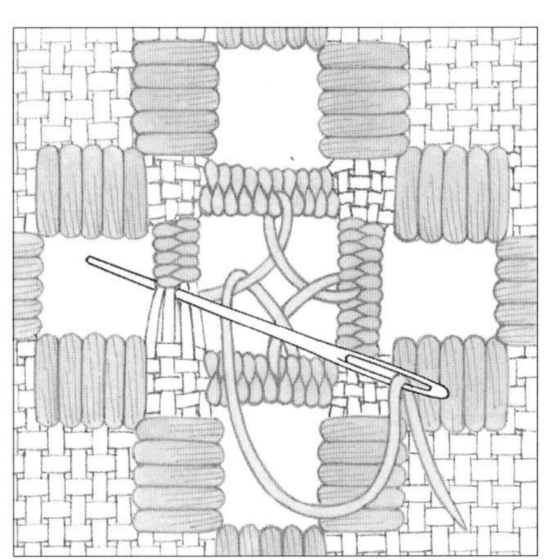

Working lace filling inside the bars

Completed lace filling stitch is one of the most delicate and attractive embellishments to Hardanger work (*see photograph below*).

Sample of simple lace filling

Working dove's eye filling

Dove's eye filling is used to embellish openwork squares.

• Overcast the right-hand bar from top to bottom, always working toward the centre point.

• At the centre, take the needle up to the diagonally opposite corner, then work three or four overcasting stitches over the thread back to the centre (*see illustration below*).

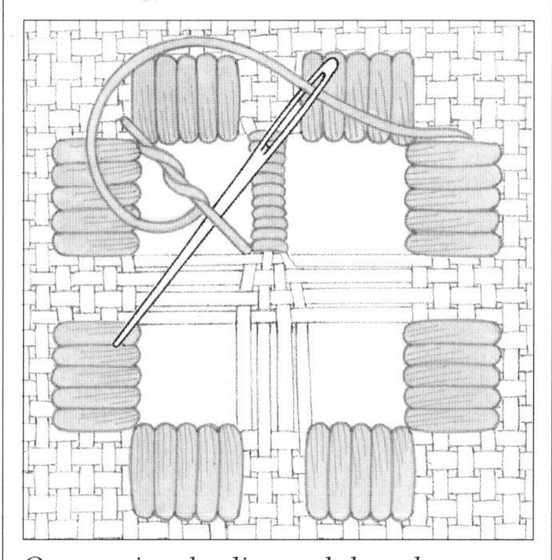

Overcasting the diagonal thread

• Overcast the next bar, then lay another thread across the first from the lower left-hand corner to upper right-hand corner of the square that is being filled.

• Overcast the laid thread to the centre. Then carefully make a single buttonhole stitch over the crossing point (*see illustration below*).

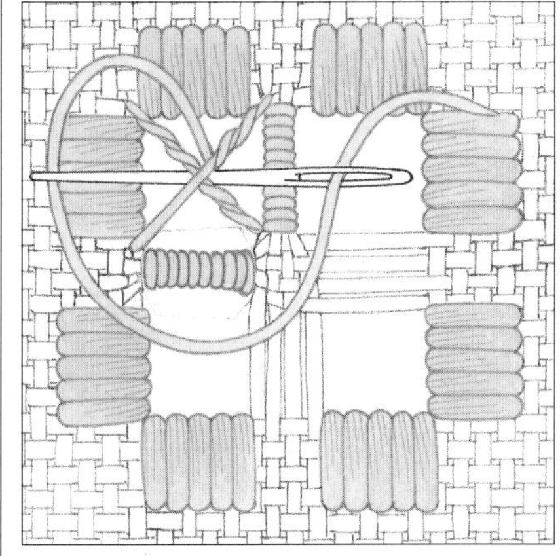

Working a single buttonhole stitch over the crossing point

• Take the needle under and over the threads alternately in a counterclockwise direction for one or more rounds.

- Overcast the lower end of the second crossing thread (*see illustration below*).

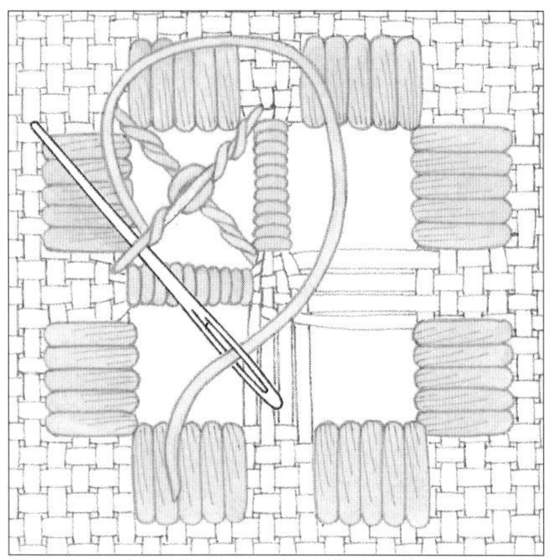
Overcasting the crossing thread

If you are working a dove's eye within four bars, you should then complete the remaining two bars. Work around the motif to fill the squares (*see photograph below*).

Sample of dove's eye filling

Working whipped spider's web filling
Use this filling for a larger square that consists of four small ones.

- Bind the fabric threads with needleweaving. Lay threads diagonally, then overcast each thread working outward from the centre (*see illustration below*).

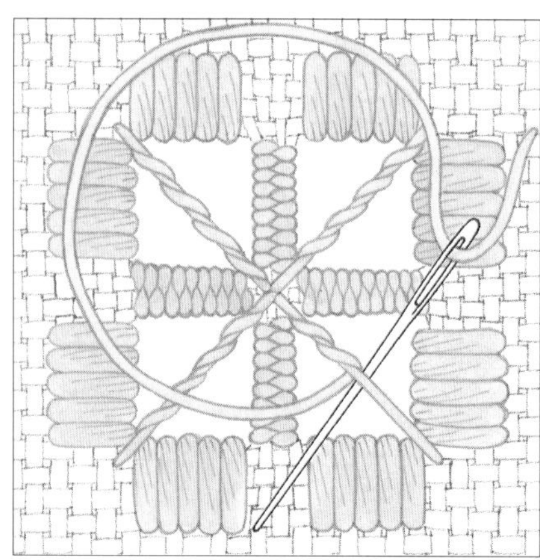
Working the overcasting

- Fasten off after you have finished overcasting the last diagonal thread of the square.
- Weave the end of the thread into the back of one woven bar. Bring the needle up into the centre where the bars meet.
- Take the needle under the first bar from right to left.
- Then take the needle under the first bar and the first thread to the left (*see illustration below*).

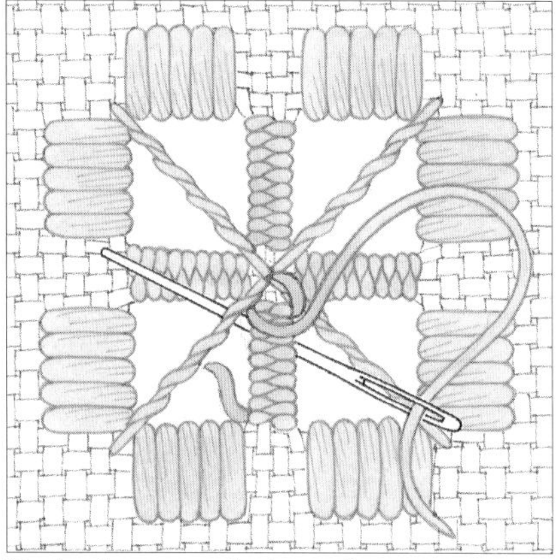
Beginning to work the web

- Take the needle back over the thread and take the needle under the next bar (*see illustration below*). This forms another strand of the web.

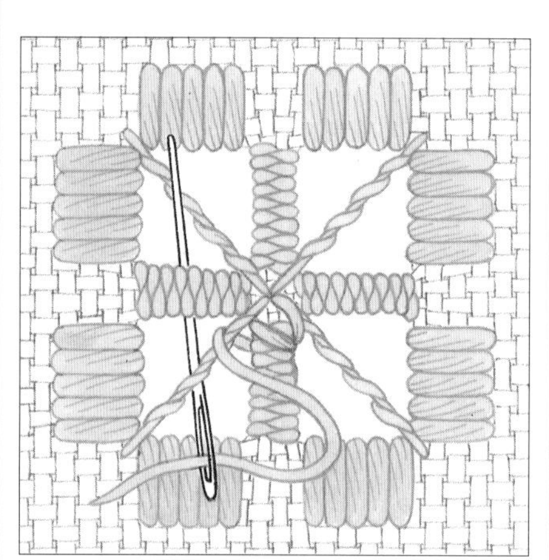
Working backstitch over the bar

- Backstitch over this bar and take the needle under the next laid thread.
- Continue backstitching in this manner, spiralling around the circle in a clockwise direction until the web is the desired size.
- To fasten off, bring the needle up into the centre of the first bar (*see illustration next column*). Then take the needle over the edge and weave the thread into the wrong side of web.

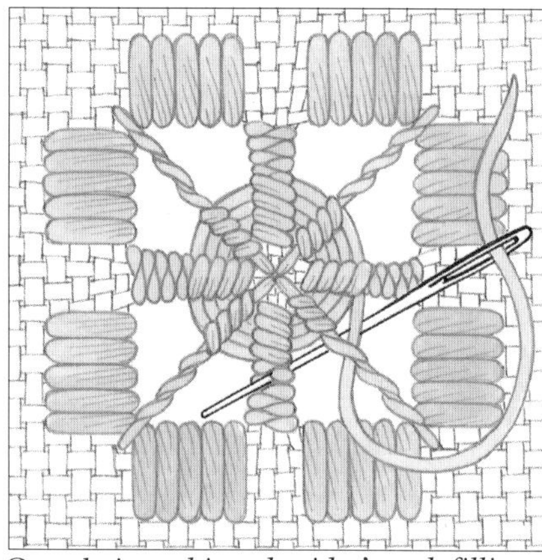
Completing whipped spider's web filling

Sequence of working bars and fillings
Although there are no fixed rules governing the order of covering bars and working filling stitches, it is often easiest to work over the bars in a diagonal direction as shown on the example of simple lace filling (*see photograph below*). You should move up and down alternately and add the filling stitches as you go.

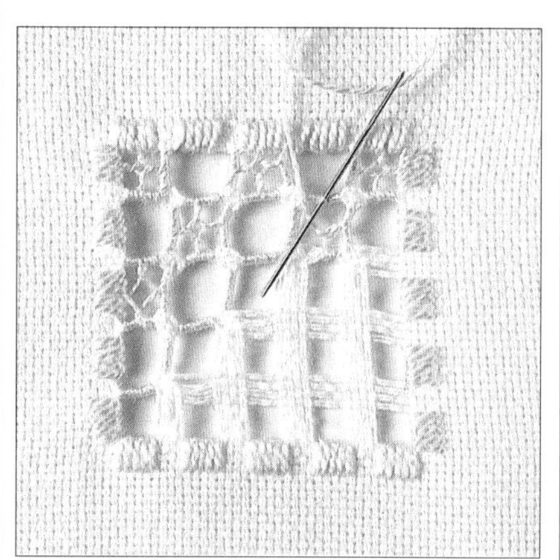
Example of simple lace filling worked over overcast bars

Golden Roller Blind

This lovely buttery yellow roller blind has a crisp openwork pattern, embellished with delicate woven bars and picots. The scalloped lower edge is finished with buttonhole stitch. The design can be adapted for any width of blind.

SIZE

Blind shown: 21½ in (54.5 cm) across
One pattern repeat (i.e. centre of one lower scallop to centre of next): 3⅛ in (8 cm)

MATERIALS

22-count Hardanger fabric, 3⅓ yds (3 m), width and length determined by individual window
Fabric shown: Zweigart "Oslo," shade 207

DMC no. 8 perlé cotton. For blind shown, 8 skeins were used; colour shown is 745

DMC no. 5 perlé cotton. For blind shown, 10 skeins were used, colour shown is 745

Tapestry needle, size 22
Roller blind kit: type shown is side-attached endless cord.
Fabric stiffening spray

Planning the blind

1 Determine the finished measurement of blind. A roller blind can be made to hang inside or outside the window frame. Instructions in the roller blind kit will help you to calculate the quantity needed. Allow 2 in (5 cm) extra along each side and below bottom scalloped edge; the kit instructions will tell you how much extra to allow at top. Trim extra fabric at bottom and sides before edges are stitched. If using an embroidery frame, allow extra fabric.

CHART FOR GOLDEN ROLLER BLIND

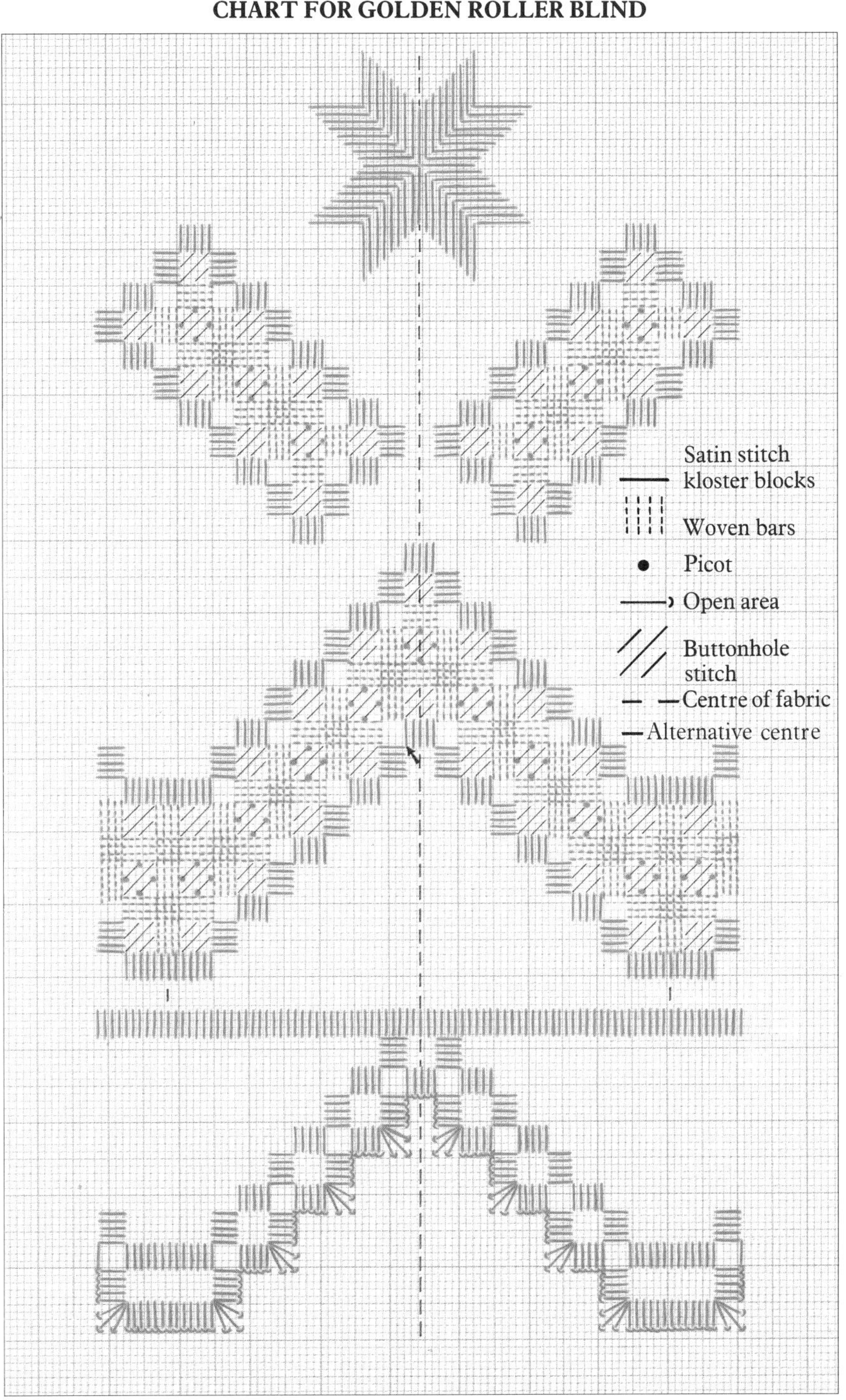

2 Decide on best way to position pattern. The blind shown has a star positioned in the centre; you may wish, for example, to place stars on either side of the centre. To help determine whether the pattern variation you wish to use will fit within the side edges, chart half of the design on graph paper.

3 Calculate the number of graph lines needed to plot half of the embroidery design. For this, you will need to work in inches. Multiply half the blind width by 22 – the number of double threads per inch in the fabric. Count and then mark off this number on the graph paper.

4 Starting at the centre of the design on page 133, copy half of it (just the kloster block outlines).

5 Continue copying the pattern to the edge of the blind. If the pattern ends awkwardly, use an alternative centre (*see chart on page 133*) or modify the design at the edge.

6 Measure outward from the new centre and carefully plot the remainder of the pattern you are using as it will appear on your fabric.

Working the embroidery

1 Cut the fabric to the required size (*see above*); then bind the edges of the fabric securely (*see page 18*).

2 Work a line of basting or running stitches along the vertical centre of the fabric from the bottom up, for about 12 in (30 cm); keep stitches between the same two fabric threads.

Use basting stitches to mark the finished side edges.

3 Mount fabric in an embroidery frame, if desired.

4 Measure up 5 in (12.7 cm) from lower edge of fabric. Starting at centre, work satin stitch over four fabric threads (paired threads are counted as one) out to the position of the finished edges of the blind. You should use no. 5 perlé cotton throughout this part of the work, unless directed otherwise.

5 Count up 36 threads along centre line. Work a kloster block (*see page 128*) at apex of lower zigzag line. Following the chart, work the rest of the line to each side edge. Or, begin with one of the 13-stitch kloster blocks at bottom of line. Do not cut threads between the blocks.

6 Work upper line of kloster blocks. Check the count; there should be 20 fabric threads between the two lines.

7 Work kloster blocks for the slanted rectangular motifs across the blind.

8 Work star motifs in satin stitch over eight fabric threads. Bring the needle up at the edge of the star and down in the centre each time.

9 Work scalloped edge. Work inner line of kloster blocks, then work buttonhole stitches. Note that stitches fan out at outer corners so that five stitches are worked into the same place (*see chart on page 133*).

10 Now you are ready to embroider the openwork sections. Before cutting threads, check the position of the kloster blocks to make sure they are aligned correctly. Then with sharp embroidery scissors, cut the appropriate threads for a small area (*see page 129*). (Cutting the threads a few at a time helps keep unworked fabric threads from snagging.)

11 Work picots (*see page 130*) on the bars where indicated.

12 Work buttonhole stitch (*see page 131*) on the sides, beginning at the top edge of the openwork and working down to the scalloped lower edge.

13 Remove fabric from embroidery frame. Cut excess fabric from lower edge, taking care not to cut stitching.

14 Work a line of zigzag stitch just inside the basted edges of the blind; this gives extra firmness to the edge. Trim the excess fabric carefully away from the side edges.

15 Using no. 8 perlé cotton, work buttonhole stitch over five vertical fabric threads, covering the zigzag and spacing the stitches two horizontal threads apart.

Making up the blind

1 Press embroidery right side down on a well-padded ironing board.

2 Lay pressed embroidery flat over a large, clean cloth. Spray with stiffener, following manufacturer's instructions; allow to dry.

3 Finish blind and hang in window, following the kit instructions.

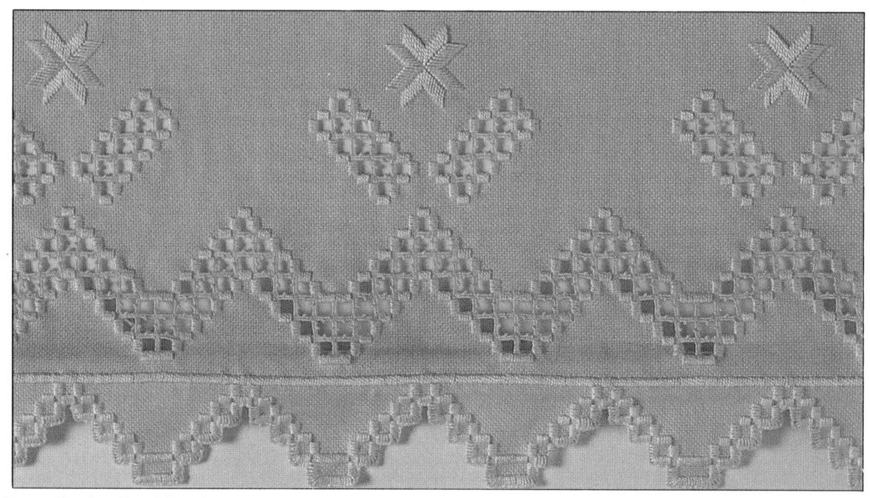

Detail of roller blind

Hardanger Pocket Motif

This lovely Hardanger motif is easy to embroider. When applied to a pocket, it adds a distinctive touch to a plain white shirt or blouse. A soft blue-violet has been used here, but any colour will work. Choose a shade to coordinate with your outfit.

SIZE
Motif: 3¼ in (8 cm) in both directions

MATERIALS
DMC no. 5 perlé cotton, 1 skein, shade 792

DMC no. 8 perlé cotton, 1 ball, shade 792

White shirt or blouse with pocket at least 5 in (12 cm) square
22-count white Hardanger fabric, at least 1¼ in (3 cm) larger all around than pocket
Tapestry needle, size 22
Tailor's chalk
Sewing needle and thread

CHART FOR HARDANGER POCKET MOTIF

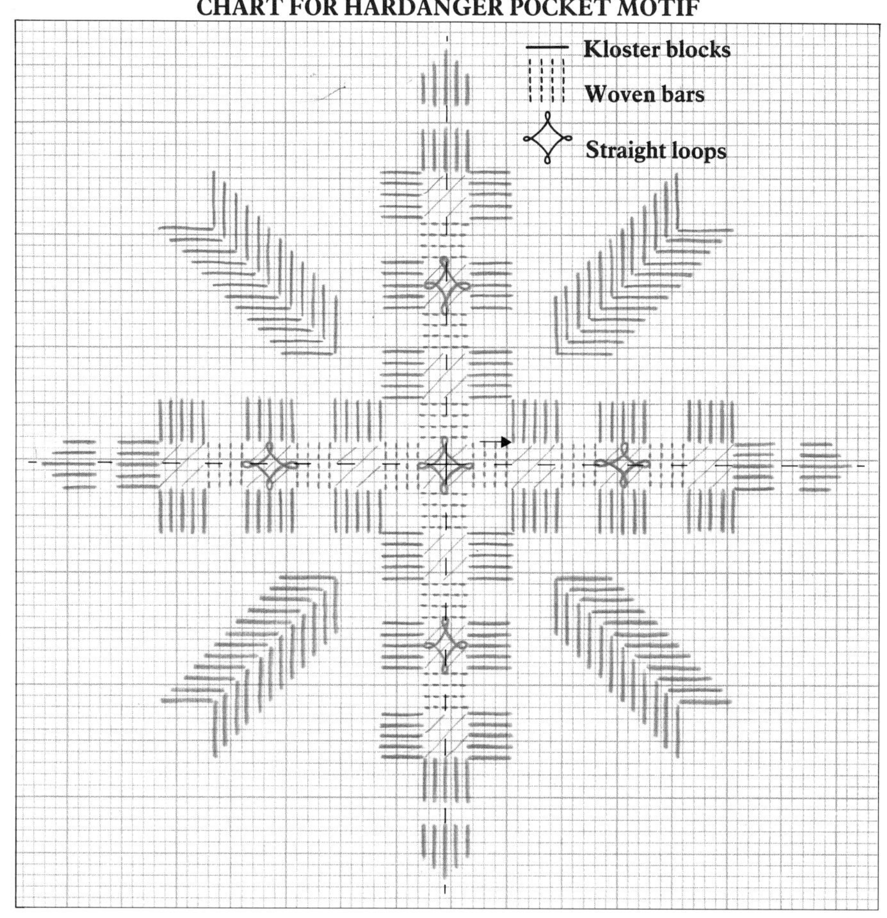

Working the embroidery

1 Bind the edges of the fabric and mark the centre in both directions with lines of basting (*see page 18*). Mount the fabric in a hoop.

2 Following the above chart and using no. 5 perlé cotton, work kloster blocks (*see page 128*). Begin at the arrow on the chart and work clockwise. Each line on the chart represents one pair of threads. Add chevron satin stitch motifs and pointed motifs at the cross ends.

3 Cut the fabric threads between the kloster blocks (*see page 129*). Using no. 8 perlé cotton, work woven bars over the fabric threads remaining between the kloster blocks. Work straight loops between the bars.

Attaching the pocket

1 Place the embroidered piece right side up over the detached pocket (also right side up). Carefully tuck under the fabric edges if necessary. Pin Hardanger work to the centre and turn the embroidered pocket wrong side up. Trim away excess fabric, leaving a margin of ⅝ in (1.5 cm).

2 Fold under the fabric edges even with the edges of the pocket, mitring square corners; baste edges in place.

3 Slipstitch Hardanger fabric pocket to the original pocket edges with white thread in small stitches.

4 Pin pocket on shirt and carefully baste. Topstitch the pocket onto the shirt, either by hand or machine, so that it is positioned ¼ in (6 mm) from side and lower edges.

Baby's Cot Quilt

This charming quilt will make an ideal gift for a new baby. It is made from soft fabric that is quite safe for young skin and can be washed if required. You can also adapt the diamonds to create your own individual pattern.

SIZE

Finished quilt: 32 × 40 in (81 × 101 cm)

MATERIALS

For quilt top: cotton fabric 38 × 29 in (94 × 74 cm)

For large diamonds: 18-count Aida cloth, 6½ × 4½ in (16.25 × 11.25 cm), 5 pieces

For small diamonds: 18-count Aida cloth, 3½ × 2½ in (8.75 × 6.25 cm), 8 pieces

Backing fabric, 41 × 33 in (104 × 84 cm)
Bias strips of quilt top fabric, 2 × 156 in (5 × 396 cm)
DMC no. 5 white perlé cotton
8 oz (230 g) polyester wadding:
32 × 40 in (81 × 101 cm), 1 piece
2 × 40 in (5 × 101 cm), 2 pieces
2 × 32 in (5 × 81 cm), 2 pieces
½ in (1.25 cm) wide edging lace, 9 yd (8.25 cm)

Follow the instructions for working the embroidery by referring closely to the charts. The numbers on the large diamond chart show your position as you work each step of the same number. On the small diamond chart, this is shown by the letter A.

Working the embroidery for large diamond

1 Fold the fabric for the large diamond carefully into quarters. Count out 10 threads from the centre of the diamond to the nearest point. Sew one stitch over six threads, then three stitches over four threads,

CHART FOR HALF OF LARGE DIAMOND

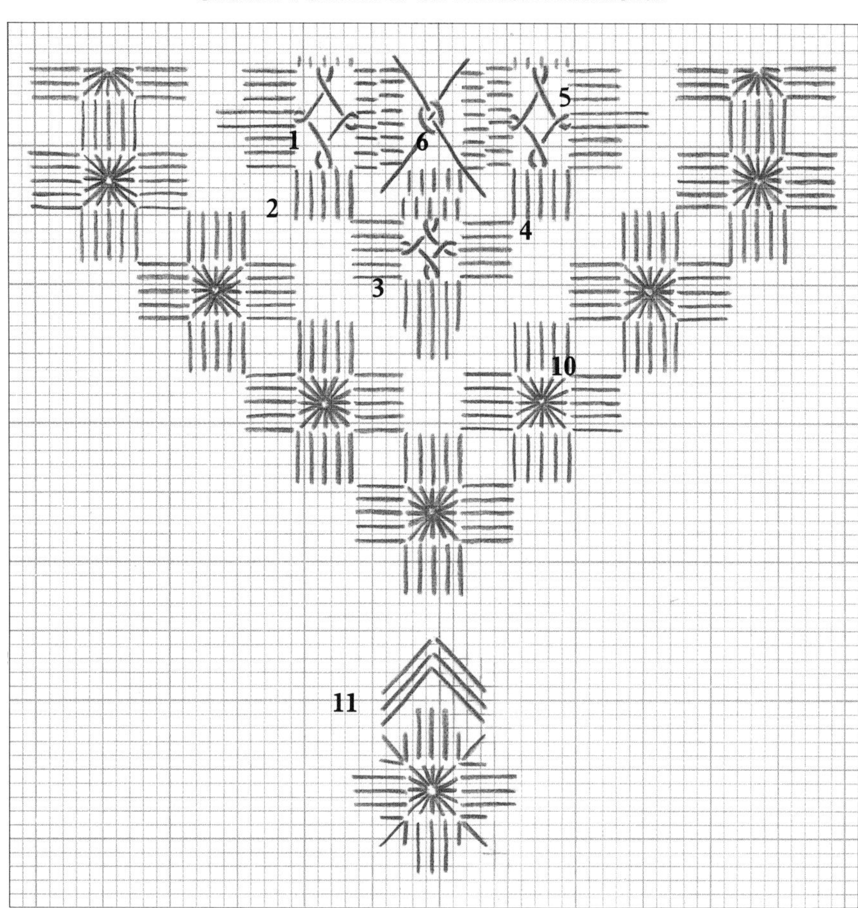

CHART FOR HALF OF SMALL DIAMOND

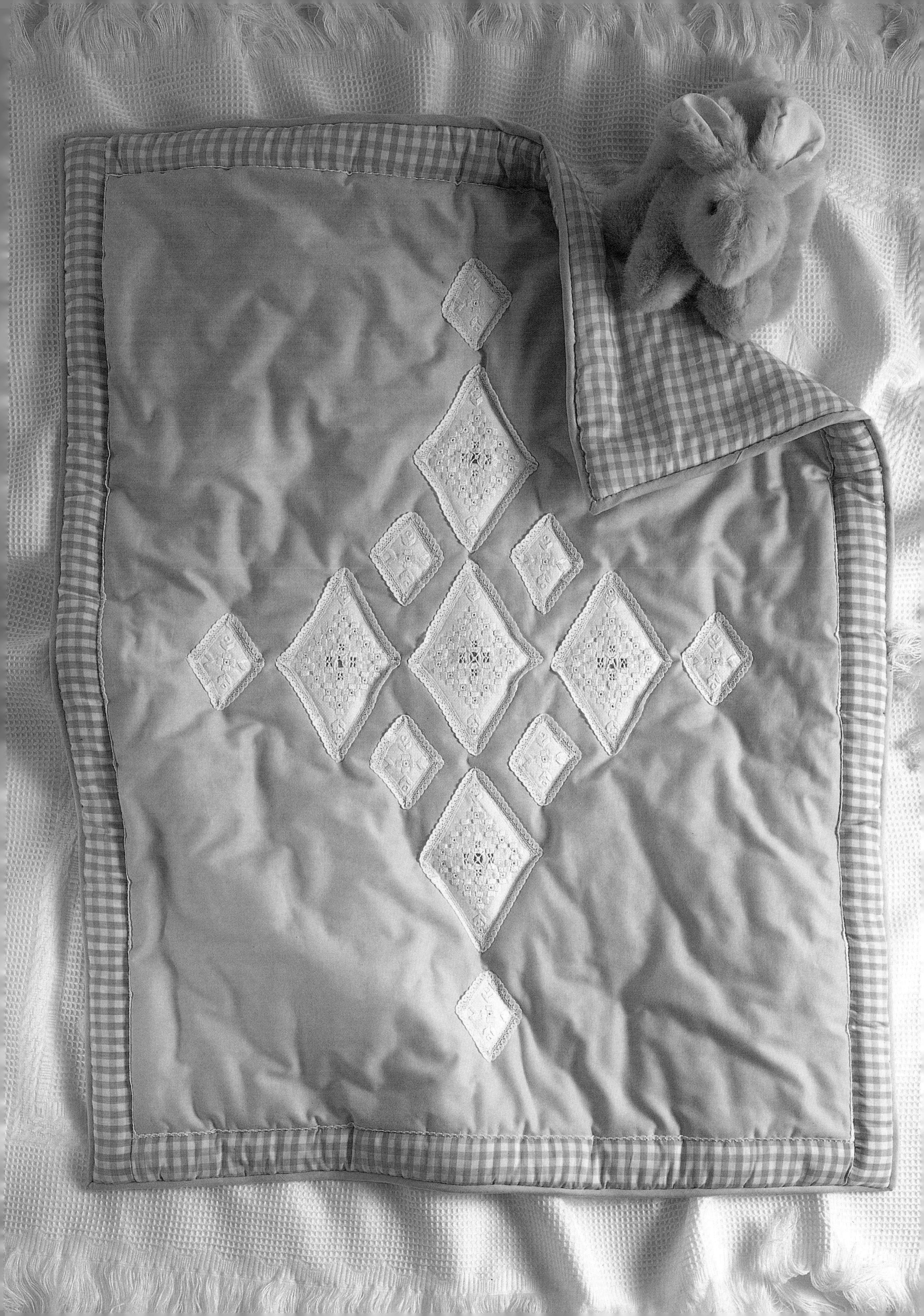

working from right to left (*see chart on page 138:* **1**).

2 At right angles to these three stitches, work another five stitches over four threads, starting at the outer edge (*see illustration below and chart:* **2**).

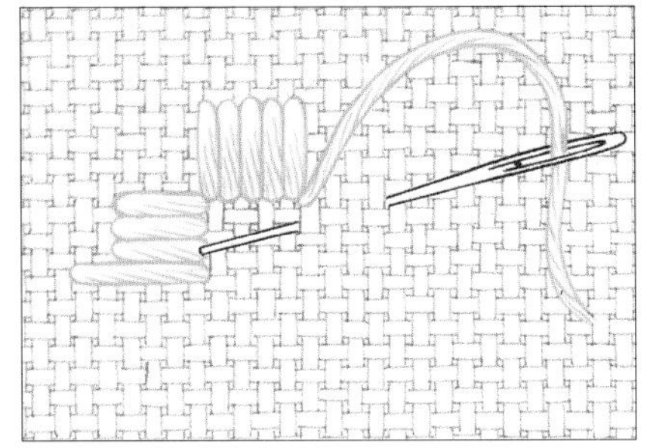

Working five stitches over four threads

3 At right angles to these and following the chart carefully, work another five stitches over four threads. Then, again at right angles to these five stitches, work one stitch over four threads, three stitches over six threads and one stitch over four threads. These last five stitches will all point to the narrow point of the diamond (*see chart:* **3**).

4 At right angles and starting on the inner edge, work a five-stitch block over four threads. Then at right angles to these and starting at the outer edge of this last block, work another five-stitch block over four threads (*see chart:* **4**).

5 Starting at the inner edge at right angles to the last block, work three stitches over four threads and two stitches over six threads. Then work a further three stitches over four threads. You have now finished half the pattern (*see chart:* **5**). Continuing clockwise, repeat steps 2–5 to complete the pattern.

6 Cut away the centre with scissors (*see chart:* **6**). Repeat on the four smaller areas. Remove loose threads from the bars, then, sewing across the bands of four threads, weave thread over and into the centre of the bars.

Continue weaving in this way over all four bars in order to complete all the four sides of the square (*see illustration below*).

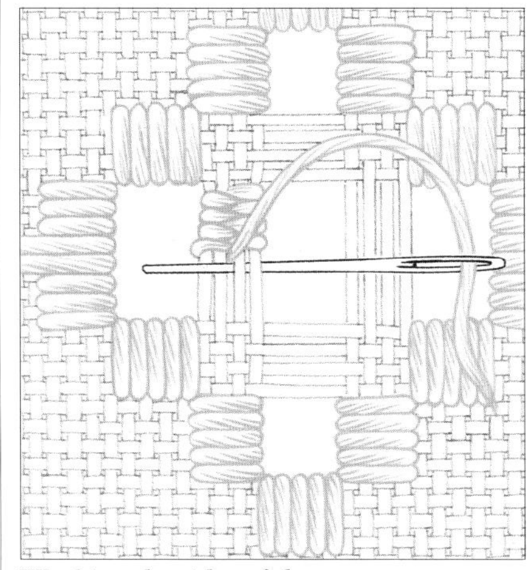

Working the sides of the square

7 Starting in the midpoint of the square, take the needle down at the diagonally opposite point.

Then bring the needle up at the nearest adjacent corner. At the centre of the previous diagonal stitch, weave the thread in and out of the three strands in a circular direction.

Finally, bring the needle up through the weaving and take it down at the final, unworked corner of the square (*see illustration below*).

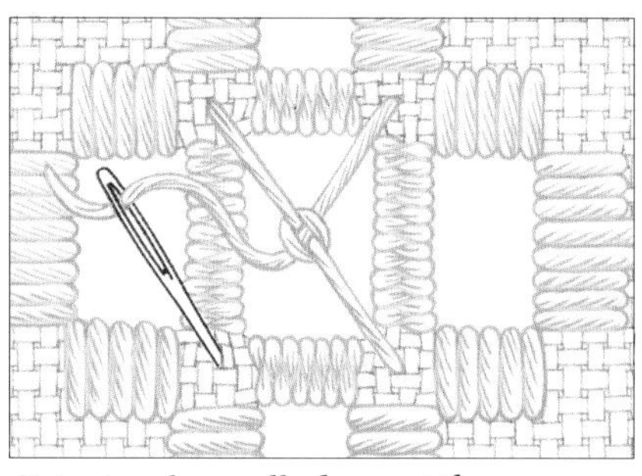

Bringing the needle down at the unworked corner after working the centre of the square

8 Bring the needle up at the centre point of the small square's outside edge. Then carefully take the needle down at the central point of the adjacent outside edge. This is indicated by the position of the needle in the diagram of working the centre (*see illustration next column*).

Working from the right of the entry point, bring the needle up. Take the thread behind the previous stitch and down on the next adjacent side of the square. Repeat the stitch on the final two sides of the square.

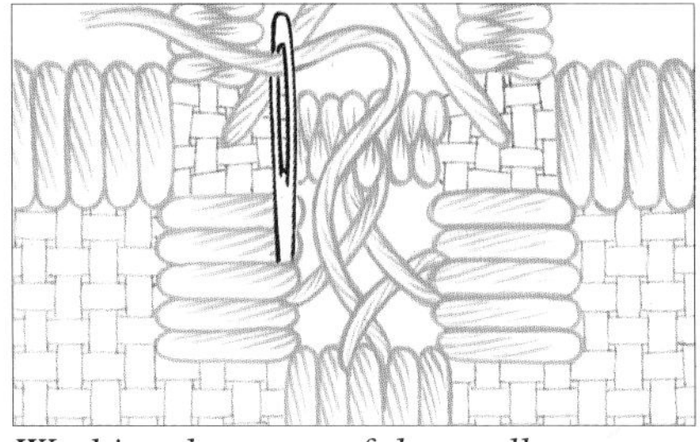

Working the centre of the small square

9 To work the flowers on the outer pattern, follow the chart. Bring up the needle and work a block of five stitches over four threads. Work these blocks of five stitches from left to right to form a square pattern of flower petals (*see illustration below*).

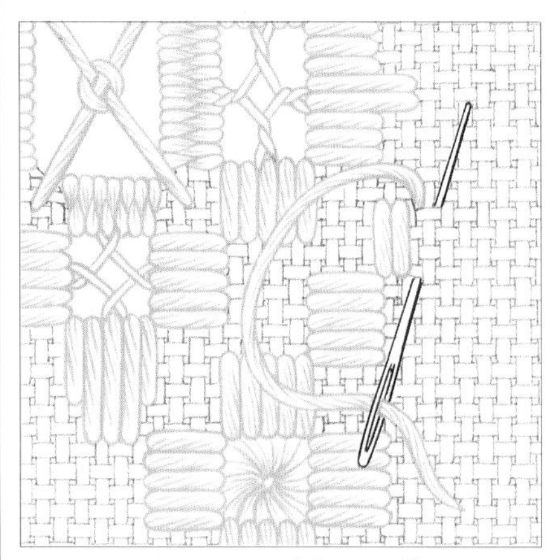

Working the centre of the small square

10 To sew the centres of the flowers, bring the needle up through the centre and into the corner, pulling the threads tight. Work four more stitches along the sides, always starting from the centre and pulling tight. Repeat along the remaining three sides (*see illustration below*).

Note that the two flowers at the broad point of the fabric share one block of stitches (*see chart:* **10**).

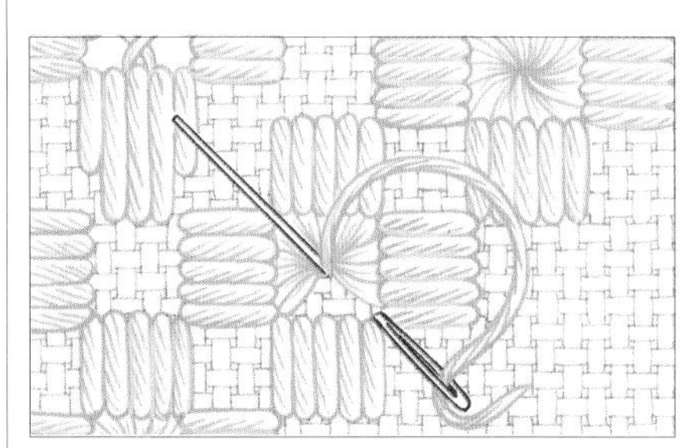

Working the flower centres

11 For the small flower leaf, bring needle up three threads out from outer edge of upper petal. Take down four threads to left and four threads down (*see chart:* **11**). Work two stitches as above to complete half the leaf. Work petals as above (*see illustration below*).

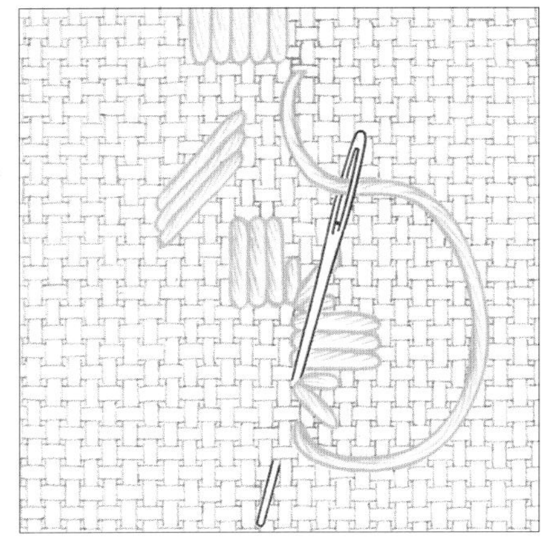

Working the small flower petals

12 Work the second half of the leaf in the way described above. Then work the centre of the small flower as in step 10.

Working the small diamond

1 Fold the small diamond fabric into quarters. Count out two threads from the centre of the diamond to the nearest point. Work three stitches over four threads. Continue as for the flowers and leaves on the large diamond (*see illustration below*).

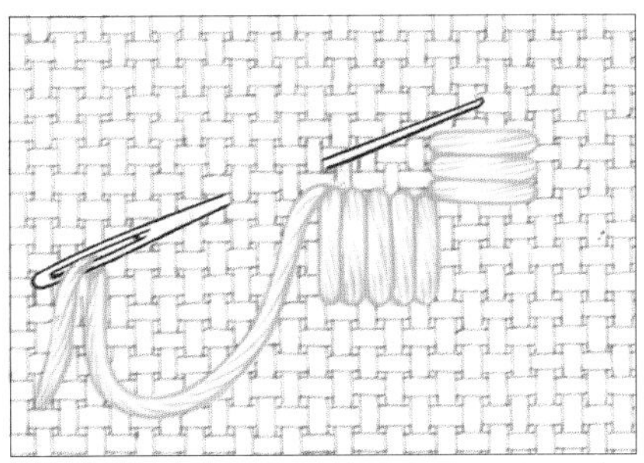

Working three stitches over four threads

2 Count two threads out from the outer edge of the petal (*see chart:* **A**) Work the four leaves as for the large diamond. Work the small flower as a square (*see illustration next column*).

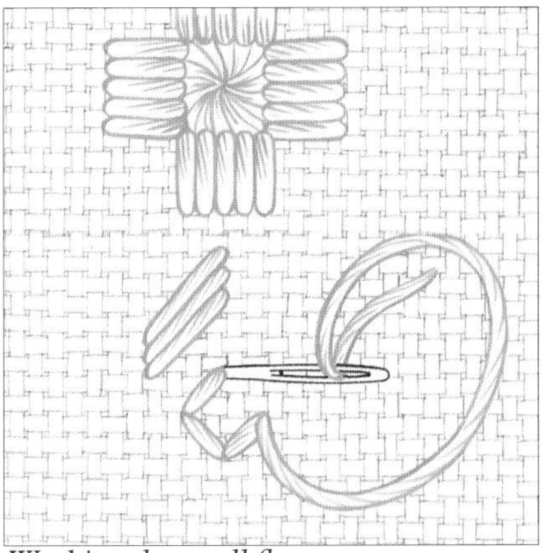

Working the small flower

Making up the quilt

1 Right sides together, lace edging inward, sew edging to quilt top.

2 Baste or machine the two short sides and then the two long sides of contrasting fabric border to lace edging, making sure that the pattern stripe runs parallel to quilt edge and lace edging lies between the two.

3 Attach wadding strips to wrong side of border fabric and baste.

4 Pin large wadding strips to quilt top matching edges. Baste in position. Trim away any surplus backing fabric. Lay quilt top on contrasting backing fabric, making sure pattern lines are straight, and baste in position. Mark crosswise and lengthwise centre lines and baste through all thicknessess.

5 Turn under ½ in (1.25 cm) on all edges of the Hardanger diamond pieces; press and open out.

6 Place diamonds and lace edging right sides together, with lace pointing inward (*see photograph of components below*). Baste, pleating at the corners. Machine or hand stitch edging and diamonds together.

7 Pin diamonds as desired on quilt top; baste. Stitch by machine or by hand around edges of diamonds.

8 Join bias strips into one strip long enough to go around outside of quilt. Turn over 1¼ in (3 cm) on one edge. Place other edge along edge of quilt top, right sides together. Baste, mitring corners, then sew.

9 Fold bias strip over to back of quilt, forming a neat bound edge. Pin, then slipstitch in place.

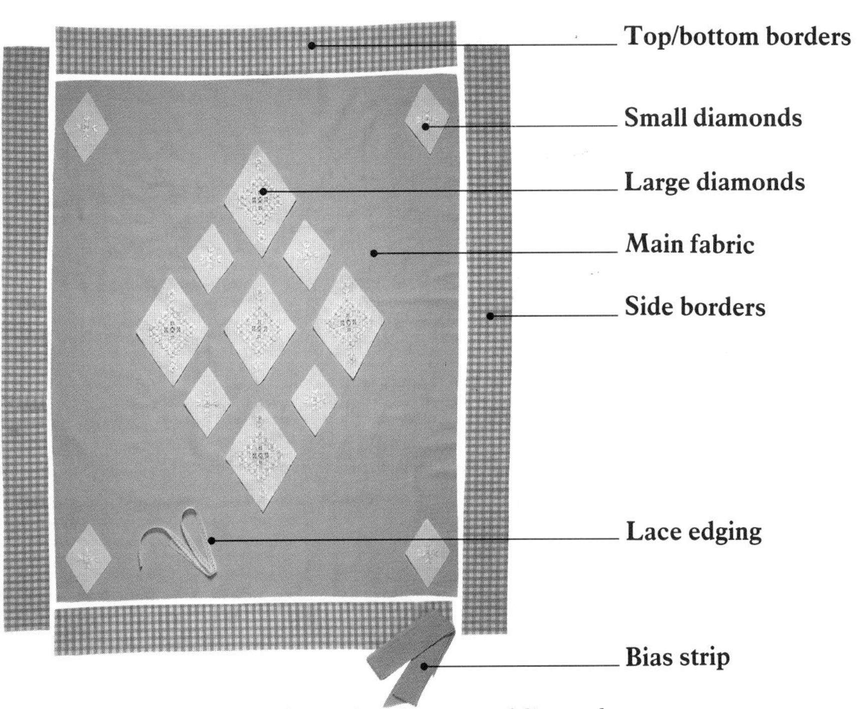

Quilt components showing alternative placement of diamonds

Drawn Thread Work Techniques

Drawn thread work has the most lace-like appearance of all the counted thread openwork techniques. Used primarily for working borders, it makes an attractive decoration for table linen and can also be used to embellish clothing.

BASICS OF DRAWN THREAD WORK

Drawn thread work is a technique that involves removing certain fabric threads, then grouping the remaining threads to form decorative patterns. The two methods of working over the threads are hemstitching and needleweaving.

In the hemstitching method, the threads are stitched together along the edge of the open area and sometimes laced or knotted together. In the needleweaving method, the working thread is used to cover the fabric threads. Where threads have been withdrawn in both directions, either to form an allover lattice or at the corner of two bands, use other forms of stitching.

Choosing materials for drawn thread work

Drawn thread work has traditionally been worked entirely in white. However, it can be worked in colour, matching or contrasting with the fabric. Drawn thread work can be adapted to any scale, provided the fabric has an even weave and the threads can be withdrawn easily.

A strong single thread is best suited to drawn thread work. Use an embroidery thread such as perlé cotton, flower thread, or soft embroidery cotton. Stranded floss is relatively weak, but could be used on a delicate item. In some cases, a thread which has been withdrawn from the fabric is the best choice.

Simple hemstitching is best worked in the hand, and even more complex forms can be worked in this way. However, for learning the techniques, an embroidery frame or hoop is recommended.

HEMSTITCHING

Hemstitch is used decoratively at the top, or bottom, or both of a band of drawn threads. It can also be used to make an attractive finish on the hem of items such as bed linen or clothing. Wide bands of hemstitch make pretty openwork patterns that become the focal decoration of the fabric. Certain areas, however, can be rather delicate.

Positioning the work

In most cases you will need to mark the position of the band of hemstitching, in order to ensure that the correct horizontal threads are withdrawn, leaving the correct number of vertical threads in place for stitching.

- Mark the vertical centre of the work with a line of basting or running stitches (*see page 18*).
- Calculate the number of vertical threads to be included in the stitching. To do this, multiply the width of the band by the number of threads per inch (centimetre), then divide by the number of threads in each group. The result can be rounded up or down. For example, a band 20 in (50 cm) wide, with 25 threads per inch (10 per centimeter), has 500 threads for working. If each group has three threads, there are 167 groups. Multiply the number of groups by the threads per group to work out the number of vertical threads needed. In our example, $167 \times 3 = 501$ vertical threads.
- Decide on the position of the lower edge of the border. Mark with basting or running stitches from end to end. Count the vertical threads to be sure that you included the correct number. To keep track while counting, insert a pin after every 40 or 50 threads. If a large item such as a tablecloth is edged with basic hemstitch, the exact number is not so important. When hemstitching near a corner, if the remaining threads are not an exact multiple, work a stitch over one thread less or one thread more to make it come out correctly.

If including two or more bands of drawn thread work, mark the lower and upper edges of each band with basting or running stitches.

Withdrawing the threads

After positioning the work, remove the required number of horizontal threads. Unless the bands will be incorporated in a seam, the ends must be secured.

Darning in the ends is the basic method for hemstitching where only two or three fabric threads need to be withdrawn. The extra threads will thicken the fabric slightly; darn carefully to keep inconspicuous.

- Cut at the centre all the threads to be withdrawn. (If threads are long, cut them in several places to make them easier to remove.)
- Ease the threads out of the fabric up to the position chosen for the end.
- Working from the wrong side, thread each loose thread into a needle and darn it back into the fabric for about 1 in (2.5 cm) (*see illustration below*). Trim the ends.

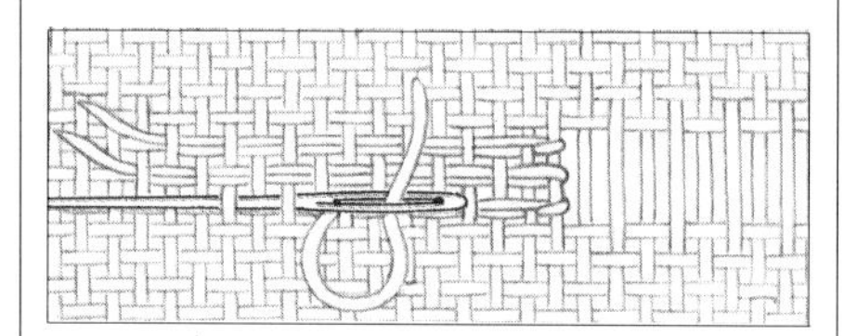

Darning the thread into the fabric

Buttonhole-stitched ends are recommended where a relatively wide band (four threads or more) is to be worked. Besides securing fabric threads, buttonhole stitching adds to the decorative effect.

Choose a working thread no heavier than the fabric threads or the effect may be lumpy. You can use a thread unravelled from the end of the fabric; run it between your fingers to smooth out the kinks.

- Decide on the number of threads to be withdrawn and the exact position of the work, then carefully cut the top and bottom threads of the band at one end.
- Withdraw these two threads for a short distance (*see illustration below*).

Withdrawing the top and bottom threads

- Fasten the working thread with a couple of running stitches in the edge to be stitched, then buttonhole stitch over this edge as shown, taking care to stitch between each of the fabric threads. You should work over the same number of vertical threads each time to keep the edges straight (*see illustration below*). After you have worked a few stitches, cut off the beginning end of the thread.

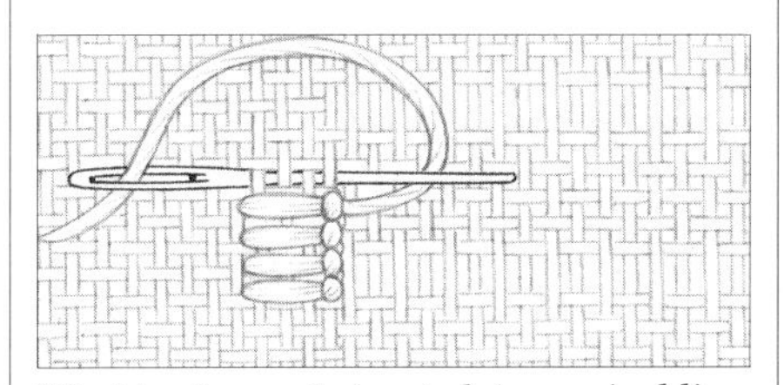

Working buttonhole stitch in vertical line

- To fasten off, run the needle under the stitching on the wrong side.
- Withdraw the top and bottom threads up to the position chosen for the opposite end of the work and cut them off. Buttonhole stitch this end in the same way.
- Cut carefully and then withdraw the remaining threads.

Working basic hemstitch

Hemstitching is normally worked from the wrong side, especially when used to turn up a hem (*see page 153*).

- Fasten the working thread temporarily at the left-hand edge with a couple of backstitches, leaving a long end.
- Take the needle from right to left under the first group of threads (*see illustration below*). Four threads are grouped in the example, but the number can be greater or smaller.

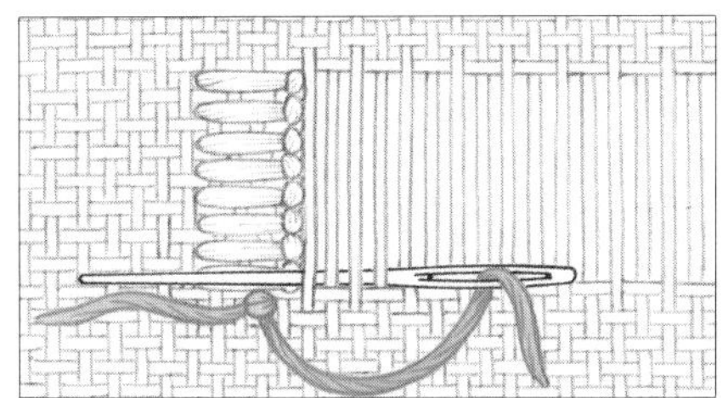

Starting hemstitch over a group of four threads

- Insert the needle vertically from back to front into the fabric edge, to the right of the group of threads as shown. Pull the thread through, bunching the vertical threads together (*see illustration below*).

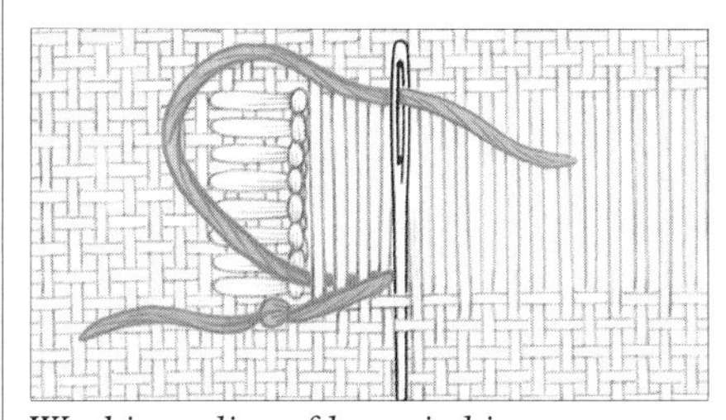

Working a line of hemstitching

- Repeat these two steps across the length of the band. To fasten off, take the needle through several of the last few stitches. Undo the backstitches at the starting point and fasten off the thread end in the same way.

The illustrations for single knotted hemstitch and interlaced hemstitch (*see page 144*) show how the completed basic hemstitch appears on the right side of the fabric.

When matching thread is used, the stitching on the right side is inconspicuous. To highlight the stitching, use a contrasting thread or work from the right side, leaving the diagonal loops visible.

HEMSTITCH VARIATIONS

Basic hemstitch can be varied by grouping the threads in different patterns and by carefully lacing or knotting them together.

Working ladder hemstitch

- To create ladder hemstitch, simply work basic hemstitch on both sides of the band of withdrawn threads.
- To turn an inner corner, take the needle around the last group of threads before the corner, then around the first group after the corner, finishing with a vertical stitch after the second of these two groups (*see illustration below*).

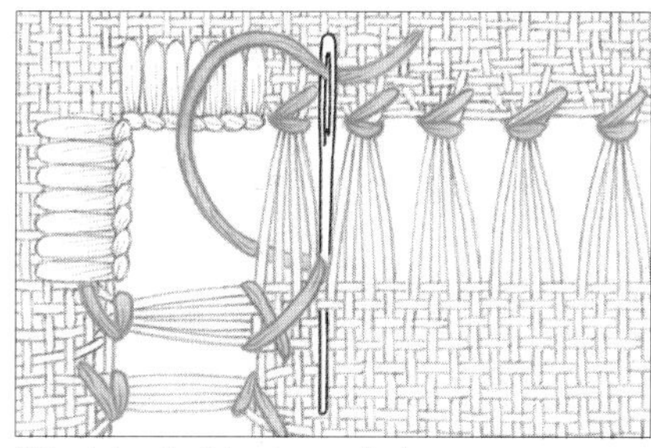

Working ladder hemstitch on a corner

Working zigzag hemstitch

This pattern requires an even number of fabric threads in each group.

- Work basic hemstitch on one edge over the chosen number of threads.
- On the opposite edge, take the first stitch over half the number, then work over the full number up to the end, where half the number of threads will remain to be stitched.

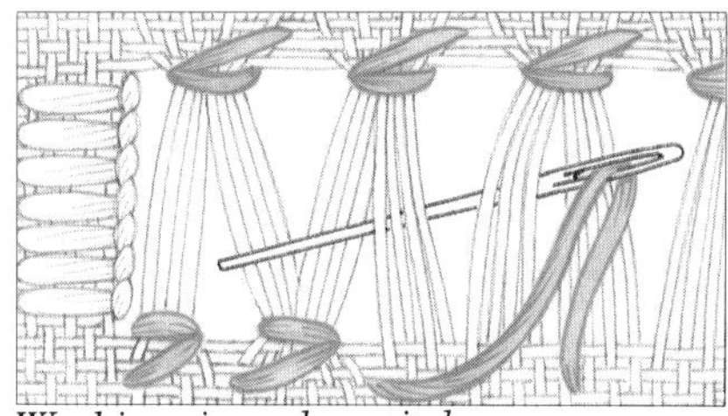

Working zigzag hemstitch

Working single knotted hemstitch

- First decide on the number of threads to be grouped by hemstitching, then on the number of groups, which must be divisible by 3. For example, 30 knotted groups of 4 threads each equals 120 threads. The band should be at least ⅝ in (1.5 cm) deep.

• Work hemstitching along both edges to form the basic groups.
• Fasten a new thread on the wrong side under the right-hand edge halfway up the band.
• With the right side of the fabric facing you, take the needle under the first three groups and loop the working thread around and under the needle (*see illustration below*).

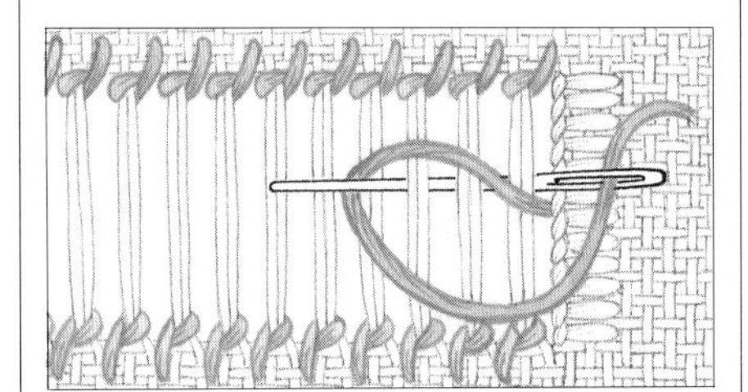

Working single knotted hemstitch

• Pull on the thread to tighten the knot (*see illustration below*).

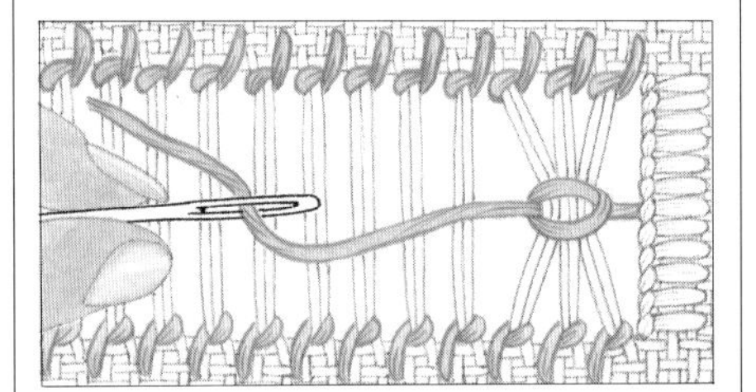

Tightening the knot

• Repeat the procedure to the end and fasten off (*see photograph below*).

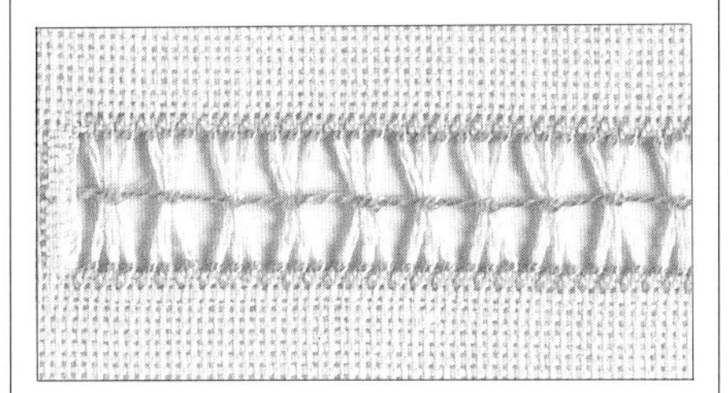

Sample of single knotted hemstitch

More complex knotting patterns can be created on deeper bands by working two or more lines of the stitching and then by staggering the placement of the knots.

Working double hemstitch

• For double hemstitch, two bands of thread are withdrawn to leave a strip of solid fabric between them. In this example, four threads were withdrawn for each band and three threads left in the centre strip.
• Anchor the working thread under the right-hand end of the strip.
• Take the needle from right to left under the first group of threads in the lower band.
• Bring the needle back over them and under the strip, taking it up to the left of the first group in the upper band (*see illustration below*).

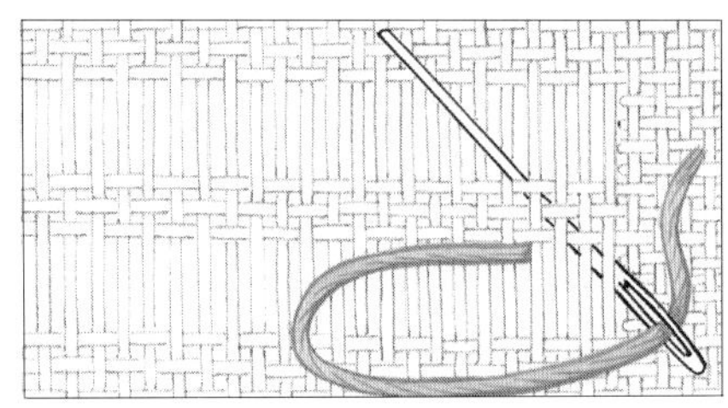

Beginning double hemstitch

• Take the thread around this group as shown, then over the strip to the lower band. Repeat to the end of the band (*see illustration below*).

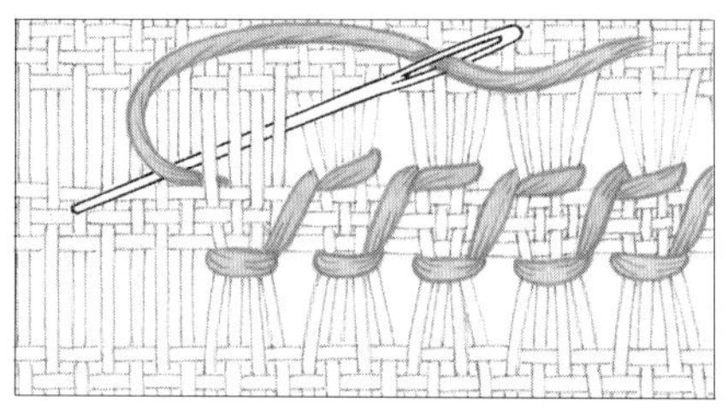

Working a row of double hemstitch

An example of a finished row of double hemstitch is illustrated here (*see photograph below*). The characteristic strip of solid fabric is left in place between the threads.

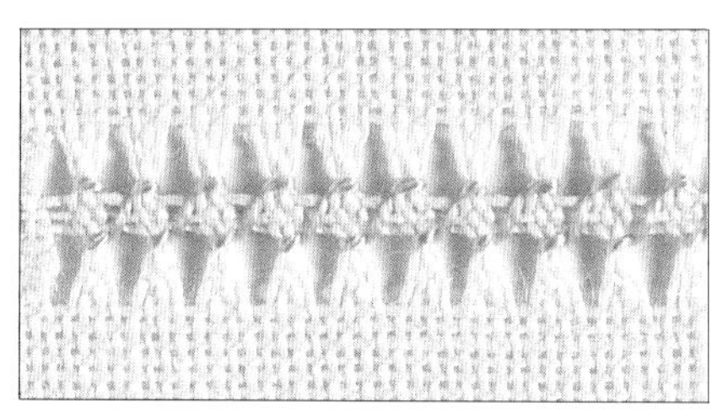

Sample of double hemstitch

Working interlaced hemstitch

• For this variation, fabric threads are withdrawn for at least ⅝ in (1.5 cm). Work hemstitch along both edges.
• Fasten a new thread on the wrong side under the right-hand edge.
• Working with the right side of the fabric facing you, take the needle across the first two groups of threads. Slip the point of the needle under the second group and over the first group (*see illustration below*).

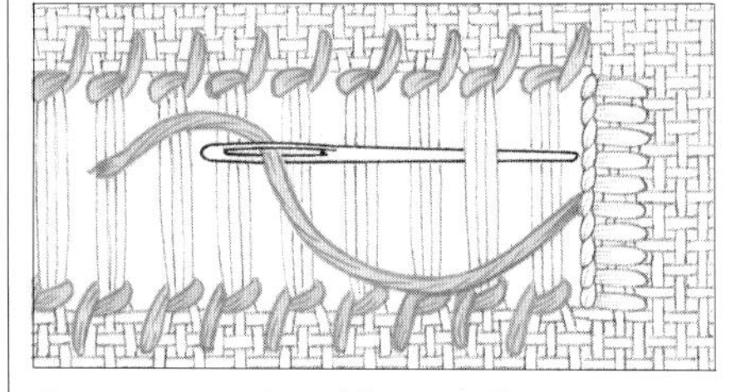

Starting interlaced hemstitch

• Turn the end of the needle from left to right, twisting the first group under the second. Draw the thread through. Repeat the twisting stitch to the end (*see illustration below*).

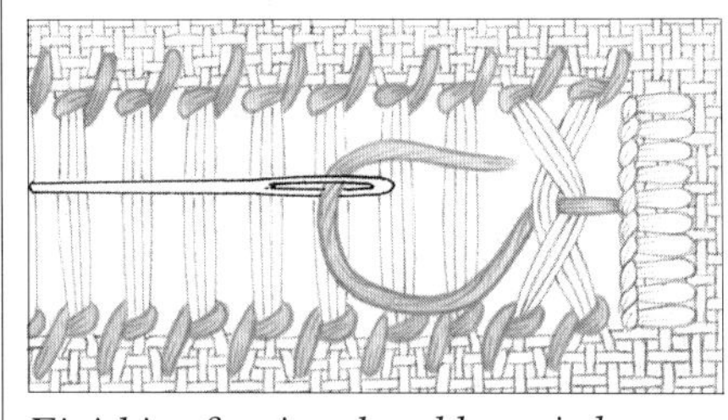

Finishing first interlaced hemstitch

Decorating corners

If a wide band of hemstitching turns a corner, fill in the empty corner space to strengthen as well as decorate it.
• Remove the threads as in the darning-in method (*see page 142*), but fasten them with backstitch (*see page 98*) on the wrong side using a fine sewing thread and a sharp needle.
• Work buttonhole stitch over edges; trim ends close to stitching.

A spider's web corner is shown (*see photograph below*). Other possible corner fillings are shown on page 117.

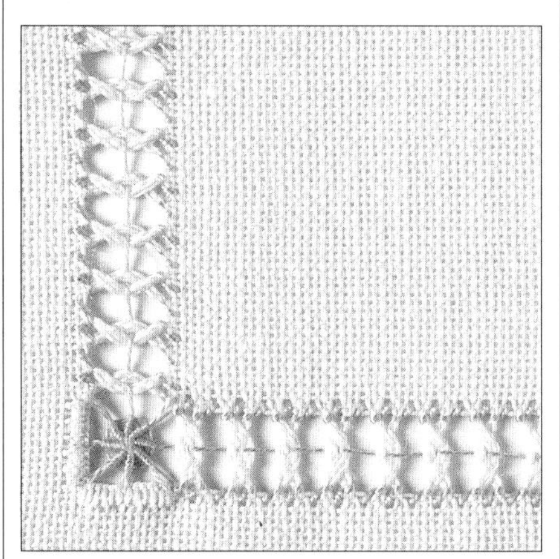

Spider's web corner decoration

NEEDLEWEAVING

Needleweaving involves wrapping (overcasting) or weaving in and out of (darning) the vertical threads in a band of drawn threads to decorate and strengthen the area. Like hemstitch, it decorates threads in a drawn thread border. Needleweaving can enhance skirts or the cuffs of a blouse.

If the needleweaving is to cover only one bar of grouped threads, no hemstitching is needed at the edges. However, for the simple parallel bar pattern shown, hemstitching may be desirable. It adds decoration and provides a stitched edge through which the thread can be passed on the wrong side from one bar to the next, eliminating the need to fasten off each bar.

When you are first practising needleweaving, fasten the thread temporarily in the edge of the embroidery with backstitches, then fasten the end into the work later. Once you have gained in experience and proficiency, you can lay the thread along the fabric threads as shown in the diagrams and work over it.

Working simple overcasting

- Lay the end of the thread along the vertical fabric threads to be overcast.
- Insert the needle from right to left under the threads, then take the needle around and under them again, just below the first stitch.
- Insert the needle, then pull tightly, thus grouping the threads securely together (*see illustration below*).

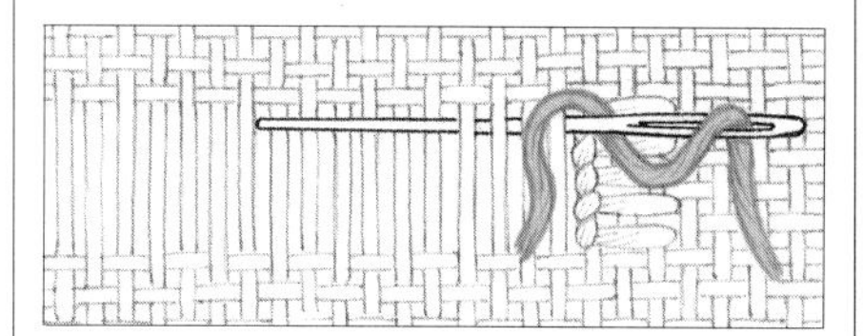

Pulling the needle to group the threads

- Continue in this way, placing the stitches close but not overlapping them (*see illustration below*).

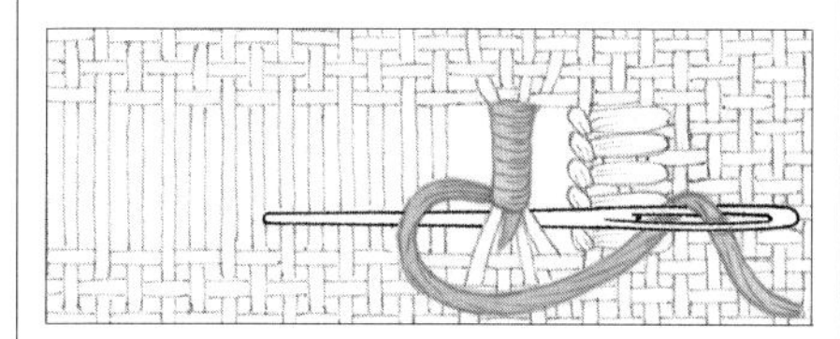

Working overcasting

- To fasten off, run thread vertically back through the bar. In the sample the edges have been hemstitched (*see illustration below*).

Completed band of simple overcasting

Working zigzag overcasting

- Begin to work the zigzags by overcasting the first group of threads almost to the bottom.
- At the bottom, work two stitches over the first group and the next group combined (*see illustration below*). Then work the overcasting back up over the second group alone.

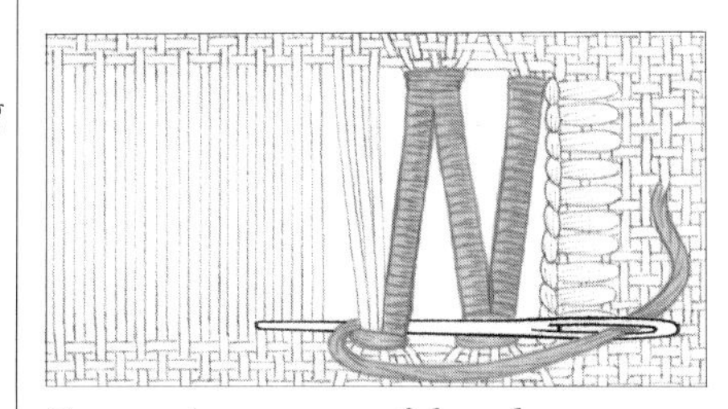

Overcasting a group of threads

- At the top, join this group to the following group as before, and work back down over the latter. Repeat to the end of the band.

Working simple darning

- Begin simple darning by laying the end of the working thread over the threads to be woven.
- Take the needle under the first two (or more) threads of the group, working from right to left and bringing the needle up over the thread end (*see illustration below*).

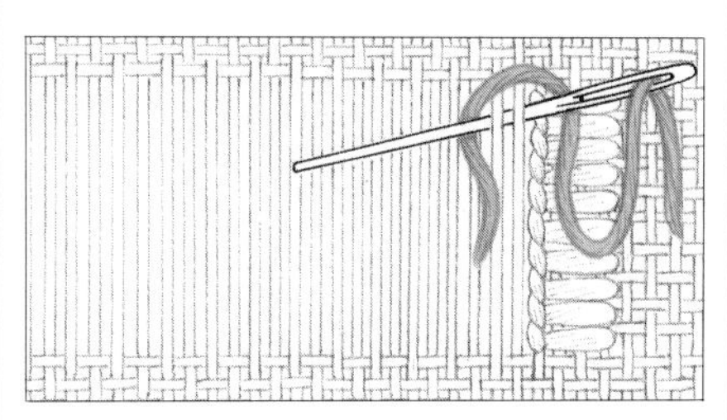

Working simple darning under the first threads

- Take the needle from left to right under the second group of threads (*see illustration below*).

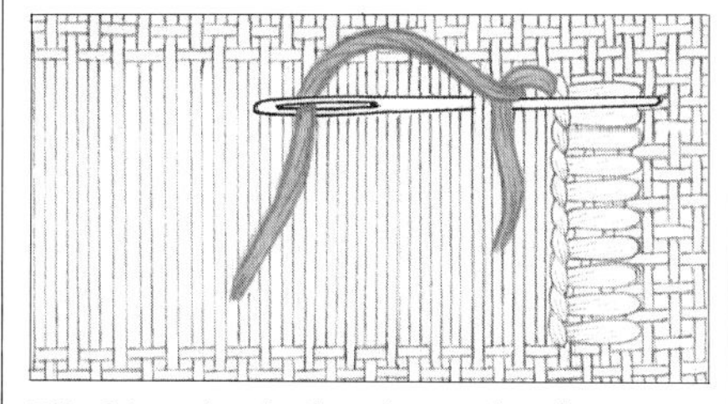

Working simple darning under the second group of threads

- Repeat to the bottom of the vertical threads being covered, then move on to the next group of threads to be darned. The completed row should have a smooth, densely woven texture (*see photograph below*).

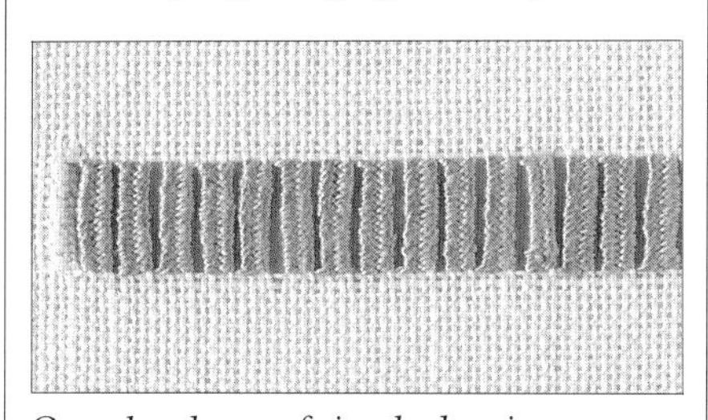

Completed row of simple darning

Working needleweaving variations

Many variations can be worked using the darning technique. The grouping can be staggered, perhaps alternating with overcast bars; the groups may include three or more groups of threads. The stitching can be done over only the middle threads, leaving the ends of the band free. Embroidery threads in a range of different colours can be used to great effect in needleweaving, creating an attractive braided finish.

Embroidered Nightdress

The embroidery on this attractive button-through nightdress is worked on a strip of linen that is then attached to the fabric. You could adapt this design to enhance borders of a skirt, the button band and cuffs of a shirt, or children's clothes.

SIZE
Linen strip: 18½ × 1⅜ in
(47 × 3.5 cm)

MATERIALS
18-count evenweave linen, 19¼ × 2⅛ in (49 × 5.5 cm)
DMC no. 5 perlé cotton, red 666, 1 skein

Working the embroidery

1 Turn under ⅜ in (1 cm) on all edges, taking care on corners; baste to hold (*see illustration below*).

Basting the hem

2 Work cross stitch over the basted hem along two long sides and one short side of the fabric (*see illustration below*). The cross stitches worked should be four linen threads wide.

Working cross stitch over the hem

3 Find the middle 14 threads running the length of the fabric and mark each end with coloured basting threads (*see illustration below*).

Marking the end

4 At one short end, count in 24 threads from the inner edge of the cross stitch hem. Mark with a line of basting. Then mark out the pattern repeats, counting in from the end marker. The pattern uses sets of nine threads, so count in multiples of nine. Continue counting down the fabric, marking with a tailor's tack each time, up to 24 or more threads from the end. Mark the end with basting stitch (*see illustration below*).

Marking out the pattern repeats

5 Starting 1 in (2.5 cm) in from the end markers, cut through the 14 middle threads. Remove the 14 middle threads.

Carefully draw the cut threads back to the "end" marker at each end, keeping them on the underside (*see illustration below*).

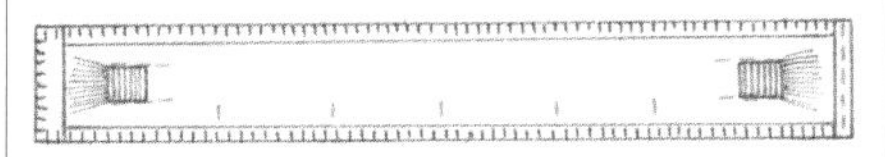

Pulling cut threads to back of work

6 Remove basting stitches and tacks. Work blanket stitch over the frayed end threads on the underside, working from the front. Trim the frayed threads back to blanket stitch (*see illustration below*).

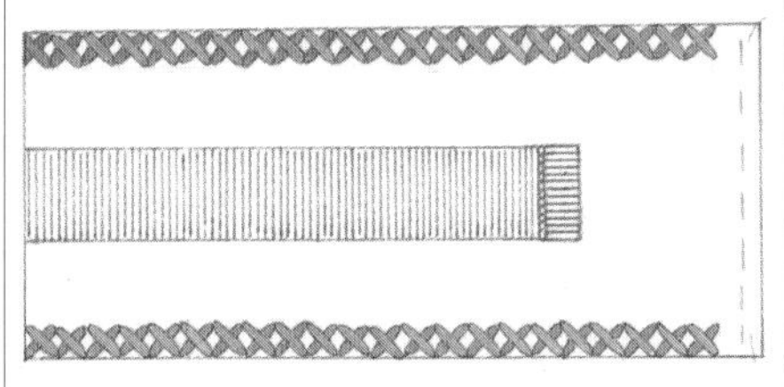

Covering cut threads with blanket stitch

7 Work hemstitching between every three threads down the long sides of the drawn thread area (*see illustration below*). The stitches should be four linen threads in depth.

Detail of the nightdress design

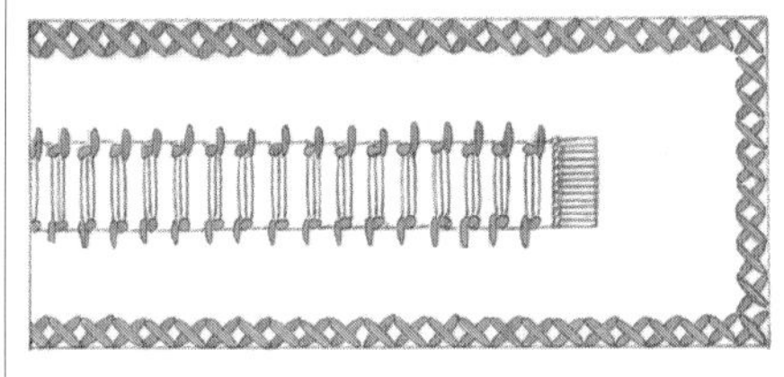

Working the hemstitching

8 Starting from the centre of the blanket stitch at one short end, begin overcasting sets of nine threads (*see illustration below*). If the thread runs out, weave it through the back knot, and start from the same point.

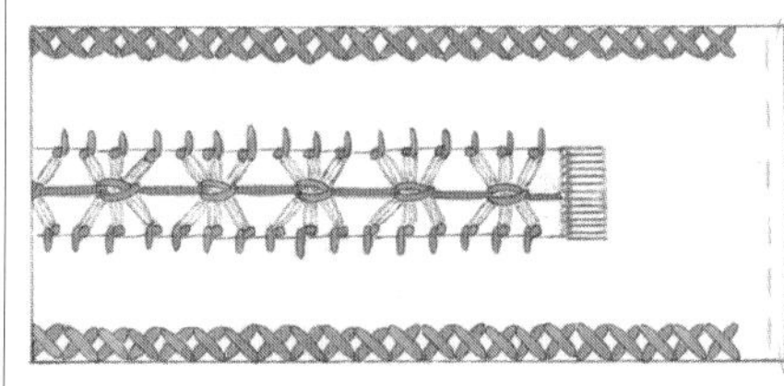

Overcasting sets of nine threads

9 Press completed work with a steam iron on a well-padded surface.

Ribbon-Lined Pillowcases

These luxurious linen pillowcases have beautiful bands of hemstitching lined with satin ribbon. Make a pair of one or both designs as a special present for a bride, or for yourself! Choose an appropriate ribbon for your own colour scheme.

SIZE
Finished pillowcases 17¾ × 27¼ in (45 × 70 cm)

MATERIALS
For both pillowcases: 36-count white evenweave linen, 1⅛ yd (1 m), at least 36 in (90 cm) wide
Fabric shown: Zweigart "Edinburgh," shade 100
For single-band pillowcase: satin ribbon, ⅝ yd (57cm), 2¼ in (5.5 cm) wide
For triple-band pillowcase: satin ribbon, 1 yd (90 cm), 1 in (2.5 cm) wide; matching ribbon, 1 yd (90 cm)
Tapestry needle, size 24

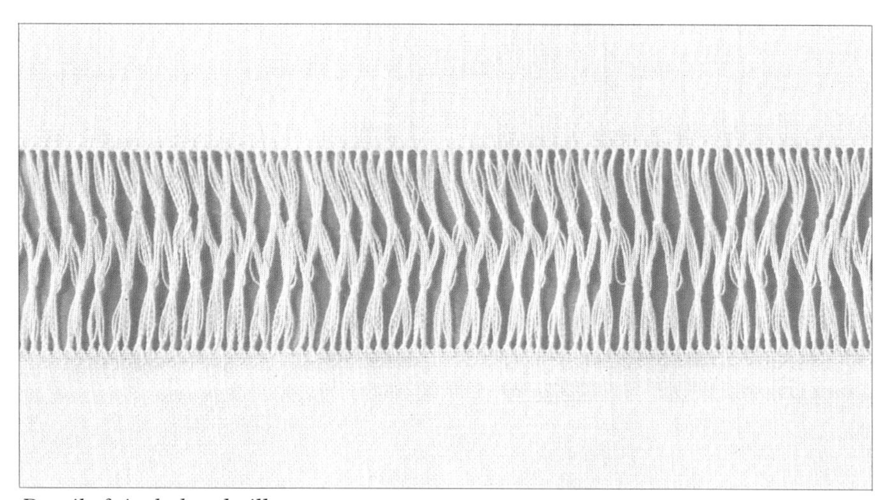

Detail of single-band pillowcase

Making the single-band pillowcase

1 Cut linen: Bottom, one piece, 35 × 19 in (89 × 48 cm); Top, one piece, 32 ¾ × 19 in (83 × 48) cm. On one short edge of each piece, baste along foldline. Foldline is 6⅞ in (17.5 cm) from edge of bottom piece, 4⅝ in (11.7 cm) from edge of top piece.

2 On top piece, measure 4 in (10 cm) in from the foldline. Then carefully pull out a single thread at line 1 (*see illustration below*).

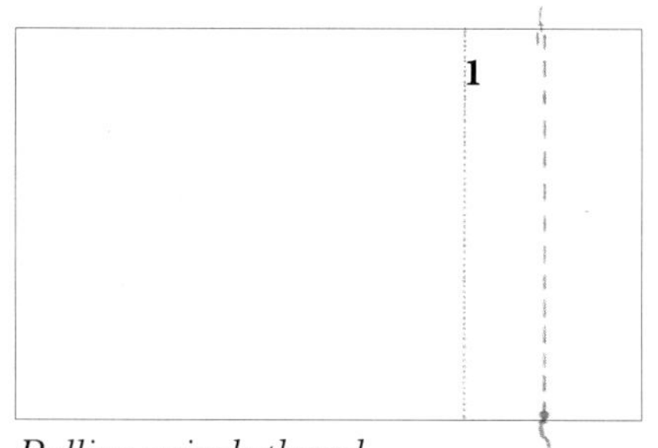

Pulling a single thread

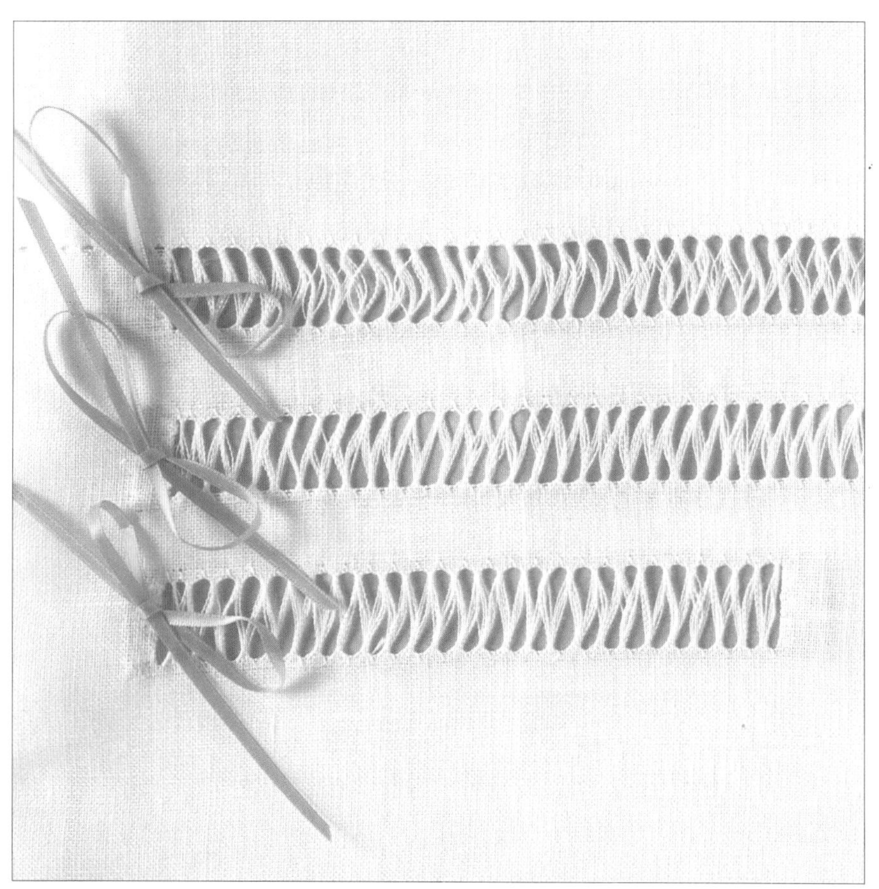

Detail of triple-band pillowcase

3 Stitch top and bottom pieces together along three sides; use ⅝ in (1.5 cm) seam allowance. Press seams open. Trim across corners; neaten edges with zigzag or overcast stitch. Turn pillowcase right side out.

4 On flap edge (bottom piece), turn under ¼ in (6 mm); press. Turn under another ⅜ in (1 cm); press. Baste hem in place. Pull out a single thread just above the hem. Work hemstitching (*see page 153*) over four fabric threads to complete the hem.

5 Turn under both top and bottom edges along the basted foldlines. On top piece, turn under raw edge at line 1; press. Baste edge in place. Work hemstitching over three fabric threads to complete the hem (*see illustration below*).

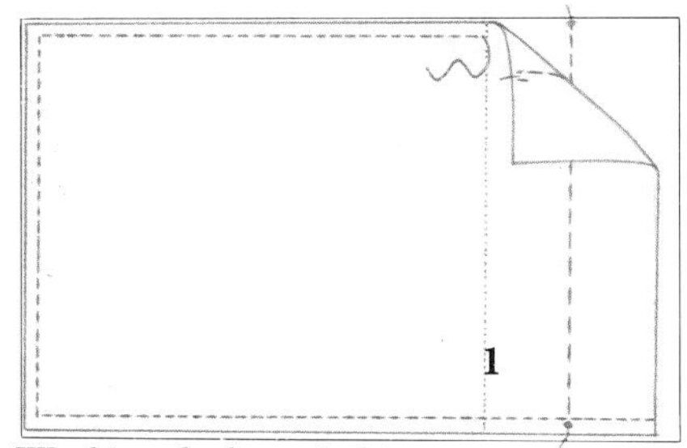

Working the hemstitching

6 Withdraw fabric threads to make a band 2 in (5 cm) wide. Position the band 5 in (12.7 cm) down from top edge of pillowcase. Hemstitch along the remaining edge. Work from the wrong side and position the stitches carefully to produce parallel groups of four threads (*see illustration below*).

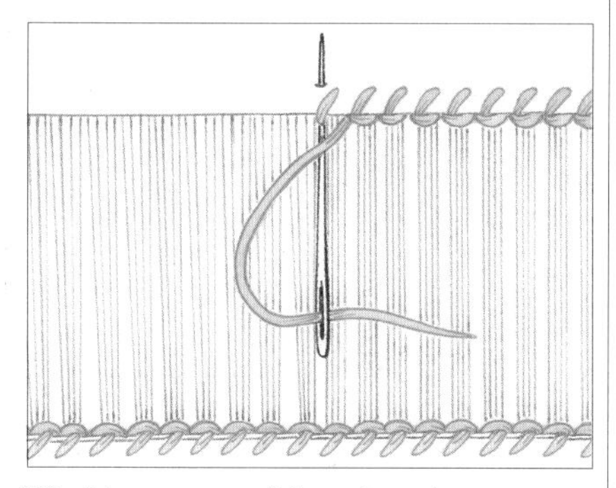

Working groups of four threads

7 Cut a 19 in (48 cm) length of ribbon. Work two lines of basting along ribbon, ¾ in (2 cm) from each edge. Pin ribbon under band of grouped threads. Baste and slipstitch the ribbon in place, catching only one fabric thread on top.

8 Work knotting (*see page 126*) over groups of threads, taking thread in a zigzag pattern and using basted lines as a guide (*see illustration guide*).

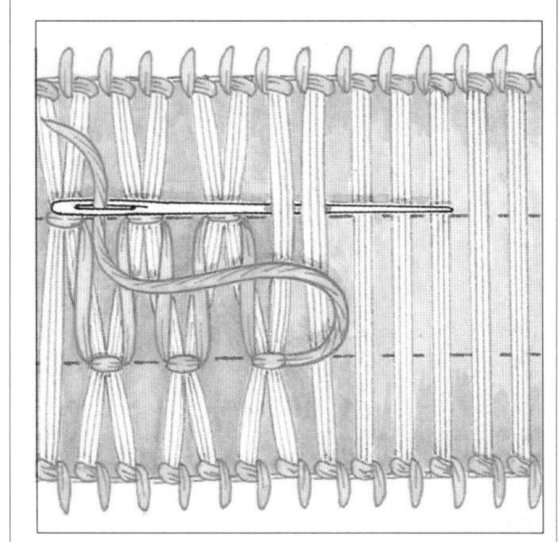

Working the knotting

9 On the wrong side, turn under remaining raw edges of the flap and slipstitch in place. The slipstitch should conceal any remaining raw edges of ribbon. Remove any remaining basting threads.

Making the triple band pillowcase

1 Follow the instructions for the single-band pillowcase, steps 1–5. On the top piece, work hemstitching over eight threads instead of four.

2 Withdraw three bands of fabric threads, each ¾ in (2 cm) wide. Space bands 1¾ in (4.5 cm) apart, or any even distance as required, starting 5 in (12.7 cm) down from top edge of pillowcase. (For a pair of pillowcases, reverse positioning on one.) The first band should be 14¼ in (36 cm) long, the second 9½ in (24 cm), and the third 6 in (15 cm). Press thread ends to the wrong side, but do not trim them.

3 Work zigzag hemstitch along all edges of bands, grouping four threads from two adjacent groups (*see illustration next column*).

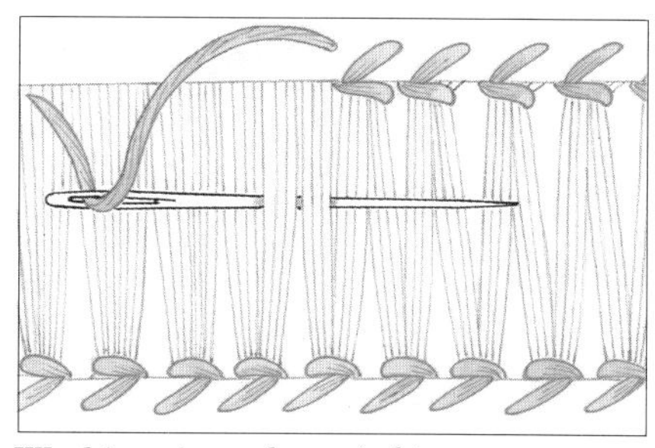

Working zigzag hemstitching

4 Cut strips of ribbon to the length of each band plus 1½ in (4 cm). Slipstitch each ribbon under the corresponding band along both edges of the pillowcase.

5 Trim the ends of the withdrawn thread to ¼ in (6 mm). Slipstitch fabric to the ribbon at each end, then turn under raw edges of the ribbon on the wrong side, enclosing the thread ends, and slipstitch in place.

6 Turn under remaining raw edges of flap and slipstitch over the seam inside the pillowcase (*see illustration below*). Remove any remaining basting threads.

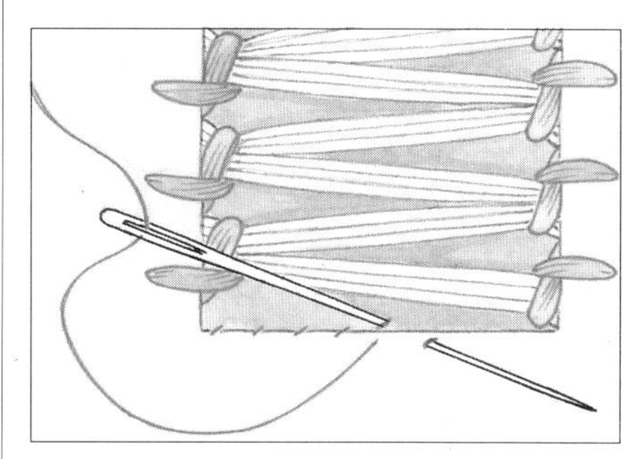

Slipstitching the seam

7 Cut narrow ribbon into three equal lengths. Sew centre of each length to the top of a band, then tie in a bow.

Finishing Techniques

When all the stitching is completed, a piece of embroidery will require one or more finishing techniques. Instructions are given here for cleaning, pressing, blocking, framing, hemming, making cushion covers, and making and attaching trimmings.

CLEANING

If you have worked the embroidery in a frame and kept your hands clean, the work should not need cleaning. However, washing or dry cleaning may be desirable for a large item like a tablecloth or a small one that has sat in your workbasket a long time.

Most evenweave fabrics are washable, as are the DMC cotton threads that are used for the projects. If in doubt about the washability of the work, ask a reliable dry cleaner.

Washing embroidery

Use tepid water and a mild soap when washing a piece of embroidery.

- Wash by hand in a basin, swishing the work gently in the soapy, tepid water; do not rub.
- Rinse again in tepid water.
- Roll in a towel to remove excess moisture and press while damp.

Pressing embroidery

To smooth out your finished embroidery, it is often sufficient to iron it gently. Some work may, however, require the blocking technique that is described in the next column.

- Place the damp work face down over a folded turkish towel and place a dry pressing cloth on top. If the work has not been washed, and thus is dry, use a damp cloth and dry iron or a dry cloth with a steam iron.
- Gently apply the iron. Lift it up and re-apply it in another area; do not drag the iron over the surface.
- Repeat as necessary until the work is smooth and dry.

BLOCKING

In some cases, especially where surface stitches have been used, you may prefer to block your finished counted thread embroidery. Blocking is a method of smoothing out fabrics by dampening, then stretching gently and leaving them to dry. It has the advantage over pressing of not flattening attractive raised and textured surfaces.

For blocking you can use either a well-padded ironing board or a specially made blocking board as explained below.

Blocking on an ironing board

If your finished embroidery is small enough, it can easily be blocked on your ironing board.

- Place the finished piece of work right side up, on the well-padded ironing board.
- Pin at intervals of ¾ in (2 cm); to make sure that the corners are completely square, it helps to use a set square.
- Spray the embroidery evenly with water from a plant sprayer (*see illustration below*).

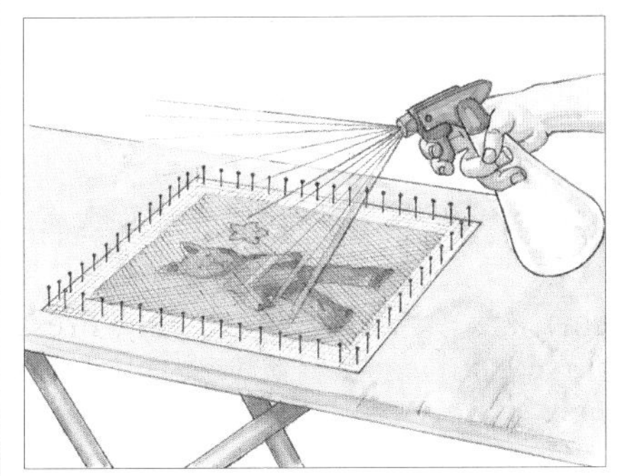

Spraying right side of the work

- Leave the work to dry thoroughly before removing from the board.

Making a blocking board

Although seldom required for counted thread work, especially if worked in a frame, a blocking board can be useful for a distorted piece. To make a blocking board, you will need a piece of soft pine about 24 in (60 cm) square, a piece of unbleached muslin (previously washed, dried and pressed), cut 2 in (5 cm) larger than the board all around, and a staple gun.

- Staple the cloth to the board on the underside, working out from the centre of each side, stretching cloth firmly and mitring the corners as shown (*see illustration below*).

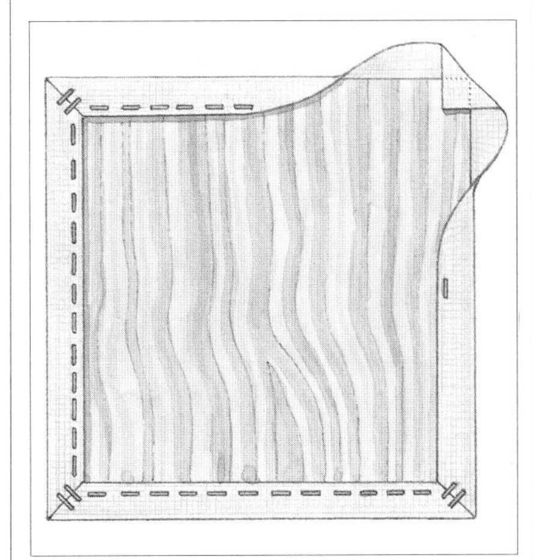

Stretching muslin over a blocking board

To block an item that is larger than 20 in (50 cm) square, you would need to make a blocking board larger than the one described above. If you decide to make a larger blocking board, be sure to cut the muslin at least 4 in (10 cm) larger than the board all around, so that you can get a better grip when stretching and stapling it over the board.

Using a blocking board

Once the blocking board has been prepared, it is used for blocking in the following way:

- Immerse the finished embroidery in cold water and lay it right side up on the board.
- Pin it to the board with large drawing pins at each corner, pulling firmly. Check that the corners are square, using the set square.
- Pin again at the centre of each side, then outward along the sides, checking carefully to make sure that the edges of the fabric are straight *(see illustration below)*.

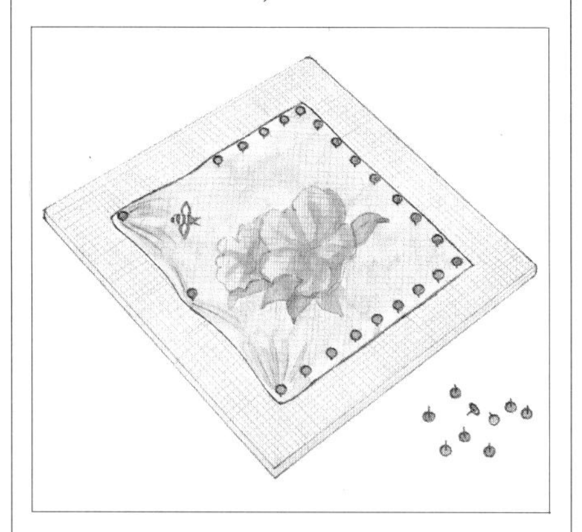

Pinning the embroidery in place

- Once the work has been evenly secured in place, leave to dry thoroughly before removing it from the blocking board. Remember that damp fabrics are always more fragile, and damage may occur to your embroidery if you try to remove the fabric from the board too soon.

Certain types of embroidery, such as bands of drawn thread work, contain areas that are particularly delicate because of the threads that have been withdrawn. This means only warp or weft threads remain in these places to hold the fabric together. They can be strengthened, for example by placing a ribbon underneath, but great care should be taken if blocking these pieces of embroidery.

FRAMING

An embroidered picture or panel should always be carefully mounted on a piece of cardboard before it is taken to a shop for framing. This will help keep the work smooth when it is framed.

When using the following method of mounting, always be sure to work on a smooth, clean surface. This will avoid the risk of snagging or soiling the embroidery.

Mounting an embroidered picture

For mounting you will need: a piece of stiff, acid-free cardboard of the required size, a piece of thin wadding the same size as the cardboard, strong sewing thread (linen thread is ideal), a large sewing needle, and some double-sided tape or fabric glue.

- Attach the wadding to the board with a couple of pieces of tape or tiny dabs of glue; this will hold it in place during the lacing.
- Lay the embroidery right side down and position the board with the wadding on top of it.
- Fold one of the two longer edges of the fabric over the board, and hold it in place securely with carefully positioned pins inserted into the edge as shown *(see illustration below)*.
- Check the positioning of the embroidery on the right side and adjust it if necessary.
- Turn up and pin the opposite edge in the same way.

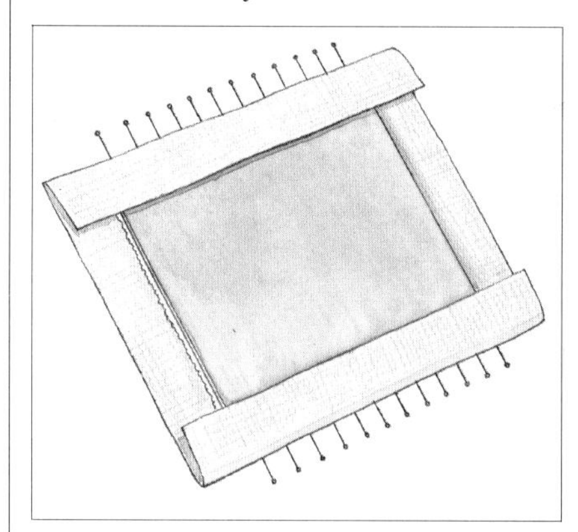

Pinning the first two sides in place

- Thread the needle with the strong thread, but do not cut it off the spool.
- Beginning at the centre, and pulling off more thread as required, work herringbone stitches between the two fabric edges out to the right-hand edge *(see illustration below)*. Then fasten off the thread securely.

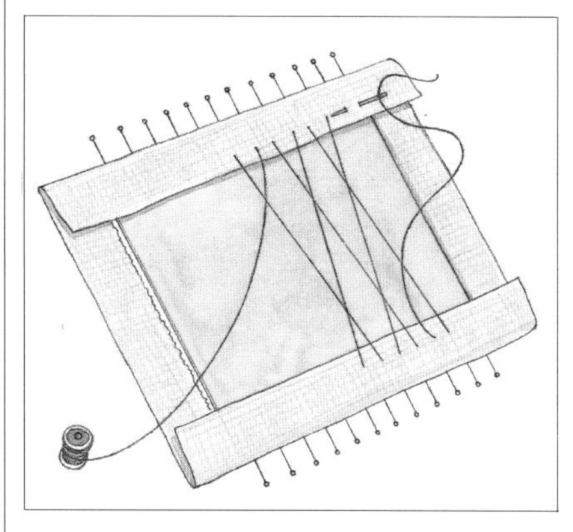

Lacing from the centre outward

- With a long thread, work to the left-hand side, but do not fasten off.
- Remove the pins.
- Starting at the right, pull each thread to give an even tension *(see illustration below)*. Fasten off.

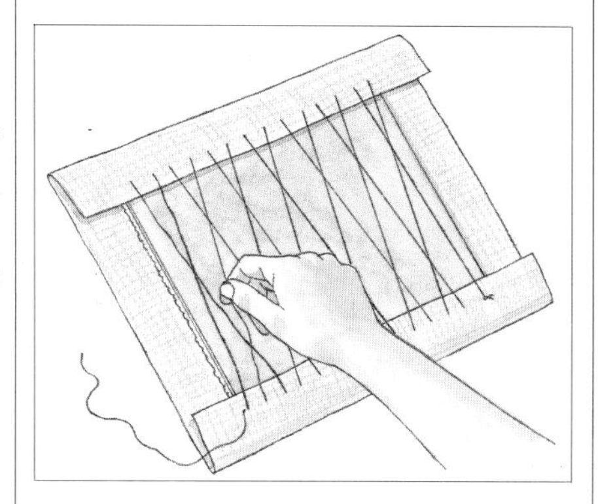

Tightening the lacing

- Turn over the work and pin and lace together the remaining edges in the same way.

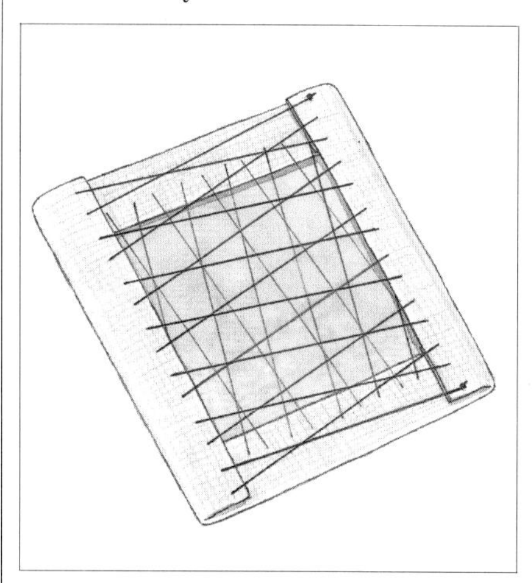

Back view of the mounted picture

HEMSTITCHING

Hemstitching creates a subtle, narrow line of openwork stitches along the top of a hem. It is an attractive way of finishing off your embroidery.

Detailed instructions for working hemstitching are given on page 142. The instructions below explain how to prepare the hem along the fabric edge and how to mitre the corners before working the decorative hemstitching along the top of the hem.

Withdrawing threads for hemstitching

If the number of threads for hemstitching must be exact or the main embroidery must be worked before hemming, you should always take care to cut the fabric larger than the size required. Then withdraw the threads for the hemstitching, leaving the correct number of vertical threads still in the fabric.

- Mark the hemfolds in reverse order to that shown below, and follow the instructions for mitring the corners and hemming.

The following method is suitable for turning up a hem for hemstitching a large item, such as a tablecloth, where the stitching will not be conspicuous and where having a precise multiple of threads is not as important as it would be in a smaller, more delicate item.

- Decide on the finished depth of the hem. Then measure in from the raw edge a distance about ½ in (1.25 cm) less than this. Withdraw a thread at this point to mark the first fold line.
- Count the number of threads before the fold line (in this example it is seven) and withdraw a thread at the same point on the three remaining sides of the fabric.
- Measure inward from the withdrawn thread the depth of the finished hem. Withdraw another thread here to mark the second fold line as indicated in the next column (there are 11 threads in this hem).
- Count the threads as before, and withdraw threads on the three remaining sides.
- Add one to the number of threads between the two fold lines and count inward this number (here 12). Then work a line of basting between this thread and the next one (*see illustration below*).

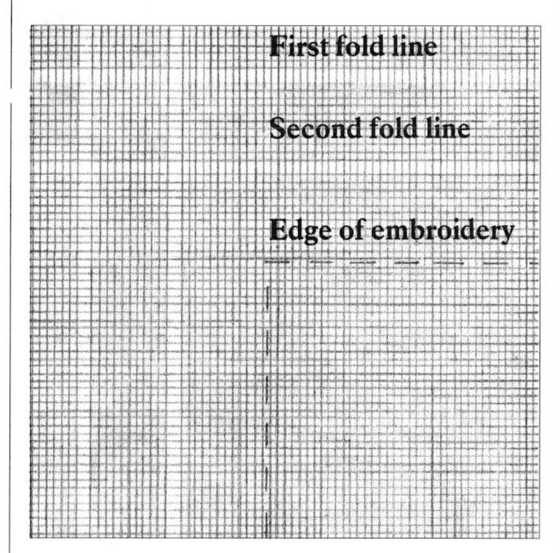

Initial threads withdrawn

- Withdraw the required number of threads for the hemstitching, and either darn the ends into the corners or turn them back and secure them with buttonhole stitch (*see page 143*).

Mitring the corners and hemming

This basic method for mitring can be used (omitting the withdrawn threads for hemstitching) with ordinary hemming stitch and with other decorative stitches such as point de Paris (*see page 117*).

- Using a pencil or fabric marker and a ruler, draw a diagonal line across the point where the outer fold lines meet.
- Then draw another line, parallel to the first, where the inner lines meet.
- Cut along the *outer* marked line as indicated (*see illustration below*).

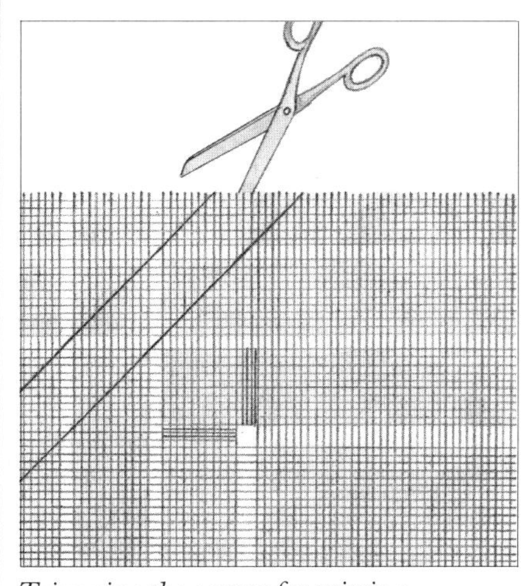

Trimming the corner for mitring

- Turn in and press along the remaining marked diagonal line.
- Fold the hem along the two fold lines as shown (*see illustration below*) and baste it in place.

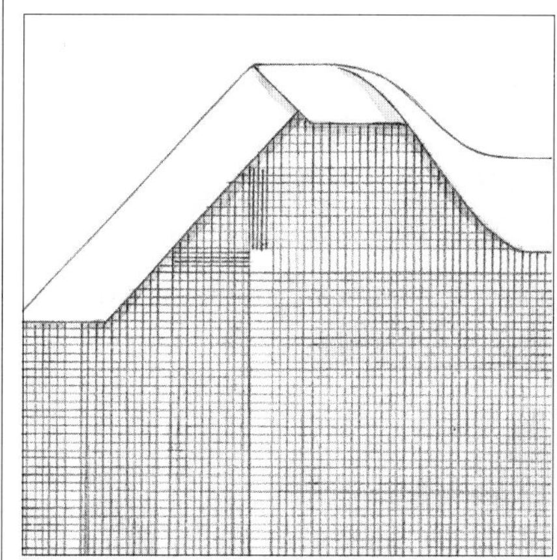

Folding the hem to the wrong side

- When both edges have been folded, the corner is mitred. Sew the edges of the mitre together as shown, then work the hemstitching along the top of the hem (*see page 142*).

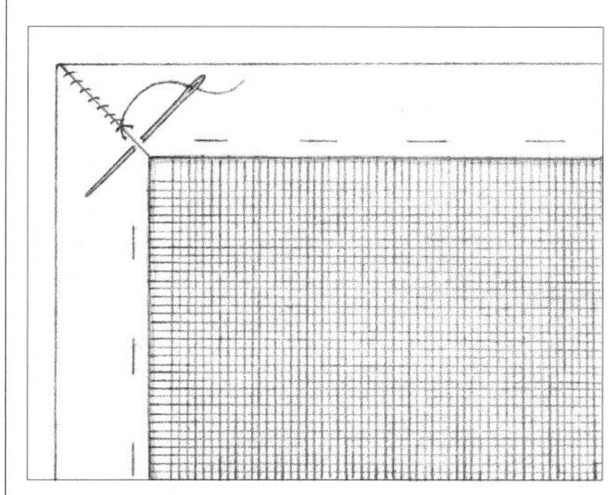

Slipstitching the mitred corner

SIMPLE CUSHION COVER

This method for making a cushion cover is perfectly satisfactory for a cover that will not require frequent cleaning. It can be removed, but this entails restitching the opening each time.

If you are going to trim the edge of your cushion cover with a decorative cord, read the instructions on page 155 for attaching a cord before sewing the cover together.

Making a simple cushion cover

- Cut the front and back pieces of the cushion cover the same size, ¾ in (2 cm) larger all around than the size of the finished cover. For a snug fit, you may wish to make the cover slightly smaller than the cushion pad.
- Machine stitch (or backstitch) the two pieces together along three sides and about 2–3 in (5–8 cm) in from each corner on the fourth side.
- Trim the corners diagonally to reduce bulk. If the fabric frays easily, work overcast stitches or machine zigzag along the raw edges of each layer of fabric.

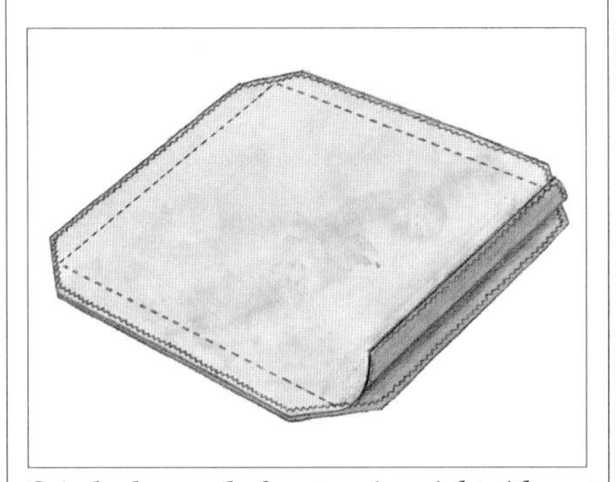

Stitched cover before turning right side out

- Turn the cover right side out.
- Insert the cushion pad and close the opening securely with slipstitch (*see illustration below*).

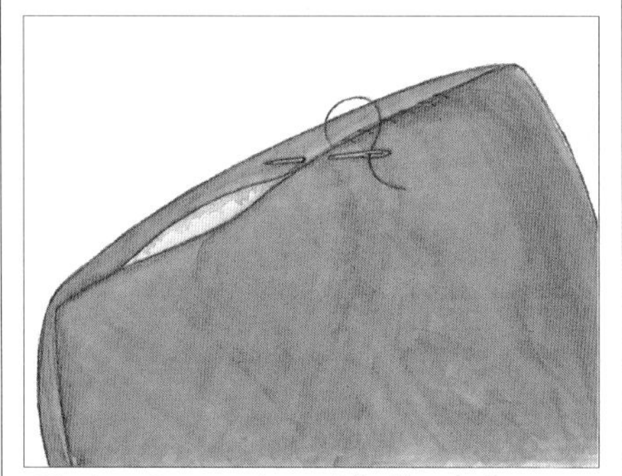

Closing the opening with slipstitch

REMOVABLE CUSHION COVER

Most removable cushion covers are made with a zip fastening. Ideally this is placed in a side seam so as to be inconspicuous; however, this is easier said than done, and often, after a lot of work, the result is less than satisfactory. An easier alternative is simply to insert the zip into a centre seam in the back, using a method that covers it with a flap of fabric; even if this is successful, the effect is not very attractive.

Another method, which is relatively easy and and also decorative, is to use buttons – fastened either with buttonholes or with thread loops. For a graceful effect, position the closing to one side, rather than exactly in the centre.

Making the paper pattern pieces

Begin by making pattern pieces for the two back sections of the cover. The instructions here are for a closing with button loops. For an opening with buttonholes, see below.

- On a large piece of paper (preferably graph paper), draw two pieces measuring, combined, the finished size of the back cover. In the example shown here, the cushion cover is a rectangular one measuring 15 in (38 cm) in width and 12 in (30 cm) in height, and the closing is to be postitioned 5 in (13 cm) from the left-hand edge. Leave about 6 in (15 cm) space between the two pieces.
- Now add a ¾ in (2 cm) seam allowance to the outer edges of each piece – *not* the two opening edges (*see illustration below*).

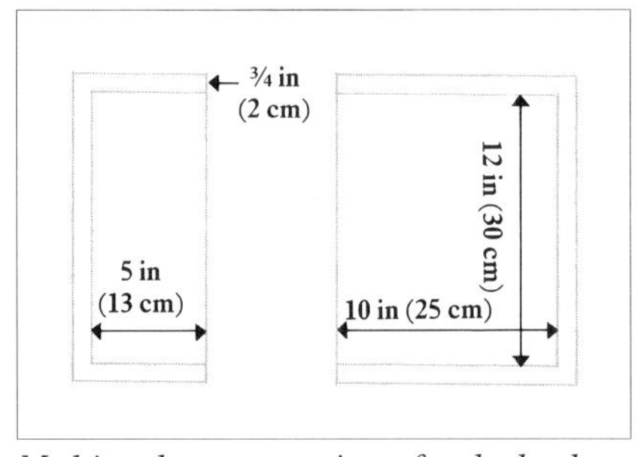

Making the pattern pieces for the back

- On the left-hand edge of the larger, overlapping piece, add a hem allowance of 1½ in (4 cm).
- To the right-hand edge of the smaller, underlapping piece add 3 in (8 cm). (Again, this is for a thread loop closing; for an example of buttonholes, *see illustration below*).

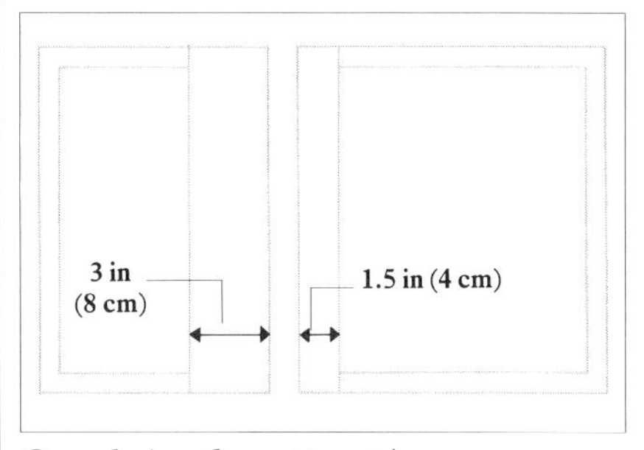

Completing the pattern pieces

- Plan the number of buttons and mark the positions of the thread loops on the paper pattern. Multiply the button diameter by the number of buttons. Subtract this from the diameter, then divide the remaining distance by the number of buttons plus one; this gives you the length of the spaces between the thread loop fastenings.
- Once you have double-checked all the dimensions on your paper pattern pieces, cut them out carefully.

Cutting and sewing the cover back

If you plan to trim the cushion cover edge with cord, read the instructions for attaching a cord (*see page 155*) before sewing the cover together.

- Using the paper pattern pieces, carefully cut out the two pieces for the back from the fabric.
- On the left-hand edge of the overlapping piece turn under ⅜ in (1 cm) and stitch.
- Turn under ⅜ in (1 cm) and stitch the right-hand edge of the underlapping piece in the same way.
- On the overlapping piece, turn under and press a further 1⅛ in (3 cm) and baste this in place at the top and bottom edges.
- On the underlapping piece, turn under and press 1½ in (4 cm) and baste this turning in place.
- Work the thread loops in the overlapping piece of the back, taking care to follow the positions marked on the paper pattern. Work three straight stitches along the edge of the fold, then work over these closely

with buttonhole stitch (*see illustration below*). Fasten the thread off securely under the fold.

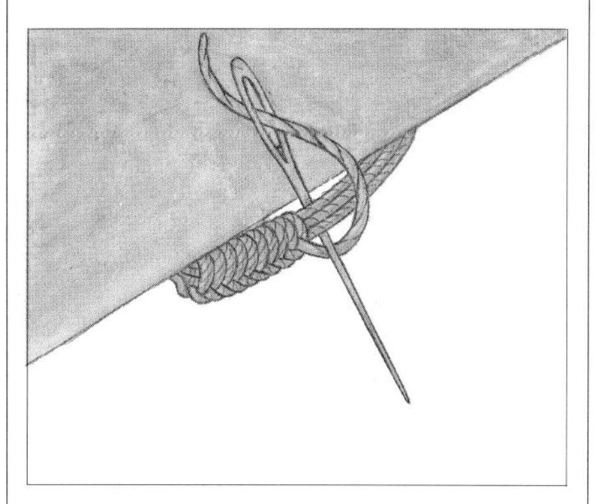

Working a thread loop

- Place the overlapping piece on a flat surface, right side down. Then lay the other piece on top, carefully overlapping the first piece so that the width equals the finished width of the cover plus 1½ in (4 cm) – twice the seam allowance. In this example, this will be 16½ in (42 cm).
- Baste the pieces together at the top and bottom along the seamline where they overlap. (If the fabric has a nap or an "up" or "down" ("one-way") design, remember to position the pieces carefully so that they will match up correctly.)

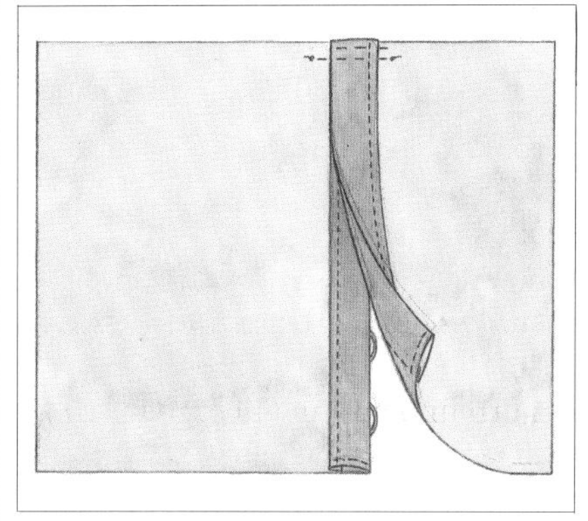

Joining the back cover pieces

- Place the back pieces and cushion cover front together with right sides facing and edges matching. Stitch around all sides, taking ¾ in (2 cm) seam allowance.
- Neaten edges as for simple cushion cover, and turn right side out.
- Insert the cushion pad and mark the positions of the buttons with pins.
- Remove the form and sew on the buttons opposite the loops.

Working a buttonhole fastening

The back for a cushion cover with a buttonhole fastening should be made in the same way as the one with thread loops, but the turning allowances for the two pieces of the back need to be slightly wider to accommodate the buttonholes. You should first plan the paper patterns before working the buttonholes, using the following instructions:

- On a large piece of paper, draw the two pieces of the back cover as described on page 154, but leave about 7½ in (19 cm) space between the two pieces.
- Add a ¾ in (2 cm) seam allowance to the three outer edges of each piece.
- On the left-hand edge of the larger, overlapping piece, add a turning allowance equal to the buttonhole width plus at least 1¼ in (3 cm). For a ¾ in (2 cm) wide buttonhole, for instance, the turning allowance would be 2 in (5 cm).
- To the right-hand edge of the smaller, underlapping piece add either once or twice the required underlap (depending on whether a double thickness is required; on a heavy fabric a single layer may be preferable) plus ⅜ in (1 cm) for finishing the raw edge.
- Complete as for the paper pattern pieces for the removable cushion cover with thread loops, but substitute buttonholes for the threads loops.

CUSHION TRIMMINGS

Cords and tassels can be used to trim the edges of an embroidered cushion cover. You will usually be able to find a wide range of ready-made cords and tassels in stores that sell furnishing fabrics. Alternatively, you could make your own quite easily if you prefer.

Attaching a cord

If you are going to attach a cord to your cushion cover, leave a gap of about 1¼ in (3 cm) in the bottom seam when making the cover.

- Cut the cord about 2 in (5 cm) longer than distance around cushion.
- Wrap a piece of sticky tape securely around one end of the cord to prevent it from later unravelling.
- Insert the other end of the cord into the gap. Lay the cord along the seam, and, using a sewing needle and thread to match the cord, sew the cord in place as shown.
- Work from alternate sides, going through the underside of the cord each time and catching only a few fabric threads on either side of the seam (*see illustration below*).

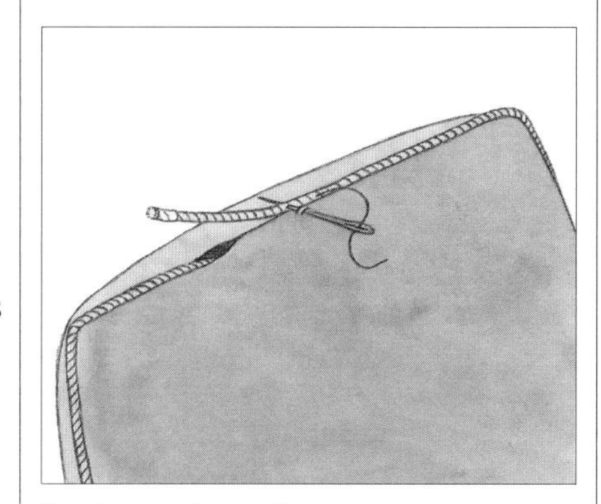

Sewing on the cord

- When you reach the starting point, trim the free end to about 1¼ in (3 cm) and insert it into the opening so that it crosses the other end at a slant. Sew the ends in place, closing the opening at the same time.

Making a twisted cord

Instead of purchasing a cord for trimming your embroidered cushion cover, you could make your own. Perlé cotton, wool embroidery thread, or knitting yarn are good choices for making such a cord.

• Estimate the number of strands you will need by twisting a few together to see the effect.
• Cut the chosen number of strands into lengths three times the finished length of the cord.
• Knot the strands at each end, taking care that they will then lie smoothly together.
• If possible, get someone to help you twist the strands. Insert a pencil through each knot, and pull the strands out to their full length. Turn the pencils in a clockwise direction to twist the strands.

You can also tie one end of the strands around a doorknob or similar fixed object and then turn the strands yourself.

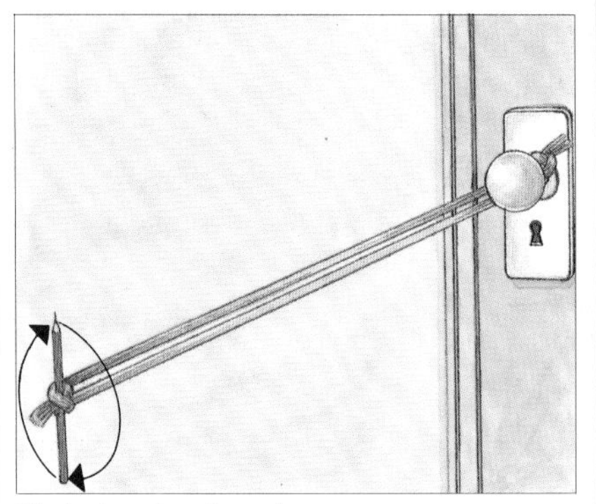

Twisting the threads

• When the strands are very tightly twisted – so that they kink up as soon as the tension is released – fold them in half. The cord will twist around itself. Give it a shake and run it between your fingers, if necessary, so that it twists evenly; long cords may require a bit of coaxing.

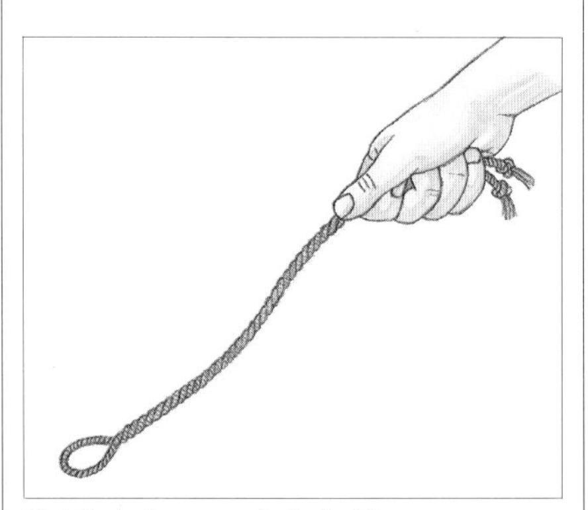

Folding the strands in half

• Tie a knot in the folded end of the twisted cord. Cut the ends and fluff them out. Then tie a knot at the other end where the two original knots are. Fluff out that end as well.

Making a tassel

• Cut a piece of cardboard to the required depth of the tassel and a convenient width for winding. A utility knife is the most helpful tool for this *(see next column)*.
• Cut a piece of thread for tying the tassel at the top, and keep it handy.
• Wind the thread around the cardboard until the tassel is the desired thickness.
• Holding the strands in place at the top with your free hand, cut through them at the lower edge. Then slip the additional strand under the tassels as shown to hold them together; form the tying strand into a loop as shown *(see illustration below)*.

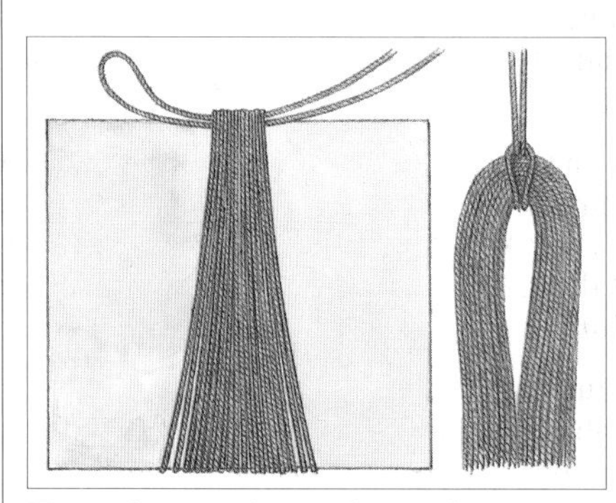

Tying the strands together at the top

• Cut another, longer piece of thread for binding the strands. Make a loop in one end, and lay this loop along the tassel as shown *(see illustration below)*.

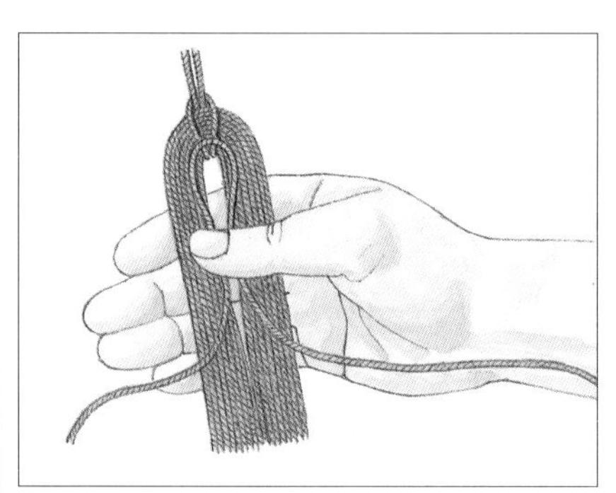

Beginning the binding

• Wind the thread tightly around the tassel, holding the loop in place for the first few rounds. When the binding is the required depth, slip the end through the loop. Pull firmly on both ends, thus drawing the join into the centre. Trim the ends and push them into the tassel.

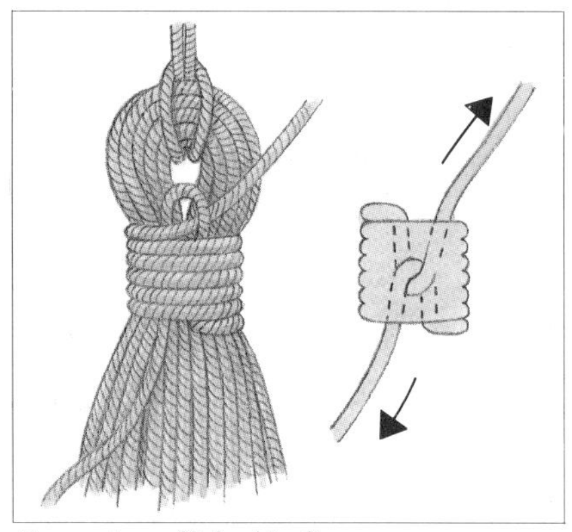

Fastening off the binding

Using a utility knife

A utility knife is the most convenient tool for cutting pieces of poster or cardboard. It should be used with a steel ruler and, ideally, a self-healing cutting mat; otherwise, place a piece of thick, strong scrap cardboard under the work. Make sure that the blade is sharp; replace it if not.
• When cutting, hold the steel ruler firmly in place with your free hand, keeping your fingers well away from the cutting edge. Draw the utility knife smoothly and firmly toward you, keeping it vertical and always close to the steel ruler.

Obviously a utility knife is a dangerous tool in the wrong hands. Make sure that it is always stored safely on a shelf out of children's reach, and is kept firmly closed when not in use.

Glossary

Aida cloth a type of *evenweave* in which the *warp* and *weft* are composed of groups of threads – normally of four

basting large running stitches used to mark positions on fabric or to hold two or more fabric layers together temporarily

bias the direction running at a 45° angle to the weave of the fabric, having the greatest amount of stretch

box chart a type of chart in which each square on the grid represents a single stitch; commonly used for cross stitch embroidery (see *line chart*)

count the number of fabric threads per inch; used to describe the fineness or coarseness of the fabric

counted thread work or **counted thread embroidery** a form of embroidery in which stitches are worked over given numbers of fabric threads

crewel needle a needle with a sharp point and relatively large eye

double darning a type of pattern darning in which the fabric is solidly covered with superimposed lines of running stitch

evenweave a type of *plain weave* fabric having the same *count* in both directions; also applied to *single-thread* evenweave, as opposed to *Aida* or *Hardanger* fabric

Hardanger fabric a type of *evenweave* fabric woven with pairs of threads and used for Hardanger embroidery

kloster block a group of upright satin stitches, normally five; a distinguishing feature of Hardanger embroidery

line chart a type of chart used for counted thread embroidery in which the grid represents the fabric threads (see *box chart*)

mitre to turn under the corner of fabric in one of several ways that avoid placing a seam or fold at the turned edge, generally distributing the bulk evenly for a smooth, flat finish. A mitred corner joins two pieces of material exactly in a 45° angle

oversew or **overcast** to work stitches by hand or machine over a raw edge to prevent it from fraying; also to join two or more edges by this method

perlé cotton a twisted, lustrous cotton embroidery thread with a beaded appearance

plain weave the simplest type of fabric weave, in which the *warp* and *weft* threads go over and under each other singly

ring frame an embroidery hoop or frame consisting of two tightly fitting rings, between which the fabric is held taut

scroll frame or **slate frame** an embroidery frame in which the top and bottom edges of the fabric are attached to rollers and the sides laced to slats

selvedge the firmly woven side edges of fabric

single-thread a term used to describe *evenweave* fabric in which the *warp* and *weft* are composed of individual threads (see *Aida cloth and Hardanger fabric*)

soft embroidery cotton a relatively thick, matt-finish cotton embroidery thread

stretcher frame a rectangular embroidery frame composed of four canvas stretchers, to which the fabric is attached with pins

stranded cotton a lustrous cotton embroidery thread composed of six fine threads that may be used singly or combined

tapestry needle a needle with a blunt point and large eye, used for counted thread work

wadding a lightweight, spongy fabric, often made of polyester or cotton, generally used as a middle layer in quilted articles

warp the vertical, or lengthwise, threads of the weave, running parallel to the *selvedge*

weft the horizontal, or crosswise, threads of the weave, running perpendicular to the *selvedge*

INDEX

Acknowledgements

Many people contributed to the making of this book; however, I should like to single out a few for special recognition. First of all, thanks to my British publishers, Collins & Brown, especially to Gabrielle Townsend and to Catherine Bradley, who saw the project through to completion.

Warm thanks to Cara Ackerman of DMC for her help and encouragement, and to Maria Diaz, for supplying the materials so efficiently. Special thanks to Reader's Digest, whose experience in needlework publishing has been of great value.

I am indebted to Carol McCleeve for planning the projects on pages 94–97, 118–120, 138–141 and 146–147.

Above all, I am grateful to Linda Doeser, Sally Harding, and Maggi McCormick, for their first-class editorial skills, and to the embroidery designers whose work I commissioned, for their creativity and cooperative spirit.

Eleanor Van Zandt

The author and publishers would also like to thank the following embroiderers who conceived or worked the samples and projects in this book:

Projects: pages 50–52 Joan Bray; pages 53–55 Gisela Banbury; pages 56–58 Elizabeth Stuart Designs; pages 59–61 Caroline Davis; pages 62–64 Sandra Sullivan (Homespun Elegance Ltd.); pages 65–67 Chris Timms; pages 68–71 Chris Timms; pages 72–73 Dorothea Hall; pages 74–77 Gisela Banbury; pages 78–81 Geraldine Marchand (original painting), Caroline Davis (embroidery); pages 82–83 Janette Sawyer; pages 85–87 Sandra Sullivan (Homespun Elegance Ltd.); pages 92–93 Anna Griffiths; pages 94–97 Doreen James; pages 102–104 Anna Griffiths; pages 105–107 Moyra McNeill; pages 118–120 Doreen James; pages 121–123 Grace Lister; pages 100–102, 124–127, 144–145 Eleanor Van Zandt; pages 133–135 Hanne Pentith; pages 136–137 Joanna Churton; pages 138–141 Doreen James and Shirley Coleby; pages 146–147 Doreen James and Shirley Coleby; pages 148–150 Caroline Davis.

Samples and finishing projects: Gisela Banbury; Rachel Bowyer; Joanna Churton; Caroline Davis; Penny Hill; Grace Lister and Helen Parsons.

Cross Stitch Motif Library: page 33 Dorothea Hall; pages 34–35 Gisela Banbury; page 36 Gisela Banbury and Dorothea Hall; pages 37–38 Anna Griffiths; page 39 Chris Timms; page 40 Gisela Banbury; pages 41–42 Caroline Davis; pages 43–45 David Ashby; pages 46–47 Eleanor Van Zandt; pages 48–49 Gisela Banbury.

Suppliers

All of the following suppliers offer a mail order service.

The Campden Needlecraft Centre
High Street
Chipping Campden
Gloucestershire
(0386 840583)

Creativity
37/45 New Oxford Street
London WC1
(071 240 2945)
Mail Order: 15 Downing Street
Farnham
Surrey
(0252 714856)

Homespun Elegance
11047 Pierson Drive
Suite I
Fredericksburg
Virginia
U.S.A.
(0101 703 371 6377)
(kits by Sandra Sullivan in traditional American style)

John Lewis
Oxford Street
London W1
(071 629 7711)

Liberty
Regent Street
London W1
(071 734 1234)

Mace & Nairn
89 Crane Street
Salisbury
Wiltshire SP1 2PY
(0722 336903)

The Stitch Shop
15 The Podium
Bath
Avon BA1 5AL
(0225 481134)

Voirrey Embroidery Centre
Brimstage Hall
Wirral L63 6JA
(051 342 3514)

For the name of your nearest stockist of DMC threads and Zweigart fabrics, contact:
DMC Creative World Ltd.
Pullman Road
Wigston
Leicestershire LE18 2DY
(0533 811040)